THE NON-AMISH NEIGHBORS WERE THUNDERSTRUCK BY THE SLAUGHTER...

They told reporters and police investigators that he'd suffered a recent brush with mental illness but had never exhibited tendencies toward violence.

For the first time in American history, an Amish man stood accused of homicide, raising a host of bewildering questions. What had driven this quiet, easygoing man to commit a crime so ghastly as to defy description? Who *was* Edward Gingerich? *What* was he? How would his family, the Amish community, and Pennsylvania's criminal justice system deal with this unique and disturbing case?

• • •

Jim Fisher, a former FBI agent and current professor of criminal justice at Edinboro University of Pennsylvania, has been nominated for two Edgar Awards, first in 1997 for *Fall Guys* and again in 1999 for *The Ghosts of Hopewell*. He is also the author of *The Lindbergh Case*. He has written extensively about writing scams involving phony literary agents, book doctors, and vanity publishers. He is a graduate of Vanderbilt University Law School.

CRIMSON STAIN

John —

Best Wishes —

Jim Fisher
nice hearing
from you again.

JIM FISHER

B
BERKLEY BOOKS, NEW YORK

CRIMSON STAIN

A Berkley Book / published by arrangement with
the author

PRINTING HISTORY
Berkley edition / May 2000

The Penguin Putnam Inc. World Wide Web site address is
http://www.penguinputnam.com

ISBN: 0-425-17433-6

BERKLEY®
Berkley Books are published by The Berkley Publishing Group,
a division of Penguin Putnam Inc.,
375 Hudson Street, New York, New York 10014.
BERKLEY and the ''B'' design
are trademarks belonging to Penguin Putnam Inc.

PRINTED IN THE UNITED STATES OF AMERICA

11   10   9   8   7   6   5   4   3   2

Jesus paid it all
All to him I owe;
Sin had left a crimson stain:
He washed it white as snow.

Mrs. Elvina M. Hall, 1865

Contents

Introduction

Between 1693 and 1697 a Swiss Mennonite bishop named Jakob Ammon broke free of the Mennonites, bestowing his name upon his followers—the Amish.

Ammon's people fled to North America to escape religious persecution in Europe. They drifted in clusters across the continent, occupying parcels of land in some twenty-six states, concentrating in central Ohio and eastern Pennsylvania, where more than one-quarter of this nation's 150,000 Amish reside.

The Amish are honest, hardworking people known for their self-sufficiency and simple uniformity of dress. The women wear bonnets, shawls, heavy black shoes, black stockings, and plain, dark-colored dresses. The men grow beards (they do shave their upper lips) and dress in blues and blacks. The most conservative sects, referred to as Old-Order Amish, avoid the use of electricity and do not own motor vehicles or telephones. Their dwellings are unpretentious, furnished in spartan fashion and do not feature modern indoor plumbing. Members of this male-dominated society refer to those outside their faith as "the English." The Amish worship in clusters of twenty-five to thirty families led by an ordained elder called the bishop, the spiritual and cultural leader of the group. The bishop's authority is great and his word, in matters of Amish life, is law.

The Amish are stoical, keep their feelings to themselves, abhor violence, and loathe publicity. They do not abide departures from their principles of conformity, humility, devotion to God, and detachment from the modern world. Excommunicated transgressors are "shunned," sometimes permanently.

There is no such thing as an Amish divorce, and there has never been an Amish murder—until now.

The Gingerich Family

Atlee D. Edward's oldest brother. Born 1963. Wife: Susie. Three children. Sawmill worker and farmer.

Clara D. Edward's younger sister. Born 1968. Single, living at home.

Dannie E. Edward's father. Born 1938. Wife Mary née Shetler. Eleven children. Farmer, sawmill owner. First to settle in Brownhill. Farm: both sides of Frisbeetown Road. Brownhill minister.

Daniel D. Edward's younger brother and closest friend. Born 1967. Wife: Fannie. Two children. Farm: Sturgis Road across from sawmill.

Daniel E. Edward and Katie's first child. Born 1987.

Eli Edward's paternal grandfather. Five children from first wife, six children from second wife. Farmer, Apple Creek, Ohio.

Eli D. Edward's younger brother. Born 1969

Enos E. Edward and Katie's second child. Born 1989.

Joe D. Edward's older brother. Born 1964. Wife: Annie. Three children. Farm: Frisbeetown Road.

John D. Edward's younger brother. Born 1972.

Lizzie D. Edward's younger sister. Born 1971. Second Sturgis School teacher.

Mary E.   Edward and Katie's third child. Born 1990.

Mary J.   Wife of Dannie E. Her maiden name Shetler, a distant relative of Levi and Rudy Shetler. Edward's mother. Born 1941.

Noah D.   Edward's younger brother. Born 1974.

Rudy E.   Edward's paternal half uncle.

Simon D.   Edward's younger brother. Born 1976.

The Shetler Family

Emma A.   Katie's mother. Née Slabaugh. Born 1938. Husband: Levi N. Shetler. Sixteen children. First Porter School teacher.

Emma L.   Katie's younger sister. Born 1973.

Enos L.   Katie's younger brother. Born 1980.

Lovina L.   Katie's younger sister. Born 1971.

Lovina J.   Katie's paternal grandmother. Maiden name: Coblentz.

Levi L.   Katie's younger brother. Born 1977.

Levi N.   Katie's father. Born 1933. Wife: Emma A. Sixteen children. Bishop Rudy Shetler's older brother. Dairy farmer. Farm: 300 acres on both sides of Townline Road. Died, May 1994.

Lydia L.   Katie's younger sister. Born 1981.

Marie L.   Katie's older sister. Born 1961. Husband: Samuel R. Hershberger. Two children.

Mary L.   Katie's oldest sister. Born 1960. Husband: Emanuel R. Hershberger. Eight children.

Andy L.   Katie's younger brother. Born 1969. Wife: Susie. One child.

Barbara L.   Katie's younger sister. Born 1965. Husband: Ben Coblentz. Four children.

Clara L.   Katie's younger sister. Born 1968. Husband: Eli Yoder. Three children.

Daniel L.   Katie's older brother. Born 1963. Wife: Sarah J. Four children.

David R.   Katie's cousin. Bishop Rudy Shetler's son. Second head of the Gingerich sawmill. Born 1965. Wife: Mary C. Three children.

Drucilla L.   Katie's younger sister. Born 1975.

Elmer L.   Katie's oldest brother. Born 1960. Wife: Soloma. Three children. First head of Gingerich sawmill.

Emanuel L.   Katie's younger brother. Born 1967. Wife: Anna. Four children.

Mose N.   Katie's paternal uncle. Wife: Ella. Five children.

Noah L.   Katie's younger brother. Born 1979.

Noah L.   Katie's paternal grandfather.

Rudy N.   Katie's paternal uncle. The Brownhill bishop. Born 1940. Wife: Fannie. Three children. Farm: Townline Road.

Prologue

E dward Gingerich killed his wife, Katie, at dusk on
March 18, 1993, a cold gray Tuesday preceded by
several days of snow. The twenty-eight-year-old Amish
man attacked his spouse in front of two of their children
who witnessed the atrocity in stunned horror. In the
kitchen of their western Pennsylvania farmhouse, he
knocked her down, crushed her skull by stomping her face,
ripped off her clothing, and then opened up her belly with
a kitchen knife. Through the gaping, seven-inch gash, he
removed her heart, lungs, spleen, liver, kidneys, ovaries,
and intestines, stacking these in a neat pile beside her
corpse. Within an hour, volunteer ambulance personnel
from a nearby village stared at the bloody shell sprawled
nude on the kitchen floor and at the knife plunged into the
dripping mound of organs.

The tall, pale-skinned lumber-mill operator was arrested
by the Pennsylvania State Police at a dirt road intersection
near his house. Bearded, denim-clad, wild-eyed, blood-
spattered, and virtually incoherent, the Amish man mumbled biblical passages and made vague references to the
devil.

Gingerich's non-Amish neighbors were thunderstruck
by the slaughter. They told reporters and police investigators that he'd suffered a recent brush with mental illness
but had never exhibited tendencies toward violence.

For the first time in American history, an Amish man
stood accused of homicide, raising a host of bewildering

questions. What had driven this quiet, easygoing man to commit a crime so ghastly as to defy description? Who *was* Edward Gingerich? *What* was he? How would his family, the Amish community, and Pennsylvania's criminal justice system deal with this unique and disturbing case?

1

The Brownhill Amish

Edward D. Gingerich was eighteen when he and his family, from the small Amish enclave clustered around the town of Norwich in southeastern Ontario, moved to the 150-acre farm located in Crawford County, Pennsylvania, thirty miles south of the town of Erie. The nearest town, Mill Village, was nothing more than a handful of buildings, a few dozen houses, and a blinker light a couple miles north on Route 6, a two-lane highway that cut across the northern part of the state. Fourteen miles to the west, I-79 connected Erie, a lakeside community of 130,000 to Pittsburgh, 125 miles to the south.

Edward's parents, Dannie and Mary Gingerich (themselves born and raised in central Ohio), and his seven brothers and two sisters were the first of seven Amish clans to move to this remote section of northwestern Pennsylvania, a place that would come to be known as the Brownhill settlement. Dannie Gingerich had brought his family to Pennsylvania because, unlike Ontario, there were no government-enforced regulations on dairy farming. It was spring 1983.[1]

Ed, or Eddie as he was called, had completed his eight grades of formal Amish education in a one-room schoolhouse outside of Norwich. He had been an average student who had preferred to read rather than join in schoolyard games of baseball and soccer. Because he was moody, had a short temper, and was thin-skinned, Eddie got into more than his share of schoolyard fights. Being taller and stronger than most of the kids his age, and having a fierce determination never to give up no matter what, Ed won all his fights and became known and feared as something of a bully and a show-off. He became an unpopular loner who wasn't even liked by his teachers.[2]

Even as a child, Eddie made no secret of the fact that he hated farm labor. He used every trick in the book to avoid his share of the chores. As a result, he also earned the reputation of being a slacker and, because he often pretended to be sick, a malingerer. Mr. Gingerich, a soft-hearted dairy farmer and ordained Amish minister, saw through all of this but indulged his son in hopes he would outgrow his laziness, his tendency to lie, and his lack of interest in religion and living the good Amish life.[3]

The Gingerich farm, in the heart of Rockdale Township, a thinly populated region of hardwood forest and rolling pastures, spread along the north side of Sturgis Road, a dirt line parallel to and a half mile south of the Crawford–Erie County line. Frisbeetown Road, narrow and unpaved, cut north and south, dividing the farm in half. The farm featured three main buildings, the most impressive being the massive red barn. The two-story, gray fiberboard-sided house, across Frisbeetown Road from the barn, was small and run-down. Between the little gray house and Sturgis Road sat an odd-looking structure sided by unpainted clapboard with multipaned windows all around. Mr. Gingerich figured he'd use this building for a woodshop.

Within a mile radius of the Gingerich land were six small English farms. Their nonfarming neighbors, mostly blue-collar folks and the rural poor, lived along Sturgis and Frisbeetown in small houses or in trailers with haphazardly added garages, cement-block steps, closed-in porches, wooden decks, and possession-cluttered yards. In this place, it wasn't unusual to see a flower bed surrounded by a tractor tire painted white or a gravel driveway lined with painted rocks and rods bearing red reflectors. Rabbit cages, outdoor swing sets, aboveground swimming pools, snowplow blades, firewood piles, and a variety of store-bought and homemade lawn ornaments were also evident. This was the land of riding mowers, pickup trucks, motorcycles, and snowmobiles.

That April, following the arrival of the Gingerichs, it would be a matter of days before members of the other seven families moving to the area started showing up. One clan was on its way from the Amish enclave around Greenville, Michigan; another from the Conewango settlement near Jamestown, New York; and the rest from Fryburg, an Amish colony located sixty-five miles to the southwest in Venango County on the other side of Oil City, Pennsylvania.

The Gingerichs, and those who were following them to Brownhill, had every reason to believe they had found the perfect place to raise their families and start a new community. There were fertile farms accessed by a network of dirt roads used only by the locals, who seemed delighted to have them as neighbors. The surrounding forest provided lumber for new homes and barns, as well as fuel for heating and cooking. Moreover, the woods were teeming with game, including deer. Union City, a town of four thousand, a few miles to the east, had everything Amish families needed in their daily lives. The town wasn't too close nor was it out of reach by buggy.

When the last of the Amish moved to Rockdale Township that spring, the Brownhill settlement, a rectangular area of roughly nine square miles, consisted of a community of eight families of forty-three children and sixteen adults. Since twelve of the children were between six and thirteen, a schoolhouse would be built in the fall on Sturgis Road not far from the Gingerich barn.

The Amish, like everyone else, move because they are searching for something better. Although the Brownhill settlers were leaving their homes for a variety of reasons, they were all seeking a fresh start in a place where they could raise their children away from the threatening influences of the modern world. That was their dream; this was their new land.

Compared with their Amish counterparts, the older Gingerich boys—Atlee, Joe, Ed, and Danny—were on the rowdy side. Occasionally things got out of hand and someone would get hurt—or angry. Ed enjoyed a good, rough practical joke as long as it wasn't on him. Shortly after arriving in Brownhill, the boys wrestled Ed down, tied him to a pole in the barn, and covered his mouth with duct tape so he couldn't summon help. Early the next morning, Mr. Gingerich found Ed in the barn still lashed to the pole. Ed was so furious his father wouldn't untie him until he promised not to retaliate. Ed kept his word, but his brothers watched their backs for a month.[4]

Ed was nothing like his father, who believed in and followed the *ordnung* (pronounced ott-ning), the social and behavioral rules and values that define and govern the Amish way of life. Like all good Amish men, Mr. Gingerich obeyed the bishop, who was the spiritual and social leader of his church district, a group usually composed of thirty or so families. He was a good husband, a proud father, and a helpful neighbor. Ed respected his father's Amishness, but didn't approve of his soft heart, especially when it came to his dealings with the English. For example, when offered too little money for one of his prize hogs, Mr. Gingerich would accept the price rather than risk offending the man who made the offer. Ed considered this a terrible weakness and hated this trait in his father. He vowed that he would never let anyone take advantage of him in business or otherwise. Just because he was an Amish man didn't mean English people could intimidate him. He was not going to be a patsy or a sucker. He would be strong and, if he had to, even stand up to the bishop.[5]

The Amish talk to relax; they therefore keep their conversations light, avoiding weighty topics such as politics, religion, philosophy, and complicated personal relationships. For the Amish, psychology is something beyond their comprehension. For this reason, Ed never told his father how much he detested, and was embarrassed by, his capitulation to the English and to the bishop. Instead, Ed let these feelings eat away at him.

Mr. Gingerich hoped that Ed was merely going through a phase. He had seen this in other families—kids who were restless, moody, sullen, lazy, and contemptuous of church and their elders. Most of these children grew up, found women to marry, became fathers and, ultimately, pillars of the Amish community. Contentment and peace of mind came from hard, physical work, a good wife, many children, and the love of God. Mr. Gingerich had to believe that all of these blessings would eventually come to Edward, his most troubled son.

By June of 1985, the Brownhill settlement, composed of thirteen families, boasted a population of ninety-three. Mr. Gingerich, with the help of his four oldest boys, had built a sawmill on the northeast corner of the Sturgis-Frisbeetown crossing, the geographical center of the enclave. Sitting next to the unpainted building that now housed a woodshop, the mill assembly featured a five-foot saw blade driven by a diesel-powered motor. The abundance of timber in the region had made logging a major industry. Locally, with the influx of Amish families building new houses and barns, a need had been created for rough-cut lumber. Mr. Gingerich, with Bishop Rudy Shetler's permission, would supply some of the building material for the community. Bishop Shetler had approved of the venture because it would provide jobs for local Amish men.

Following the construction of the mill in July, Mr. Gingerich hired Levi Shetler's oldest son, Elmer, an experienced sawmill operator, to run the business. Levi Shetler was one of the bishop's brothers and the owner of the biggest farm in the settlement. As part of the deal, Elmer and his wife and their baby boy would move into the gray farmhouse vacated by the Gingerichs following the construction of the new and much larger family dwelling on the northwest corner of the Sturgis-Frisbeetown intersection. Ed's oldest brother, Atlee, now twenty-two, would be Elmer Shetler's assistant. More of a farmer than a mill-worker, and shy around the English, Atlee was not enthusiastic about his new position. He hoped to have his own farm someday, but in the meantime he'd do what his father wanted and work at the mill. In the Amish community, sons obeyed their fathers.

Ed, now twenty, was enthusiastic about the new mill and particularly interested in the mechanical end of the operation; he was spending a lot of time tinkering with its motor and the other mechanical components. He took it upon himself to keep the machinery running smoothly, and if something broke, he was there to make repairs. Before long, he knew more about sawmill mechanics than anyone in Brownhill. He enjoyed amazing his fellow Amish men with his mechanical knowledge and skill.[6]

That summer, Ed and his brother Joe, the second-oldest Gingerich son, began spending time with Richard Zimmer, the owner of the horse-and-cattle farm adjacent to the western border of the Gingerich land. Joe Gingerich, with perhaps more guts than common sense, impressed Zimmer with his uncanny ability to break wild horses. Ed, on the other hand, spent day after day keeping Zimmer's trucks, tractors, and farm machinery in good working order.

As the summer wore on, Ed spent less and less time on the family farm. When he wasn't at the sawmill, he was at Zimmer's place fixing trucks and motors brought to him by Zimmer's friends and neighbors. Ed took pride in knowing Zimmer and his English friends, and he clearly enjoyed the reputation he had earned as a mechanical wizard.

Ed avoided church as much as he could. Every other Sunday morning (the Amish worship on alternating Sundays), Ed would fake an illness then sneak across to Zimmer's farm instead of joining his family in church. Zimmer, a fiercely independent man himself, admired the young Amish man for his willingness to break the rules and defy the bishop. Zimmer often remarked that he could never live under the thumb of a Rudy Shetler.[7]

During his visits to Zimmer's farm, Ed confided to his English friend that he didn't understand why the Amish limited themselves by doing everything the hard way—the slow way. Why, for example, plow a field with horses when a tractor could do the job in a fraction of the time? What did all of these limitations—forbidding electricity and so on—have to do with morality? Were English people evil simply because they drove automobiles and watched television? Amish folks were allowed to hire drivers and ride buses and trains, but they couldn't drive or own a car or even a truck. Did this make sense?

Richard Zimmer had to admit that he found the Amish aversion to modern technology a bit strange, but he understood the power of tradition. He told Ed that in 1943, when his father bought his first tractor, his mother nearly threw a fit. The family had managed perfectly well with horses, why did they need a tractor? Horses were a lot cheaper to run and maintain and much more reliable. Ed told Zimmer straight out that he'd been thinking about leaving the Amish faith. The trouble was, he wasn't exactly sure how to go about it.[8]

One afternoon, as Ed and Zimmer were drinking sodas in Zimmer's driveway, where Ed had been working under the hood of a truck, Ed asked his English friend if he had a daughter he could marry. Ed's plan was this: He'd leave the Amish, marry Zimmer's daughter, build a little house on Zimmer's land, and start a sawmill. Richard said he liked the idea, but there was a problem—he didn't have a daughter, quickly adding that if he had, he would be proud to have Ed as a son-in-law.[9]

That fall, Ed met a thirty-two-year-old English woman

named Debbie Williams. A private-duty nurse, she lived with her husband, Hank, on Mackey Hill Road about a mile south of Mill Village. Hank Williams, a local carpenter, did business at the Gingerich sawmill. Hank, a black man (his wife was white), had been born and raised in Mill Village. He was an easygoing fellow, popular around the sawmill with Elmer, Atlee, and Ed. Ed met Debbie at the mill one afternoon when she came for a truckload of free sawdust she used as bedding for her horses. A horse lover himself, they became friends and were regularly seen attending local horse auctions together.[10]

Ed found Debbie Williams, like his friend Richard Zimmer, someone he could confide in. Debbie knew how much Ed hated farm life and how badly he wanted to leave the Amish and start a sawmill or become a certified automobile mechanic. But he couldn't force himself to make the break. As a result, he was unhappy, trapped in a world he could not abide.[11]

2

Ed Meets Katie

Elmer Shetler, one of the bishop's nephews and the man in charge of the Gingerich sawmill, became, on October 26, 1985, the father of a baby girl. He and his wife, Soloma, named the child Drucilla after one of Elmer's younger sisters. Their first child, Samuel, was almost two. Soloma didn't have family in the Brownhill settlement that could help her with Sammie and the brand new baby. For that reason, Elmer asked one of his younger sisters, Katie, to stop by the little gray house once a day to lend his wife a hand. Having helped care for eight of her eleven younger siblings, Katie, at twenty-one, was an old hand at feeding, bathing, and watching after babies and toddlers.

Katie Shetler's baby-sitting at the little gray house on Frisbeetown Road next to the sawmill brought her into Gingerich territory. Ed, working around the mill every day with Katie's brother Elmer, took notice of the petite young Amish woman playing in the leaves in front of Elmer's house with her nephew Sammie. One fall afternoon, Ed walked up to Katie and formally introduced himself. In the days and weeks that followed, he'd stop by the house he had once lived in to talk to the pretty young woman.[1]

Katie had been mildly acquainted with Ed before he had introduced himself that fall. She had known Ed's younger brother Danny a little better. Katie liked Danny, everybody did, and she enjoyed talking to him, but Danny, like his older brothers Atlee and Joe, had a girlfriend back in Canada. Katie had heard stories about Ed. She knew, for example, that he was something of a rebel who was not on very good terms with her uncle Rudy, the bishop.

Unlike Ed, the thought of not being Amish had never entered Katie's mind. She came from a big, hardworking family that exemplified what it meant to be Old-Order Amish. Her father, Levi, was perhaps the most respected and best-liked elder in the community. Emma Shetler, Katie's mother, was a tightly wound bundle of nonstop energy. Katie, like her mother, was an energetic person who helped raise her younger siblings, cleaned the house, helped with the cooking, and was out in the barn every morning at daybreak milking thirty cows by hand.

On November 25, 1985, a cold snowy Tuesday, Katie's twenty-five-year-old sister, Marie, married Samuel R. Hershberger, a twenty-one-year-old farmer from the Fryburg settlement. Bishop Rudy Shetler presided over the ceremony. The all-day event, held at the home of the bride, Levi and Emma Shetler's farm on Townline Road, and attended by everyone in the Brownhill settlement plus three dozen up from Fryburg, was the social happening of the season.

Katie Shetler had two brothers and two sisters older than she. With Marie's marriage to Samuel Hershberger, she became the oldest unmarried child in the family. Her sister Barbara, one year younger, already had a steady boyfriend. Although Katie was next in line chronologically, her prospects for marriage didn't look promising. She was in danger of being passed over by a younger sister, the first indication that an Amish woman was destined to be an old maid, a fate, in the Amish community, worse than death. None of this was lost on Ed, who, at the age of twenty-one, was beginning to feel the heat.[2]

Twenty-one and single, Katie had a boyfriend but not a suitor. She wasn't sure if Ed would ever pop the question. Marriage was one of the few subjects that didn't come up in their conversations. If Katie got too pushy, she might scare Ed off, but if she didn't get at least a little aggressive, he might string her along for years. If she wasn't careful and didn't play her cards right, she would wake up some morning and find him gone, along with her youth and her future.

Katie's fear of being passed over in marriage by a younger sister turned into reality in January when she learned that Ben Coblentz had asked her nineteen-year-old sister, Barbara, to marry him. Barbara and her fiancé would be married on February 10, 1986, at her parents' house. This would be the second Shetler daughter in four months to get married. Katie could only hope that Ed would catch the marriage bug and keep the ball rolling with a proposal of his own. The next few months would be critical.[3]

Atlee and Joe Gingerich married their Canadian girlfriends that fall. The wedding ceremonies, conducted on different days in October, were held in the Norwich settlement homes of their brides, Susie and Annie Miller. Katie did not make the trip to Ontario to attend the weddings with Ed and the rest of his family.

Atlee returned to Brownhill with his new wife, Susie, and moved into the little gray house recently vacated by Katie's brother Elmer and his family. Elmer had moved his wife and children to the Amish settlement around Fort Plain, New York, where he was operating a sawmill. Mr. Gingerich had offered Elmer's old job to his oldest boy, Atlee, but Atlee had refused. He would continue to work at the mill, saving his money for a farm, but he didn't want the responsibility of being in charge. Mr. Gingerich gave the job to his nephew David Shetler, the bishop's oldest son. With the bishop's boy running the mill, Ed would have to be careful. He wasn't pleased with this development.[4]

Joe Gingerich, the son between Atlee and Ed, would be moving that fall to a hundred-and-twenty-acre farm along the east side of Frisbeetown Road, one mile south of Sturgis. Joe, who had never worked at his father's mill, was living with his wife, Annie, in the temporary house built by his father and his grown brothers. By spring, he would be ready to start farming.

Besides tending and tinkering with the sawmill machinery, Ed interacted with the growing number of English people coming to the mill to buy custom-cut lumber. David Shetler and Atlee, much more comfortable with their own kind, were happy to let Ed deal with the English. As a result of his daily interaction with these customers, Ed unofficially maintained a sort of Amish liaison with the local English population. It was perhaps a bit ironic that the one person who least represented the Brownhill Amish was becoming, in this respect, their spokesman. This was not a development that gave comfort to Bishop Shetler.

Regarding Katie, Ed was now in the position of having to fish or cut bait. He had been seeing her regularly for almost a year; in his own family, he was next in line to get married; and for Katie, the marriage clock was ticking loudly. If Ed quit Katie, he wouldn't be excommunicated, but in a very real sense, he'd be shunned, at least for a while. Dumping Katie would put him on the bishop's blacklist for a long time. It came down to this: Ed would either have to marry Katie or jump ship altogether. He didn't like either choice; it was a matter of deciding which was worse—getting married or trying to make it in the English world.

3

A Short Honeymoon

It rained on the day, December 2, 1986, that Ed married Katie. Levi and Emma Shetler hosted the daylong wedding celebration attended by friends and relatives from Canada, western Pennsylvania, Ohio, and New York. The vans and minibuses that brought the guests crowded the driveway leading back to the house and the turnaround in front of the hay and milking barns. Standing before Bishop Rudy Shetler, Katie, in her dark blue dress, and Ed, wearing his crisp white shirt and black go-to-church suit, made a strikingly handsome couple. When Bishop Shetler pronounced them man and wife, one could almost hear a collective sign of relief coming from their parents.

Mr. Gingerich, now that his third-oldest son was married, would pay Ed three dollars an hour as an official employee of the sawmill. Since Ed and Katie would move into the basement apartment in the Shetler house, room and board would be free. He would have preferred to live in the little gray house next to the mill, but his brother Atlee and his family were living there.

It had been slow that winter at the sawmill. David, Atlee, and Ed spent most of their time trying to keep warm around the huge wood-burning heater. But with the advance of spring, business picked up considerably. In March 1987, Atlee and Danny Gingerich, helped by Katie's brother-in-law Emanuel Hershberger, constructed, behind the little gray house next to the mill, a one-story chipboard house for Ed and Katie. The structure was intended as a temporary dwelling until the babies started coming. At that point, a bigger, permanent house would be built. Emanuel, a carpenter and the man in charge of the project, built the little house on skids so it could be moved when Ed and Katie grew out of it.[1]

In May, Rudy Shetler's son David bought some land on the west side of Townline Road on the eastern boundary of the enclave a few miles north of the bishop's farm and Levi and Emma's place. A few weeks later, he quit the sawmill to farm full-time. Mr. Gingerich hated to lose David Shetler at the time when business was so good at the sawmill. Atlee, dreaming of his own farm, didn't want the head job and Ed wasn't ready. He replaced David Shetler with Dan N. Stutzman, a thirty-nine-year-old farmer who had come to Brownhill in the spring of 1985 from the Lucknow settlement one hundred and fifty miles north of Norwich, Ontario. Dan owned a hundred-and-nine-acre farm on Dean Road in the southern part of Brownhill. Business was so good, Mr. Gingerich also hired Dan Stutzman's oldest son, fourteen-year-old Noah. A bright, hardworking kid who was already an experienced sawyer, Noah looked forward to earning three dollars an hour, forty to fifty hours a week. At the mill, like all Amish businesses, employees earned the same wage regardless of their experience or longevity.[2]

A month after they had moved into the little house on skids, Katie came to suspect she was pregnant. She told her mother first, then two weeks later broke the news to Ed. While Ed didn't jump with joy, he didn't hang his head in despair. He took it calmly and said he hoped that Katie would have a boy. When Mr. and Mrs. Gingerich got the news, they couldn't have been happier.

At seven in the morning on Sunday, September 20, 1987, Ed walked down Frisbeetown Road to George and Charlotte Brown's house to fetch a ride to the birthing clinic. A few minutes later, with Charlotte Brown behind the wheel of the GMC Suburban, Ed and Katie were heading south on Brownhill Road toward the tiny village of Little Cooley.

That afternoon, Katie gave birth to a seven-pound boy they named Danny E. after Ed's father. The next morning, after Katie spent the night in the birthing clinic, Charlotte Brown drove Ed, Katie, and the baby home. For the next week or so, Katie's younger sisters Clara and Lovina would come to the little house to help her care for Ed and the baby.

Ed discovered that being a father was a lot more demanding than simply being married. He couldn't stay in the tiny house with Katie and the baby for more than a few hours at a time. Although the mill closed at five, Ed seldom came home before eight and occasionally stayed out until ten or eleven. He didn't tell Katie when he was coming home late, so the meals she made for him grew cold while she ate dinner alone. When he did walk through the door, he demanded a hot meal. Katie often refused to put a second dinner on the table, and that's when they fought. He never apologized and complained bitterly to some of his friends that his wife was lazy. He also refused to explain why he was late, where he had been, or whom he had been with. It was none of her business. She had no right to ask.[3]

At the sawmill, Ed had gone back to his old habit of coming and going as he pleased. Dan Stutzman and his son Noah found that the operation ran more smoothly when Ed wasn't there horsing around with a band of English teenagers who hung around the place to watch Ed defeat some of the kids in wrestling matches. Still the schoolyard bully and show-off, he seemed to enjoy humiliating his young opponents. When he wasn't beating up on fourteen-year-old mill groupies, he disrupted the operation by showing his friends around the mill and unnecessarily tinkering with the machinery.

In June, Dan Stutzman informed Mr. Gingerich that he was leaving the mill so he could devote more time to farming. Noah would take over the day-to-day operation of the business. His younger brother Henry, fresh out of school, would assist him at the mill. Atlee also left the sawmill that June. He had rented a small farm three miles southeast of the mill. He and his wife moved out of the little gray house on Frisbeetown.

The departure of Dan and Atlee reduced the mill crew to three—the Stutzman brothers and Ed. This meant that Ed, at the urging of his father, would have to stick around the mill and actually pitch in with the work. Instead of pulling his load at the mill, Ed started a machine shop in the unpainted building with the all-around windows and the corrugated steel roof. This allowed him to pursue his interest in mechanics and to spend large blocks of time with his English friends driving around the region buying motors and mechanical parts. Ed also scouted for timber, visited other sawmills, and made calls on loggers.

The shake-up at the mill was in one respect good news for Katie. She, Ed, and little Danny moved out of the temporary house and moved into the gray house vacated by Atlee and his family. The move, however, didn't improve Ed's performance as a husband. He continued to ignore the baby and came and went as he pleased. He and Katie seldom spoke and Katie wondered if maybe there was something wrong with her husband. Maybe he was sick. Whatever the cause of his behavior, she wasn't giving up. She didn't complain to anyone; if she saved her marriage, she would have to do it alone.

Katie's efforts notwithstanding, her relationship with Ed continued to deteriorate. By midsummer 1988, they had been married less than two years. Little Danny was approaching his first birthday. Fearing that she might lose Ed, Katie went out of her way not to incur his wrath. Still, he only spoke when spoken to and kept his responses short and to the point. She couldn't coax more than a few words out of him at a time. He just wasn't interested in her, the house, or the baby.

Toward the end of July, Ed lost his appetite, started losing weight, and complained of dizziness. He started coming home in the afternoon, closing the bedroom door, and taking long naps. Katie began to think that he suffered from some kind of strange and hidden disease that sapped his strength and made him surly. She wanted to speak to Mr. Gingerich about this, but Ed wouldn't let her. If anyone spoke to his father about such personal matters, it would be him.

That summer, Ed became so depressed and exhausted from the effort it took to masquerade normality that he sought out his father for advice. On many evenings when the chores were done and the animals settled in for the night, he and his dad would take long walks or go to the barn. They talked and they argued, and although Mr. Gingerich never lost his temper, Ed would go home upset and confused.

It slowly dawned on Katie that perhaps Ed's behavior—his remoteness, indifference, exhaustion, and all the rest—had nothing to do with her or the baby. Maybe Ed was simply sick. Maybe there was something wrong with his stomach. Maybe that's why he didn't eat and felt dizzy all the time. Ed, skinny and pale, was starting to look sick and people were asking him how he felt.

Amish people who get sick receive a lot of attention, sympathy, and help.[4] Bishop Rudy Shetler and his deacon, Ben Stutzman, suspected that Ed was faking illness to get out of work and make people feel sorry for him. They viewed him as a slacker and con man. It didn't occur to them that Ed was truly ill and that his sickness was mental rather than physical. As far as the bishop and the deacon were concerned, Ed's problem had to do with his relationship with God and the church. Once he reconciled himself to God and the Amish way of life, his appetite would come back, the dizziness would go away, and he'd become a decent husband and father. What he needed was a spiritual kick in the pants, not sympathy, homemade soup, and long afternoon naps.[5]

4

The Pennsylvania Doctor

I n the Amish community, whether an illness is physical or psychological, simply going to the doctor is, for many patients, itself therapeutic. This is particularly true when a van is hired and lunches are packed for members of the patient's family going along to keep the sick one company. A motor trip to the physician's office can kill the better part of a day and is a welcome break from daily chores. It's like taking a holiday. The excursion itself can do more for the patient than the actual medical treatment.[1]

Many Old-Order Amish avoid medical doctors, wellness clinics, and hospitals, viewing these conventional health care services as treatments of last resort. Although a majority of Amish people avail themselves of lifesaving surgery and the kind of intensive care only hospitals can provide, they tend to prefer, when the problem isn't life threatening, the less conventional health-care options such as reflexology (feet manipulation), homeopathy, and chiropractic. Practitioners of these "alternative" and controversial health-care services appeal to the Amish because they reject pharmaceutical drugs and in their place dispense vitamin supplements, special foods, teas, and herbs. Because the Amish do not believe in or place a value on higher education, they find it easier to identify with and trust health-care practitioners whose methods and techniques are simple, direct, and low-tech. They put their faith in the doctor himself rather than in his science, education, or standing in the medical profession. The Amish expect to be treated with concern and sympathy, as individuals rather than medical studies or insurance accounts. They are, therefore, much more interested in a doctor's character and personality than in his educational background, training, and experience. They respond to doctors who lay hands on them, who take the time to visit and to chat. The practiced aloofness of medical doctors puts them off and drains their confidence and trust.[2]

There are "doctors" who are Amish, Mennonite, or ex-Amish who administer to their own kind and practice a natural and ancient brand of health care based upon "sympathy curing"—a form of faith healing that encompasses a variety of diagnostic techniques, physical manipulations, and, in some cases, magic in the form of charms, amulets, and incantations. These sympathy healers, also called "powwow doctors," have been around since the early 1800s when immigrants from the Rhineland and Switzerland brought these healing practices to America. Not unique to the Amish, powwowing was a common healing art among Germans who settled in Pennsylvania.[3]

In August 1988, Katie Gingerich decided it was time Ed saw a doctor. When she mentioned this to her parents, Levi and Emma, they suggested a medical doctor who had offices in the nearby town of Waterford. Katie wasn't interested in this physician; she had already made an appointment with Dr. Merritt W. Terrell, a chiropractor who practiced out of a tiny, one-story house off Route 19 below the town of Cambridge Springs, fifteen miles south of Brownhill. Doc Terrell's office, marked only by an unpretentious sign nailed to a telephone pole along the highway that read DRUGLESS THERAPY, and fronted by a sprawling graveled parking lot, was easy to drive by without seeing. On a typical office day (Monday, Tuesday, and Thursday), the sixty-six-year-old folk doctor who stood five-foot-five in his cowboy boots, saw between forty and fifty patients. The energetic, fast-talking chiropractor with the close-cropped gray hair, square head, piercing blue eyes, and jogger's build, had a military bearing that radiated authority and confidence. Although his office was spartan and cramped and he never wore a tie or white coat, Doc Terrell was so certain of his ability to heal, his patients felt better the moment they stepped into his crowded waiting room. Referred to as the "Pennsylvania Doctor," Terrell treated hundreds of Amish patients from Michigan, Indiana, Ohio, New York, Pennsylvania, and Ontario.

The Amish, far from being put off or suspicious of Doc Terrell's simplistic, nonscientific method of treatment, actually appreciated the fact that he didn't shoot them up with drugs, expose them to X rays, make them pee into a jar, drain out their blood, remove their clothing, or subject them to all the other humiliating and embarrassing procedures regular doctors put one through. Compared with the typical medical doctor, Doc Terrell was a walk in the park.

Patients entered the office through what once had been the front door to a dwelling. The former living room had been turned into a waiting room and the receptionist sat behind a tiny desk in what used to be a hallway leading back to the bedrooms. The receptionist handed each patient a little slip of paper upon which he or she carefully wrote his or her name, date of birth, mailing address, and symptoms. Patients were treated in a little examination room on the other side of the hallway from the waiting room. The examination area was dominated by a leatherette lounge chair, the only piece of furniture in the room. As the patient settled into the big chair, Terrell disappeared behind a blue curtain that hung at the other end of the room. It was here that Doc Terrell fed the paper bearing the patient's name, birth date, address, and symptoms into an instrument the size of a small copy machine. Reacting to the slip of paper, the machine displayed a series of numbers or codes, which, upon interpretation, provided the appropriate diagnosis. The handwriting on the slip of paper revealed to the diagnosis machine what was wrong with the patient. By manipulating the patient's scalp, shoulder, neck, or toes, Doc Terrell administered the treatment. Having been treated, patients paid twenty-five dollars, picked up a jar of blackstrap molasses (to purify the blood), and walked out the door to the parking lot. This was the drill, three days a week from eleven in the morning to nine at night.[4]

Thanksgiving came and went, taking with it Katie's hope of a quick, drugless cure for Ed. If anything, after follow-up visits to Terrell in August, September, and December, Ed seemed to be getting worse. The toe pulling, foot rubbing, and blackstrap molasses didn't seem to be working.[5]

On March 21, 1989, four days after Katie's twenty-fifth birthday, she had another baby, a boy they named Enos, after one of Katie's younger brothers.

Because Ed wasn't carrying his weight at the sawmill, Noah and Henry Stutzman couldn't keep up with the business. This forced Mr. Gingerich to hire, as a full-time hand, twenty-two-year-old Emanuel Shetler, one of Katie's younger brothers. Emanuel, much like his sister and his mother, was tightly wound, intense, and bursting with energy. He was a reliable worker who made it possible for Noah to fill his orders on time. Unlike his sister and his parents, Emanuel didn't have much to say, keeping his thoughts and opinions to himself. Friendly but shy, particularly around the English, the tall, thin, bespectacled Amish man seldom smiled in public and seemed much too serious and mature for someone his age. He did not think much of his brother-in-law Ed, and gave him a wide berth, but never let on to Katie how he felt. It was none of his business.

As long as Ed stayed away from the sawmill, things ran smoothly. It was no secret among the millworkers that he wasn't living up to his role as a worker, husband, or father. They figured he was faking his illness to get out of work. But for now, everybody was minding their own business, keeping their low opinions of Ed to themselves. Still, rumors had drifted back to Bishop Shetler, who was keeping an eye on Ed. One false step and the bishop would move in. The bishop considered Ed a bad apple, and he was worried about the entire barrel.[6]

5

The New Sawmill

In August 1989, Ed hired a local English woman, who earned a few extra bucks driving the Amish to stores, bus stations, doctors' offices, and the like, to drive him about the region in search of standing timber he could purchase for the sawmill. Pulling her van up to the little gray house a few minutes early, the driver stuck her head in the door to say hello to Katie. She found Enos crying in the high chair, Danny fussing over something, and Ed in a foul mood because he had just found his favorite coffee cup in the dry sink beneath a pile of dirty dishes. He was complaining about having to wash his own cup. Embarrassed for Katie, the English woman retreated to the van. When Ed joined her a few minutes later, he was upbeat and apparently in high spirits. He had turned into a completely different person.[1]

• • •

Just before dark on Saturday, December 3, 1989, an English farmer, while driving his pickup west on Sturgis Road, saw, as he approached the Frisbeetown intersection, flames shooting wildly into the darkening sky. The blaze had erupted through the roof of the Gingerich sawmill. By the time the fire trucks got to the scene, it was too late to save the mill. Ed, Katie, and several members of the Gingerich family, along with their Amish neighbors and a dozen or so English residents, stood along the west side of Frisbeetown as the mill burned, collapsed, then quickly disappeared amid the dying flames and billowing smoke. Buried beneath the smoldering debris—charred wood and sections of twisted and partially melted tin roof—lay two saw blades, the deformed diesel engine, the log carriage, its tracks, and assorted bits and scraps of metal. The fire had reduced the mill to a huge, stinking pile of rubble. There was nothing to salvage. Mr. Gingerich was suddenly out of business and the Stutzman brothers and Emanuel Shetler were unemployed. Ed still had his machine shop, but without the mill, he didn't need it.

The cause of the fire was no mystery. On Saturday afternoon, just before closing shop for Sunday, Noah and Henry loaded the heating stove, a converted five-hundred-gallon fuel tank, with firewood. The idea was to keep the big, drafty structure warm until work resumed on Monday. The tank stove overheated the tin chimney, which set the rafters on fire. Chunks of burning wood dropped to the floor, igniting more wood. When the flames reached the oily rags and the diesel fuel, the fire, whipped up by the wind whistling through the cracks in the structure, kicked into high gear. In a matter of minutes, the building burst into a crimson ball of heat.[2]

Katie was pregnant again, seven months so, which meant the baby was due sometime toward the end of March. Ed did not consider this good news and relied on his illness to disguise his profound unhappiness over the prospect of a third child. Katie and Ed had been arguing over his promise to build them a bigger house to accommodate his growing family. Had he kept his word, they would have moved into the new house a year earlier. Mr. Gingerich had promised Ed a four-acre tract of land on the north side of Sturgis Road, a half mile east of the Frisbeetown intersection. Now that the sawmill was down, Ed would have plenty of time to build the new house. He had run out of excuses.

Without the sawmill, Ed was lost. It had been his anchor and the main justification for his beloved machine shop. The loss of the mill also meant there were no more English customers to horse around with. Ed was losing his identity, his purpose, and his refuge from Katie and the kids. Without the sawmill, he had no life, no future. He hated carpentry as much as farming; the last thing he wanted to do was build a new house.

Because the Amish do not believe in insurance, the sawmill had not been covered. Mr. Gingerich, if he were to build another mill, would have to do it from scratch with his own money. In January, Ed made it his mission to talk his father into building a new sawmill, one that Ed could design from top to bottom. The new plant could be constructed on the four-acre plot on Sturgis Road. This time, besides finding a safer way to heat the place, Ed would modernize the operation, increasing production and profit. Mr. Gingerich was not opposed to the idea; he had the money and the desire to start over. But before they could go any further, he would have to consult with Bishop Shetler. A project this big could not go forward without the bishop's blessing. Ed could barely contain his anger and frustration. What business did Rudy Shetler have in their sawmill?

The idea of a new sawmill did not offend Bishop Shetler's vision of the Brownhill community. Mr. Gingerich was given permission to build the mill as long as he agreed to hire Amish workers and not to make the operation too modern. Bishop Shetler knew of Ed's fascination with electricity and his obsession with modern mechanics, things forbidden by the *ordnung*. As long as the mill was truly Amish in construction and operation, it would enjoy the bishop's approval and support.[3]

Construction of the mill would get under way in the spring, which meant that Katie would have to wait another year for her new house. Notwithstanding Bishop Shetler's conditions restricting Ed's technology, the new operation would give Ed the chance to showcase his superior knowledge of sawmill and diesel mechanics. He'd design a fully automated plant where the logs would be mechanically loaded onto the sawing carriage and the sawdust would be hauled out of the plant on a conveyor belt. With the new five-foot saw blade, featuring three-inch, replaceable carbide-tipped teeth, Noah Stutzman would be able to make all kinds of cuts and rip into any size log. If a part broke or had to be replaced, Ed would be able to repair it or make a new cog in his new machine shop. Eventually, he'd acquire the knowledge and capacity to design and build his own diesel-powered engines. Together, the mill and the machine shop would be the envy of every person, Amish and English, who visited Ed's mechanical empire. Even Bishop Shetler would back off when he came to appreciate Ed's mechanical masterpiece and its contribution to the Brownhill settlement.

In the months leading up to the actual construction of the mill, Ed lived the life he had always dreamed of. He was a working mechanic, an entrepreneur, an inventor, and a man with a mission. He traveled western Pennsylvania in search of sawmill parts, equipment, ideas, and information. Suddenly he was healthy, robust, and bursting with energy. His appetite came back, the dizziness left, and took with it the back pain, skin problems, and the headaches.

Late in Katie's pregnancy, at a time when she needed Ed the most, he was gone. He had hired, to drive him around, a shy, quiet retiree named Lawrence Kimmy who lived with his wife, Pearl, on Miller's Station Road a few miles east of Cambridge Springs. Lawrence drove Ed to parts stores, junkyards, farm auctions, sawmills, and hardware stores in northwestern Pennsylvania and parts of New York. He rarely came home for supper and, on many occasions, didn't roll in until after midnight.[4]

On Tuesday evening, March 13, 1990, four days before her twenty-sixth birthday, Katie had the baby, a seven-pound girl she named Mary after her oldest sister and Ed's mother. Katie's mother, Emma, and her younger sisters Lydia and Lovina would help with little Danny, now two and a half, and Enos, who was almost one. Ed was too busy with the mill to pay much attention to the kids or worry about Katie, who, after being cooped up all winter in the gloomy little house, was exhausted and depressed.[5]

Of the four adult Gingerich brothers, Danny, the youngest at twenty-three and the closest to Ed, was still unmarried and living at home. That spring he moved to the Amish settlement near Conewango Valley, New York, where he rented a small farm and took up residence in the old house that sat on the land. He had moved to New York to be closer to Fannie Shetler, a distant cousin of Katie and Dan's future wife.[6]

Ed and Dan were a year and a half apart, had the same parents, and had been raised in the identical way in the same environment. Ed was self-possessed and independent, with English-like ambitions and tastes, while Dan put others first, was religious, and looked forward to starting a family and establishing his own farm. Ed had a cruel streak, liked to show off, and was not above whining, while his brother was kind, modest, and stoic. Dan was the kind of man who would make a fine husband and father. Ed was already a husband and father, and that was a shame.

6

The Sidekick

Mr. Gingerich hired Emanuel R. Hershberger, the thirty-year-old carpenter who was married to Katie's oldest sister, Mary, to head up the construction of the building that would house the new sawmill on Ed's four acres off Sturgis Road. Although Noah Stutzman, the head sawyer, was only seventeen, he had worked at the mill two and a half years (up until the fire) and now would help Emanuel Hershberger build a new plant, along with his sixteen-year-old brother, Henry, and Katie's younger brother Emanuel Shetler. Ed, having collected all of the mechanical parts he needed, including the diesel-powered engines, would supervise the assembly of the sawing equipment.[1]

In 1990, winter stuck around until March, so they couldn't start building until April. Mr. Gingerich wanted to help the Stutzman brothers and the two Emanuels put up the structure, but with Dan now living up in New York, he had too much work to do on the farm.

The unpainted, wooden building, a hundred and fifty feet long and twenty-five feet wide, ran parallel to Frisbeetown Road, with the open end—the loading-dock area—facing Sturgis. The loading dock, sixty-five feet back from the road, was accessed by a gravel driveway forming an upside-down U. On a sunny day, the mill's glistening steel roof could be seen shimmering in the valley from the top of Mackey Hill a mile west of the Frisbeetown-Sturgis intersection. The sun-sparkled roof marked the geographic and cultural heart of the Brownhill settlement.

Amish sawmills are not particularly complex mechanically. Beneath a maze of diesel-powered belts and pulleys that would have impressed Rube Goldberg, the logs are delivered to the cutting blade on a tiny-wheeled carriage that runs like a trolley on a pair of rails that stretch twelve feet across the cement floor. A second, smaller saw blade is used to cut off the ends of each log according to the desired length of the boards. Not unlike the loading, chambering, and ejection of a shell casing in a semiautomatic firearm, logs are mechanically loaded onto the carriage, pushed through the spinning blade, then slice by slice, ejected onto a pile. The by-product of this process, the sawdust, is ridden out of the building on a specially designed carrier belt. Although relatively low-tech, the operation requires high-powered motors, a complicated network of belts and pulleys, constant upkeep, and, on the cutting end of the process, precision.[2]

The new mill, with Noah Stutzman as the head sawyer, bookkeeper, payroll clerk, buyer, order taker, order filler, and maintenance chief, opened for business late that May. Emanuel Hershberger would stay on as a full-time mill employee. Once the mechanical bugs were worked out, Ed disengaged himself from the day-to-day operation of the plant. He worked in his machine shop, scouted for timber, sought out new business, searched for and purchased more sophisticated motors for the mill and the shop, and, when physically at the mill, schmoozed with the English customers. Mr. Gingerich was the official owner of the mill, but Ed, the entrepreneur, was a partner, sharing equally in the profits.

The mill employees, the people who actually performed the work, were paid every week by check, and in 1990 were earning four dollars an hour. Working an average fifty-hour week for pay that was all take-home money—nothing was withheld (income tax, workers' compensation

insurance, Social Security, or unemployment insurance)—
the mill hands considered these paychecks big. There were,
however, no English-style employment benefits such as
paid vacations, sick leave, health insurance, or overtime
pay. There was still no fire insurance on the plant; if the
plant went up in smoke, they would all be out of work
again. As bookkeeper and payroll clerk, Noah Stutzman
didn't have to bother with W-4s, W-2s, accountants, and
all the other complications and distractions that can make
running a business such a headache.[3]

The combination of Noah's skill as a sawyer and Ed's
well-designed equipment produced a lot of business that
summer at the mill on Sturgis Road. Ed took pride in the
fact that, unlike his softhearted father, no one took advantage of him in business. Customers paid his price or took
their business elsewhere, and when someone was a little
slow in paying what they owed Ed, particularly when they
were English, he'd send his older brother Joe to collect.[4]

Ed had been feeling so good physically he hadn't been
down to Cambridge Springs to see Doc Terrell in six
months, and he had no plans to do so.

Ed wanted, in the worse way, to buy a used pickup truck
and to install a telephone in the sawmill—just for business.
He was tired of hiring English drivers and using George
Brown's personal telephone all the time. The time it took
to make all the transportation arrangements and to run
down to George's house for the telephone was more than
just inconvenient—it was costing the mill business. Ed had
been to Amish sawmills all over the western half of Pennsylvania and most of them had telephones. Everywhere he
went, he saw Old-Order Amish men driving forklifts,
backhoes, and even bulldozers around the wood lots. What
was the harm of one telephone and one old truck?

Ed tried the idea out on Katie first and, when he hit a
brick wall with her, ran it past his dad, who, although a
bit more diplomatic, was just as opposed. It was thumbs
down all the way. "But I wouldn't be buying it for style,"

Ed argued, referring to the truck. "I'd never drive it for pleasure or on Sunday. I'd only use it for business or for emergencies." Regarding the need for a telephone: "Our customers would be able to call in their orders. It would be more convenient for them and bring in a lot more business for us. We could hire more Amish men." They weren't bad points, but it was still no dice.[5]

When Ed had ideas like this, it frightened Katie and kept her awake at night. She begged Ed not to let the bishop find out he was even thinking about such things. It bothered Mr. Gingerich as well; he was afraid if the bishop got wind of Ed's wild desires, Rudy Shetler might shut down the mill. Ed was getting carried away with himself—he was forgetting who he was, what he was. It didn't matter what they did in other Amish settlements and districts, in Brownhill, Rudy Shetler led the way, and Bishop Shetler would never allow an Amish man to own and drive a truck. The phone idea was just as absurd.[6]

At an Amish sawmill, the first stage of converting a big log into boards involves squaring it off. The four slabs of bark and underlying wood are then cut into various lengths and sold to the English, who burn it in their fireplaces. At the Gingerich mill, some of this so-called slab wood was also purchased by the Amish, who used it in their wood-burning cooking and heating stoves. It was the slab wood that brought a man named Jake Powers into Ed and Katie Gingerich's life.

Jake Powers was an unemployed ex-farmhand who lived with his father, Harold, on Gillette Street in Mill Village. Jake started coming to the sawmill that summer for the slab wood. The small, forty-six-year-old with the full, orange beard and freckled face and arms, made a few extra bucks selling the firewood, at a small profit, to the local English. He met Ed at a time when Ed was looking for a person he never thought he would find—someone who owned a pickup and wouldn't mind hanging around the mill every day so that whenever Ed needed a lift, he'd have a driver on the spot ready to go—and all for the price of the gasoline and a little oil. In Jake, Ed got all of this and more. He acquired a loyal friend and sidekick who helped out for nothing at the sawmill when he wasn't driving Ed around in his faded, red, 1981 Ford Ranger pickup. It was a match made in heaven.

Meanwhile, Ed and Katie continued to fight. Now that he had Jake, the truck issue wasn't as big, but he still fumed over being denied the telephone. Every time he went to George Brown's house to use his phone, Ed felt inferior, like a child asking an adult for permission to do something. He wasn't a child, he was a successful business operator, but because he happened to be Amish, he couldn't be trusted with his own telephone.

Katie and Ed were fighting about other things as well. It seemed Ed was never home, and when he was, he ignored her and the children. He simply refused to do any work around the house, which was in serious need of repair. He said he didn't want to waste his time fixing up the old place because he was going to build the family a new house. When Katie pressed him for a construction date, he'd lose his temper and stomp out of the house.[7]

In Jake's eyes, Ed and Katie and their beautiful children constituted the perfect family, a family blessed by God. They never fought or exchanged an angry word in his presence and gave no clue whatsoever that there were problems in the marriage. Katie didn't mind adding another plate for Jake when Ed invited him for dinner. In fact, she rather enjoyed his company. Jake was wonderful with the kids and even fixed a few things around the old house. He was also willing to run errands for her, such as picking things up at the grocery store.[8] She knew it wasn't Jake's fault that Ed was never around; Jake was just the driver.

Beware of Loggers with Bibles

Although the Amish keep to themselves and associate with their own kind, they are not completely isolated from the English world. Most of the non-Amish people they rub shoulders with are, like themselves, poorly educated, rural, blue-collar types who share interest in the practical, day-to-day things such as the weather, the price of groceries, and their children—not necessarily in that order. In Brownhill, most of the non-Amish men are farmers, factory workers, loggers, construction workers, carpenters, or truck drivers. The women are mostly housewives, part-time postal workers, nurses, beauticians, store clerks, school-bus drivers, and waitresses. Ed Gingerich, a well-read Amish man with an eighth-grade education and a self-taught trade, was no less erudite than most of his non-Amish neighbors, people he found just as boring as his fellow Amish. Ed rarely exchanged words with college-educated people—teachers, managers, ministers, lawyers, or other white-collar, professional types.

The Amish do have contact with certain elements of the white-collar, middle-class community—small town merchants, real-estate people, dentists, and medical doctors—but have no use for, and therefore rarely interact with, lawyers, reporters, politicians, business executives, psychologists, scientists, computer experts, and insurance people. The folks who populated Ed's world, even from his point of view, were not particularly stimulating, intellectually. Although the Amish do not live in walled enclaves, they would wall out, if they could, two classes of people—criminals and Bible-thumping evangelists. They are afraid of the evangelists.

Amish bishops and their ministers see themselves as shepherds protecting their flocks from evangelistic predators lurking at the edge of the forest ready to pick off sheep that have strayed from the herd.[1]

Bishop Rudy Shetler and Minister Dannie Gingerich had heard frightening stories of how certain evangelists had penetrated Amish settlements and converted, at big tent rallies, entire families. They viewed these people as religious fanatics—soldiers of the devil—whose ideas of God and sin challenged their theology and threatened the very existence of Amish culture. The Amish believe that sinners must be held accountable for their transgressions and that the Lord is forgiving, but only to a point. God also punishes, and to simply say, "I'm sorry" every time one sins is not the road to heaven. Born-again Christians, on the other hand, think that faith alone guarantees eternal life. The Amish, who believe getting into heaven requires faith *and* good works, scoff at the notion that faith alone will do the trick.[2] The Amish consider the evangelist message one of false hope—there is, in their view, no easy way, no shortcut to the promised land. To say otherwise is carrying water for the devil.

Bishop Shetler realized that most members of his congregation were devout Amish, impervious to the evangelical message. But he did worry about those on the margins—some of the younger members of the settlement going through their rebellious phase, and people like Ed Gingerich—moral slackers and spiritual backsliders who had trouble living up to the standards enunciated in the *ordnung*. The idea of guaranteed salvation—the easy road to heaven—would appeal to sinners looking for the easy way out. An Amish man like Ed drew evangelists the way spilled blood attracted sharks.

In August, Ed ran into a young English fellow named

David Lindsey who came to the sawmill with a truckload of logs to sell.[3] Dave made it obvious he was interested in the sawmill, which led to a guided tour in which Ed explained, in detail, how everything worked, including many of his own innovations and inventions. Dave was clearly and sincerely impressed and said so. He also had a lot of questions, confiding to Ed that one day, God willing, he would build his own sawmill in the Corry area. He said he wanted to own a business, be his own boss—like Ed.[4] Ed was obviously flattered to be seen in that light.

Although Dave lived among the Amish around nearby Spartansburg, Pennsylvania, he had never met an Amish man like Ed. Ed was friendly, knowledgeable about the English, interested in people, and certainly knew his way around machinery. For an Amish man, he was also well traveled. Dave was impressed by how many of the same people he and Ed had done business with. Realizing that Ed was proud of his mechanical skills, Dave asked him how he had come to know so much about motors, him being Amish and all. Did he learn it from his father? No, Ed said, his father was just a farmer and a minister. An English neighbor, a diesel mechanic on Frisbeetown Road, taught him a lot. He picked up the rest on his own by reading and visiting machine shops and sawmills in the region. Dave said that Ed must be a born mechanic, a natural. Ed agreed that this was a distinct possibility. That meant, Dave said, that Ed was doing just what God wanted him to do.[5]

Hoping that he wasn't being too inquisitive, Dave asked Ed what his bishop thought of him being so mechanically inclined and being the owner and operator of such a large and modern sawmill. Dave said the only reason he asked was because Rudy Shetler, among the Sparty Amish, had a reputation for being rather strict. Dave couldn't help wondering, if that were true, what Bishop Shetler thought of a man like Ed who read books and built fancy sawmills. Careful not to say too much, Ed said just enough to leave the impression that all was not as well as it should be between him and the bishop.

Before Dave pulled away that day in his empty truck, he asked Ed if he could stop by the following week, you know, just to talk. "Sure," Ed said, "anytime."

"If you don't mind," Dave ventured, "I'd like to talk about something that changed my life; something wonderful."

"Sure."

"It's about Jesus; accepting Him as your personal Lord and Savior."

"All right," Ed replied. His response was not enthusiastic, but it wasn't tinged with disgust either. "I'll see you next week."[6]

David Lindsey, the Spartansburg logger, was a born-again Christian, an evangelist and self-described missionary to the Amish. A member of the Bible Believers' Baptist Church in Corry, Pennsylvania, he was convinced that he had been called upon by God to rescue Amish men, women, and children from what he called the "bishop's cult."[7] Dave believed that Amish people, like heathens in the darkest jungles of Africa and South America, were destined for eternal damnation unless someone brought Jesus into their lives and showed them the way to salvation. Lindsey liked and respected Amish people; they were decent, God-fearing folks who deserved his concern and attention. It was tragic, in his view, how these poor, ignorant people were blindly following their religious leaders down a road to hell. Rather than worship power-hungry bishops who controlled their minds and souls, Amish people had to break free so they could discover Jesus Christ, the one who had died for their sins. Dave would begin his Brownhill crusade by slowly and carefully bringing his new Amish friend closer to Jesus. Once he converted Ed, others would follow. Once he broke the bishop's grip, everything was possible. Dave saw himself as a behind-the-lines commando in a holy war.[8]

A few days after their first meeting, late on a Monday afternoon, Dave Lindsey pulled into the Gingerich mill behind the wheel of his car. This time he brought his Bible. Ed happened to be there, saw him drive up, and walked over to the car. "Do you have time to talk?" Lindsey asked through the rolled-down window.

"Sure," Ed said, sliding into the car. "What do you want to talk about?"

"Would you mind if we talk about Jesus?"

"No," Ed replied.

Dave scanned Ed's face for signs of discomfort, embarrassment, or disgust and saw nothing but an Amish man sweating in the August heat. If Ed was uncomfortable with Dave, he certainly didn't show it. Dave started off by telling Ed how finding Jesus had changed his life for the better. As he spoke, he observed Ed closely to see how he was reacting to his message, hoping for a slight nod in the affirmative or maybe a brightening of the eyes. Ed remained deadpan, neutral. But he listened and Dave kept talking, preaching. Dave zeroed in on the Amish: "You know, Ed, Amish bishops don't have all the answers. They don't tell you everything; it's better for them to keep their followers in the dark about some very important things. Did you know that?"

Ed turned to Dave and looked him square in the face. Dave had obviously sparked his interest. "I didn't know that," he said.

"Well, it's true," Dave replied. "There are spiritual truths the bishops don't want you to know, because if you did know these things, you would know you didn't need *them*."

"What truths?" Ed asked.

"Guaranteed salvation," Dave replied. He let those two important words sink in for a moment, then continued: "The very second, the moment you accept Jesus Christ into your heart—as your personal Lord and Savior—you are *guaranteed* eternal salvation. The message is simple, Jesus loves *you*."

Ed thought that over for a few seconds, then asked, "What if you had been bad?"

"Well, that doesn't matter, Ed. You know why?"

"No."

"Because, Ed, Jesus died for *your* sins. Bishop Shetler did not sacrifice himself on the cross for you. He cannot forgive your sins; that's what you're not supposed to know. That is why he's afraid people like me will tell you the good news—if you accept Jesus Christ, it doesn't matter what the bishop says or does. Now do you understand why the bishop wants to keep you in the dark?"

"I guess."

"Tell me if I'm right—if you disobey the bishop, you can be thrown out of the Amish church. That means no heaven for you until the bishop takes you back. Right?"

"Yes."

"What I'm trying to tell you, Ed, is that Rudy Shetler is just a man, his rules don't matter. He is not Jesus Christ. As long as you are Amish, your spirit will not be free; you will be cut off from Jesus, your only hope. You are being controlled by the leader of a cult."

"But Rudy Shetler is a man of God, ordained."

"That's what he wants you to believe. Ed, if Rudy Shelter doesn't accept Jesus Christ as *his* Lord and Savior, *he's* not going to heaven; he will not be saved. He is just a man, like you and me."

Ed looked a bit startled; it must have been the vision of Rudy Shetler burning in hell. "How do you know these things?" he asked, emerging from his thoughts.

"It says so in the Bible," Dave said. "Do you believe in the Bible?"

"Of course," Ed replied. "I was brought up on the Bible. But I don't remember anything in the Bible about what you've been saying. All Amish people believe in the Bible."

Dave was a bit worried he had pushed too hard, gone too far. It was good he had drawn Ed into the conversation, but he didn't want to risk offending him. Amish people weren't stupid, just misled. "I have great respect for the Amish people," Dave said. "I'm only critical of the bishop, and I don't mean it personally. I'm sure Rudy Shetler is a fine man."

"You've given me a lot to think about," Ed replied.[9]

A week later, in midafternoon, Dave returned to the mill with Bible in hand to pick up where he had left off. Ed made no effort to hide the fact that he was glad to see him. This time the two men gathered in the sweltering machine shop, where they wouldn't be seen by Katie or the millworkers. "Listen to this," Dave said, opening his Bible to a place he had marked. " 'These things have I written unto you that believe on the name of the Son of God; that ye may know that ye have eternal life, and that ye may believe on the name of the son of God.' " Dave slammed the Bible shut and said, "There it is—proof that you are guaranteed salvation the moment you accept Jesus Christ as your Lord and Savior. It's right in the Bible, Ed."

"What verse is that?" Ed asked.

"It's John, five: thirteen. 'That ye may *know* that ye have eternal life,' " Dave said. "That is your guarantee. All you need to have, Ed, is *faith*! If you love God, if you accept Jesus, everything will be fine. God will not forsake you, Ed." In the hazy half-light of the machine shop, Dave could see, by the stunned look on Ed's face, that he had been affected by that piece of Scripture.

"I've never heard that verse before," Ed said.

"I'm not surprised," Dave replied. "Like I said before, your bishop isn't telling you everything. You have not been told the full story. Now do you believe me when I say that?"

"I'm not sure what to believe," Ed said. "This has me thinking."

"He died for you, Ed, Jesus did. That's what you have to believe. Once that happens, everything will be all right."[10]

Summer finally got tired of itself and turned into fall. Dave and Ed had been holding clandestine religious meetings at least once a week, in Ed's machine shop. October was approaching and Ed, although he had not officially declared Jesus as his Lord and Savior, had at least come around to the idea that the Amish might not have all the answers—that their way might not be the way to heaven. It was a disturbing yet exhilarating thought—an idea that played on his mind night and day. He wanted to talk to his father about this in the worst way, to confront him with that verse in John—"that ye may *know* that ye have eternal life"—and see if he had an answer to that. Bringing Dave's theology to his father's attention was out of the question. Ed couldn't risk exposing Dave to the Brownhill Amish. If that happened, Dave would be banned from the sawmill, and Ed would lose a friend and any hope of bringing to an end the war that had been raging inside him since youth—living the good Amish life and going to heaven versus pursuing the life Ed wanted to live and going to hell. Dave Lindsey was telling him that he was no more a sinner than Rudy Shetler, that his sins would be forgiven. According to Dave, if he simply accepted Jesus, he would be free to live his own life, not the bishop's way of life— and he, not the bishop, would go to heaven! This concept was so wild, subversive, and liberating, so frightening in its implications, that Ed felt pressured to make a life-changing decision, and this created more than a little anxiety. He had been thinking about leaving the Amish for years, but running out on his wife and three children, and disgracing the rest of his family, would take more strength and resolve than he could muster. Katie would never leave the Amish, never. Dave Lindsey had given him hope, but unless Ed could somehow take advantage of it in his own life, hope would turn into despair. Dave Lindsey had made life for Ed Gingerich a lot more complicated.

Ed was the bomb, hope was the fuse, and Dave Lindsey, although he had no way of knowing it, was the flame.

8

The Hard Sell

Dave Lindsey, in helping Ed find and accept Jesus Christ, had to undo a lifetime of Amish indoctrination. Sometimes converting a total nonbeliever was painstaking and difficult, but completely altering a man's belief system, pulling him out of his close-knit community, his church, and his family, was the toughest assignment an evangelist could draw. Thinking he was just one voice against a choir of Amish solidarity, Dave had decided to recruit Lazar LeMajic, a friend and fellow warrior in the battle for souls.

Bringing Lazar LeMajic into the picture was a bold but risky move. The sixty-five-year-old Serb, an ex-Yugoslav, was a Bible-spouting firebrand who came across to some as a Jesus freak. A friendly nod or mere eye contact might start Lazar preaching to a total stranger.

Throwing Lazar into the fray created a dilemma. To close the deal with Ed, Dave needed the urgency of Lazar's born-again pitch. In going for the conversion, Dave and Lazar would play the missionary's version of good cop, bad cop, only in their case it would be soft sale, hard sale. However, in letting Lazar loose among the Brownhill

Amish and siccing him on Ed, Dave risked turning Ed away and setting off evangelist alarms throughout the community. Acquiring Lazar's promise to go easy, at least at first, was a little like asking a henhouse fox to eat only one chicken. Lazar had promised Dave he would come on slow and follow Dave's lead until he established his own solid relationship with Ed.[1]

Besides being older and more experienced, forceful and charismatic, Lazar had another advantage over Dave in the quest for Ed's soul. He was an accomplished machinist and diesel mechanic who shared Ed's interest in motors. In preparing Ed for Lazar, Dave would emphasize this side of his friend and point out that Lazar could help Ed upgrade and expand his machine shop. Before unleashing Lazar, Dave would lay the groundwork carefully.[2]

On the last Friday in September, following a brief, late-afternoon Bible session in Ed's machine shop, Dave asked Ed if he wouldn't mind meeting an unusual but interesting man who talked fast and had a foreign accent. "Where is he from?" Ed asked.

"Yugoslavia. He's been here sixteen years and is an American citizen. He's very big on America. He's also a born-again Christian who goes to the First Baptist Church in Corry. I thought you might like to meet him 'cause he's a mechanic like you."

"Bring him over," Ed said.

"He speaks nine languages and was in prison under the Communists. He's sold real estate, was a textile broker, a butcher, and a bookkeeper before he became a machinist and a diesel mechanic. So it's okay?"

"Yeah."

"I'll warn you about his hand—he was cleaning a machine in a Communist sausage factory in Belgrade and had his fingers cut off. He's got a thumb and half a pinkie. So you know."

"You gotta be careful," Ed said.

"It doesn't hold him back; he can do anything. He just

retired from a big machine shop in Corry. I thought maybe you'd like to meet him."

"Sure."

"He loves to talk about Jesus, I'll warn you about that; he loves Jesus. He knows a lot about motors, too."

"I'd like to meet that feller."[3]

On Wednesday, October 3, on a sunny, unseasonably warm afternoon, Dave Lindsey pulled up the driveway that led to the sawmill with Lazar LeMajic in the car. Ed must have seen them coming because he walked out from behind a log pile to greet them. Dave's passenger, a stocky man with coal-black hair streaked with gray, scrambled out of the car and stuck out his two-fingered hand. "Ed," Dave said, "meet Lazar LeMajic." The two men shook hands.

Although he had seen it before, Dave tagged along as Ed gave Lazar a tour of the sawmill and machine shop. Lazar had seen Amish people out and about in their buggies and occasionally in a store, but he had yet to actually meet one. Dave had told Lazar a lot about Ed, including his interest in motors and how outgoing he was in personality. Still, Lazar was caught off guard by Ed's friendliness and his knowledge of machines.

Just before the three men parted company that afternoon, Lazar, in a small way, broke his promise not to preach. He simply had to let Ed know that his love of Jesus was the dominating force in his life, that he wanted others to share in that joy, and hoped that someday he and Ed would be brothers in Christ. In Lazar's mind, this was hardly preaching—just passing on the good news. Much to Dave's relief, Ed took the news in stride and made a point of inviting Lazar back to the mill. He and Lazar had a lot more to talk about, and there was a big motor Ed was thinking of buying but would now wait until Lazar had a chance to look it over. Lazar said he would be more than happy to do that and offered to drive Ed to the place where the motor was being sold. Lazar looked forward to advising Ed on such matters and helping him in his shop.

Dave Lindsey drove away from the mill that day feeling optimistic about his chances of delivering Ed to Christ. Lazar figured that it was almost a sure thing.[4]

Katie had no idea Ed was discussing religion with a pair of outsiders. She was accustomed to seeing Ed talking to English people around the mill and the machine shop, therefore, she had no reason to suspect he was the target of an evangelistic attack. Ed's parents, his brothers, and the men who worked at the sawmill were in the dark as well. Even Jake Powers, Ed's daily companion, didn't realize what was going on. Why should he? Dave Lindsey sold logs and the older guy who talked funny was a diesel mechanic helping Ed at the machine shop.

Another summer had slipped by and Katie wasn't looking forward to a freezing winter cooped up in the little gray house with the children. Mary, the baby, was now seven months old, Enos was two, and Danny, three. If Ed had kept his promise, she and the kids would be spending the coming winter in their new house. Ed's principal interest, however, did not include improving his living quarters, his relationship with his wife, or helping out with the children. He spent all of his time and energy building up the machine shop, which meant traveling around the area in Jake's truck looking for motors and engine parts. Most evenings he'd come home late for dinner and expect Katie, exhausted from a long day of housework and children wrangling, to put another meal on the table. Occasionally Katie would go along, but most of the time she'd tell him that if he wanted to eat, he'd have to feed himself.[5] Whenever that happened, there would be angry words, after which Ed would stomp off to bed and sulk. The problems in the kitchen had spread to their bedroom, where nothing had happened sexually for over a year. When a healthy young Amish man quits having sex with his wife, the wife may wonder if he's getting it elsewhere. Ed's nonperformance caused Katie to wonder if Ed was fooling around with an English woman.[6] She accused him of this and he denied it. So, Katie wanted to know, what was the problem? Ed had a simple but devastating answer: the last thing on earth he wanted was another baby.[7]

The good health Ed had been enjoying began to slip away that fall. He had picked up an earache he couldn't shake and his skin started itching again. At night, agitated by these physical ailments and visions of religious rebellion, rebirth, and redemption (ideas planted in his head by the evangelists), he had trouble getting a good night's sleep.

A few days after giving Lazar LeMajic the guided tour, Ed twisted his weak ankle and started limping again. Katie noticed this and, with Ed's unenthusiastic approval, arranged an appointment with Doc Terrell on Thursday, the eleventh of October.

Doc Terrell looked at Ed's ear, fondled his sore ankle, and to cure his other ailments (including the itchy skin) prescribed blackstrap molasses.[8]

During the winter months of 1991, Ed split his time between the machine shop and the sawmill. Dave Lindsey stopped by from time to time with logs and Lazar LeMajic regularly visited the machine shop, where Ed was converting two large motors from electric to diesel and kerosene power, an ambitious project, which required a degree of skill and inventiveness that impressed even Lazar. In February, Ed enlarged the capacity of his machine shop by spending several thousand dollars on the purchase of a surface grinder, a one-ton Bridgeport drill press, and a heavy grinder. He now had the equipment to grind, cut, and drill virtually anything, which meant he could manufacture any part he needed for the sawmill, the machine shop, or an outside customer.[9] Overcoming the technological limitations created by the Amish prohibition on electricity had made Ed a determined and innovative mechanic. Single-handedly he had designed and built, in the middle of nowhere, under the bishop's nose, a state-of-the-art machine shop, and he had done it without violating the letter of Amish law. Lazar considered Ed mechanically gifted and he told him so.

In the dead of winter, farmers spend a lot more of their time indoors working in barns, garages, and sheds. Since there isn't much going on outdoors, most farms look as though they've been shut down for the season. This is appearance only; farmwork doesn't stop in the winter, it's just hidden from public view. During the winter of '91, Lazar and Ed spent hour after hour talking to each other inside the machine shop, away from others, and out of sight. Given the topic of their discussions, this was how they wanted it.

9

The Reluctant Witness

That March, Katie, having waited all winter to start her garden, had asked Ed a dozen times to plow up a patch of ground out behind the house. Ed, still spending most of his time in the machine shop or out and about with Jake Powers, said he'd do it, but he didn't. To get her peas and onions in, Katie had dug up part of the garden by hand. Finally, on a Saturday afternoon in mid-April, Ed asked Jake to hitch one of the buggy horses to the garden plow. Ed didn't care one way or the other about Katie's garden; he made enough money to buy all the vegetables they could eat. But Katie wanted her garden and Ed wanted Katie off his back. She'd nag him to death if he didn't get out that plow and make her a garden. Katie, with hoe in hand, looked on as Ed, walking behind the plow, and Jake leading the horse, turned over the soil. They had just gotten under way when Katie yelled, "Stop!" Ed was plowing up a row of her peas!

Realizing what he had done, Ed said, "Well, we sure took care of those!" He looked at Katie and laughed as though taking pleasure in her concern over the destruction of her plants. Flushed with rage, Katie walked up to husband and, without warning, hit him across the chest with the handle of her hoe. More startled than hurt, Ed, in one continuous motion, yanked the garden tool out of her grip and backhanded her across the face. It was a lightning-quick move that knocked her off her feet and sent her sprawling awkwardly to the ground. Katie landed on her back with her dress above her knees and her lawn cap askew. Perhaps worried that someone would see her lying punched out on the ground, she scrambled to her feet and adjusted her cap, brushing the debris off her dress. Ed made no effort to help her and showed no concern over her condition. Fighting to maintain her dignity, Katie half staggered to the hoe, picked it up, and started back to where she had been gardening. As she mechanically hacked the soil between the row of onions, Ed took hold of the plow. Jake, shocked and dazed by what he had just witnessed, numbly grabbed the bridle and resumed leading the horse. They had been turning the soil less than a minute when Jake saw Katie drop the hoe and stumble toward the house. Jake sneaked a glance at Ed to see if he'd taken notice of her departure. Instead of catching Ed looking in Katie's direction, the two men, for a split second, locked eyes. Jake instantly turned his face away from Ed, hoping that his expression hadn't given him away. The plowing continued as though nothing had happened, as though Katie didn't exist.[1]

Jake grappled in vain for an explanation, an understanding that would in some way mitigate what he had just seen. But there was nothing to contemplate other than the fact that his best friend, a man he admired, had just swatted his wife like a mosquito. Ed's apparent disinterest in his wife's physical and emotional condition seemed to rule out any chance that he had involuntarily struck back after being hit with a hoe. If this had been the case, Ed would have immediately helped Katie to her feet, showing concern that he had hurt her. He would have begged her for forgiveness. He would have forgotten Jake and the garden and followed Katie into the house. Ed didn't do any of those things.

Ed didn't say a word as the two men and the horse plowed Katie's garden. Minutes crawled by like hours and finally, after a half hour or so had passed, Ed calmly announced that they had done enough. He thanked Jake for helping out and said he'd see to the horse and take care of the plow. Jake let go of the bridle, said good-bye, and, without looking at Ed, headed straight for the sawmill, where he had parked his truck. He didn't look back.

On Monday, at eight in the morning, Jake, as always, rolled up to the mill in his pickup truck. The Stutzman brothers and the two Emanuels were already hard at work. Ed wasn't around. To calm his nerves and to look busy, Jake grabbed a broom and started sweeping loose sawdust out from beneath the big blade. An hour passed and the mill had come to life: some English guy was putting in an order with Noah and another man was pulling up the driveway in a pickup truck. Another hour slipped by and Jake began to think that perhaps Ed was working in his machine shop. He walked outside to see if Lazar LeMajic's truck was parked in the area when he heard Ed speaking to one of two English fellows. Ed spotted Jake and waved him over to meet the English customer.

An hour later, Jake was in his truck with Ed at his side. They were happily on their way to scout some timber on some plot of land on the other side of Spartansburg, where they stopped for lunch at an eatery that featured Amish-style country cooking.[2]

10

Alone and Abandoned

J ake Powers had known Delberta "Debbie" Williams most of her life; Ed had known her since 1985, roughly two years after he and his family moved to Brownhill. When they first met, Ed was twenty, single, and contemplating not being Amish. Debbie Williams was thirty-two, married to a carpenter, and working as a private-duty nurse. Compared with Debbie, Ed was young, unworldly, and naïve. Since Amish men almost never establish one-on-one relationships with English women, their friendship, if not odd, was unique.

Ed's marriage to Katie and the subsequent period of his good behavior meant no more Debbie Williams beyond occasionally talking to her at the sawmill in the presence of her husband, Hank. It was common knowledge, however, that English women who came to the sawmill, either alone or with their husbands, found Ed attractive. Ed was outgoing and friendly and, with some of the English gals, country-boy charming to the point of being flirtatious.[1] Most of these women hadn't been flirted with in years, some of them never. Therefore, having an Amish man, of all people, paying attention to them was flattering and appreciated.

Debbie Williams, now a buxom thirty-nine-year-old with a head of wavy, gray hair, a red Jeep Cherokee, and an adopted ten-year-old son, lived with her husband, Hank, in a low-slung house on Mackey Hill Road between Mill Village and Ed's place. No longer a private-duty nurse,

Debbie was working at the hospital in Union City. Coincidence or not, she had slipped back into Ed's life at a time when his marriage to Katie was more of a living arrangement than an intimate and loving relationship.

That spring, Debbie started showing up at the mill without Hank and without any apparent reason other than to visit Ed. Ed didn't work regular hours at the sawmill, yet Debbie, behind the wheel of her red Jeep, only rolled up the driveway when Ed was there. This frequently observed occurrence fueled speculation by Jake and the Amish mill hands that these visits were prearranged. Debbie would park the Jeep at the top of the circle then wait for Ed, who'd open the door and climb into the passenger seat. Sometimes they'd just sit in the vehicle an hour or so and talk; on other occasions, she'd drive off with him. A couple of hours later, in the middle of the day, Debbie would bring Ed back to the mill, drop him off, then leave. All of this took place in the open, but far enough from the little gray house to be out of Katie's view. Ed never bothered to explain Debbie's visits but occasionally referred to Debbie as the family nurse.[2]

Debbie and Ed shared a friend in Richard Zimmer, the ex-marine who owned the house and cattle farm next to Mr. Gingerich's spread. Debbie's long-standing friendship with Zimmer centered around her love of horses and the fact that Zimmer bought, sold, and raised them. Most Wednesday nights, she could be found at the livestock auction at Thomases Corners, on Route 98, fifteen miles south of Mill Village. On Mondays, she could be seen looking at horses at the auction barn just north of Union City, not far from the Sugar and Spice Restaurant. Most of the time she didn't get back from these auctions until after midnight, and on many occasions, she was with Ed.[3] On the nights Ed came home past twelve, he'd find Katie in a very bad mood.[4] Sometimes they'd fight all night, waking up the children. At dawn, Katie would begin a long, hard day of chores and Ed would go to bed and sleep until she served dinner. After supper, he'd go out to the machine shop and work late into the night.[5]

Although Katie had maintained a close relationship with her family, particularly with her mother, she had not burdened them with her marital problems except to occasionally gripe about Ed's laziness around the house and his broken promises to build them a new place next to the sawmill. Anyway, her mother had more important things to worry about than one of her daughters' marriage problems. That spring, everybody was worried about Katie's eleven-month-old niece, Mary. Mary was the daughter of Andy Shetler, Katie's twenty-two-year-old brother, who lived in his parents' basement with his wife, Susie, and their other child, a two-year-old boy named Levi. Susceptible to high fever, dehydration, and respiratory problems, the baby had never been healthy. The doctors in Erie had been unable to make her well, and on May 25, 1991, following several stints in the hospital, little Mary died. One of the doctors told Andy Shetler that his daughter had an enlarged heart; there was nothing they could do to save her. They held the funeral at Levi and Emma's house and buried the baby in a tiny pine box in the Frisbeetown Cemetery, an Amish burial ground situated on a knoll overlooking a swamp a mile or so northwest of the Gingerich house. The baby joined an old man and two young women, the only other occupants of the plot.[6]

Katie lived for springtime and the beginning of summer, when she and the kids could escape the house and work and play outdoors. She loved her garden, the back-porch visits at her parents' house, and the lengthening days. (The Amish do not observe daylight savings time.) This year, however, the coming of summer was not enough to lift her spirits. She was married to a man who hated her so much he refused to have sex with her because he didn't want her to give birth to another child.[7] She was living with an Amish husband who stayed out late with an English woman and got angry when she asked him what he did

with this woman in the middle of the night. Katie had a
husband who hit her and, worse, ignored his own children.
There was no one to confide in and no one who could
help. She carried her burden alone, wearing her happy
mask and slowly but surely losing hope that her life would
get better. The death of little Mary was almost more than
she could take. She had somehow failed as a wife, but not
as a mother. *Her* life might be over, but the children's were
just starting. She would live for them and try not to give
up on Ed, because without him, she had no future.

11

Evangelists at the Gate

Dave Lindsey hadn't talked to Ed for several weeks.
On a hot Saturday afternoon in July, he was speeding
along Sturgis Road in front of a three-hundred-foot dust
cloud that drifted westward into the shoulder-high corn.
Ed wasn't around the sawmill, so Dave drove to the little
gray house, where he caught Ed walking across Frisbeetown Road toward his father's barn. Dave pulled onto the
grass in front of the barn then got out of his car to greet
Ed, who seemed happy to see him. Ed was going to his
father's to help him put up some hay.

Realizing that he had stumbled upon the opportunity to
meet Ed's father, the Brownhill minister, Dave offered to
give Ed a hand. Ed seemed hesitant at first, but when Dave
promised not to bring up Jesus, he accepted the offer.

Ed introduced Dave to his father as a logger who did
business with the sawmill. Mr. Gingerich said he certainly
appreciated the help and, after the hay had been stored

away, asked Dave to stick around for a glass of iced tea. Although he hadn't stopped talking all afternoon as they forked the hay from the wagons into the barn, Dave had kept his promise not to bring up religion. But now, as the three men relaxed in the shade around a pitcher of tea, Dave, having established a little rapport with Mr. Gingerich, mentioned how important Jesus was to him in his daily life. Wasn't it a wonderful thing to believe in Jesus? Unaccustomed to hearing a stranger utter Christ's name out loud in ordinary conversation, Mr. Gingerich, having no argument against believing in Jesus, agreed. Already, Ed was feeling a little uneasy and tried to change the subject. But Dave, curious to know if an Amish minister was aware that eternal salvation was *guaranteed* in the Bible, pressed on. Dave was also eager to prove a point in front of Ed— that Amish ministers were quite uninformed about the word of God and downright wrong in their theology. So, much to Ed's discomfort, Dave asked Mr. Gingerich point-blank if he had ever read chapter five, verse thirteen from the Book of John. The question obviously stunned Mr. Gingerich, who had never, at least as an adult, been quizzed on the Bible. This otherwise very nice English fellow, someone he hardly knew, for reasons Mr. Gingerich couldn't begin to understand, seemed to be challenging his authority as an ordained minister. It was not Mr. Gingerich's way to argue religion with a stranger.

"I was just wondering," Dave said "if you accepted that passage as guaranteeing salvation on faith alone."

Mr. Gingerich, at a loss for words, just stared blankly into Dave's smiling face. Religion was simply not a subject one argued about—it was too personal, too private— besides what was there to debate? If a man believed in something, why would someone try to get him to believe in something else?

"I think we best be getting back to the mill," Ed said, climbing to his feet.

Dave got up as well and extended his hand to Mr. Gingerich, who shook it. "It was nice meeting you, sir," he said in his upbeat way.

"Thanks for helping with the hay," Mr. Gingerich replied, after a slight hesitation.[1]

Dave drove Ed over to the sawmill, which was now closed for the weekend. He rolled up the driveway and stopped in the crescent near the loading dock, leaving the motor running and the air conditioner on. The inside of the car smelled of hay. Ed hadn't spoken since he climbed into the car and Dave hoped he wasn't angry. Maybe it had been a mistake asking Mr. Gingerich about that verse in John. "I hope I didn't offend your father," Dave said. "It's hard for me not to talk about the Bible. I don't see what's wrong with that, do you?"

"No," Ed replied.

"Why can't people talk about the most important thing there is?"

Ed asked, "What is that verse again?"

"Verse thirteen, chapter five."

"What does it say?"

" 'These things have I written unto you that believe on the name of the Son of God; that ye may know that ye have eternal life, and that ye may believe on the name of the Son of God.' These are the words that the bishop does not want you to hear. We've talked about this before. I know that you and Lazar have, too. I didn't want to show up your father; I was just trying to make a point. Are you mad?"

"No."

"There are hundreds of religions, all of them based on the Bible, their own *versions* of the Bible. The Amish and the Catholics believe that the bishop and the priest can forgive your sins. To get to God, you have to go through them. That's wrong; the Bible doesn't say that, but that's how they interpret it. That's how all religions are; they only use certain parts of the Bible. They either ignore or cut out the parts they don't like, parts that don't serve their purpose."

"What purpose?'

"To control you, to make themselves God. Your bishop doesn't study or even know about the *entire* Bible. He only knows what he's been taught, and he doesn't want you or anyone else making religious discoveries or decisions on your own. He wants to control your life; he needs you to depend on *him,* not Jesus. He doesn't want you reading verse thirteen in John, chapter five—no way. I don't think your father even knows about it. Have you ever heard of it in your church?"

"I don't think so, but I don't always listen."

"That's not your fault," Dave said. "I know that verse has not been read in your church because Bishop Shetler doesn't want anyone to believe they can get into heaven without *his* blessing. Right?"

"I don't know; you got me thinking."

"Ed, there is only one way to talk to God—one-on-one, no go-betweens. You have a direct line; you don't need to go through a Catholic priest or an Amish bishop."

"We can pray," Ed said.

"Yes, but in your faith you can't pray your way through the narrow gates of heaven without the bishop's blessing. Look, the fact is, God doesn't keep a balance sheet—surpluses of good deeds and sacrifices don't amount to a hill of beans in *His* ledger."

"Then how do you get into heaven?"

"That's easy—it's right in the Bible—*'Ye must be born again.'* It's as simple as that."

"I don't know what that means."

"It means, Ed, falling to your knees and begging God to forgive your sins, great and small. Being born again comes with renunciation of the old way of life, wiping the slate clean, a fresh start. You are born again, so to speak. It is the *only* way to save your soul. The only way."

"What happens if you're not born again?"

"You know what happens—eternal damnation—you go to hell."

"Are you sure?" Ed looked worried.

"Ed, read your Bible. If I didn't know this to be true, I wouldn't be going through all this trouble trying to save your soul. I don't want you spending eternity in hell! This is the biggest decision in your life."

"Yeah," Ed replied, almost as a sigh. "I best be getting home for supper."

The following day, at a family get-together after church at the Gingerich house, Mr. Gingerich pulled Ed aside and asked him about that English fellow who gave them a hand putting up the hay. What prompted that feller to start talking about some verse in the Bible? Why would he be asking a man he had just met if he had read a certain passage out of the Good Book? Was this man a preacher of some sort; had he and Ed been discussing religion?[2]

Dave Lindsey, Ed explained, was just a logger he knew from the sawmill. He was a nice guy, one of those English people who were curious about the Amish. He meant no harm.[3]

Early one evening in August, on one of those endless summer days, Dave Lindsey swung through Brownhill on the chance he'd catch Ed at home with Katie. It would be the first time he'd seen Ed since they gave Mr. Gingerich a hand with the hay. The moment Dave turned north onto Frisbeetown from Sturgis Road, Dave saw them—Ed and Katie—on their front porch. The two boys, little Danny and Enos, were playing out in the yard. Dave parked his car in front of Mr. Gingerich's red barn and walked across the hard, dusty road toward the little gray house. Ed and Katie were sitting on the front steps cleaning the fish Katie had caught out of her parents' pond that afternoon. Always eager to help, Dave found a place on the steps, picked up a knife lying nearby, and reached into the bucket for a bluegill.

Katie put the clean fish on ice, disposed of their heads,

scales, and guts, splashed a couple of buckets of water on the porch, and poured three glasses of lemonade. Dave, sitting in one of the Amish-made rocking chairs, sipped his drink and watched the Gingerich kids chase each other around the yard.

Since Ed had merely introduced him to Katie as a logger who sold logs to the mill, Dave decided to break the ice by providing a little more information about himself. Aware that Amish women were usually not included in the conversation when men got together to talk, Dave spoke directly to her when he said he was building a new sawmill in Corry. When Katie didn't respond, he added that Corry was also the place where he attended the Bible Believers' Baptist Church. Had she heard of it?

Katie said that she hadn't.

"I'm a lucky guy," Dave said, "since I found the Lord through Jesus. So many people lead a godless life when they don't have to. All they have to do is ask God to forgive their sins—once they accept Jesus Christ as their Lord and Savior, they are *saved*. It's so simple; it's right there in the Bible."[4]

Katie's suspicion that Ed had been secretly discussing religion with an English person was now a frightening reality. She couldn't complain to the bishop because Ed would simply deny doing anything wrong. If he admitted that he had found another religion or was even flirting with the idea, Bishop Shetler might excommunicate him. Where would that leave Katie and the children? Not wanting to burden her parents with her problems with Ed, Katie had nowhere to turn. If there was a way to keep Ed from leaving the faith, or being thrown out, and also save their deteriorating marriage, she would have to find it on her own. She was up against the lure of the English world, a quick and easy religious fix, and an anger, directed at her, that bubbled up and out of Ed like flaming lava. What had she done to deserve his hate? What could she do to make things right?

12

New Home, Old Problems

Four months had passed since Ed slapped Katie to the ground in front of Jake Powers. There wasn't much left of the garden they had been plowing that day, just her pumpkins and a handful of late, pathetic-looking tomatoes. It hadn't rained in weeks and everything looked brown, shabby, and dead. Following the hitting incident, Jake had nervously anticipated an apology from Ed or perhaps an explanation, if nothing else, to clear the air. After a couple of weeks had passed without this happening, he started to put the memory behind him. The subject had yet to surface, and although Jake was a little disappointed in Ed for not expressing his remorse, he was also relieved that he didn't have to react to Ed's apology. Now, in late August, after having spent a summer at Ed's side, it was as though the terrible act had never happened. Jake had even gotten over being embarrassed around Katie. He had noticed, however, that Ed never showed any affection toward Katie or the kids, but figured that was because Ed was Amish and Amish men don't show their affection like some English people do.

Jake and Katie had decided to do something special for Ed on August 18, his twenty-sixth birthday. It would be a surprise. The eighteenth fell on a Sunday, and when Katie, Ed, and the children got home from church, Jake was there with Ed's birthday present—a bone-handled hunting knife Jake had purchased at the hardware store up in Waterford.

It was the exact knife Ed had admired a few weeks earlier. Jake had wrapped the gift himself. After lunch, Katie presented Ed with a chocolate birthday cake she had been hiding. Jake lit the twenty-six candles and Ed, to the delight of the children, blew them all out. He then unwrapped the bone-handled knife and said how proud he was to have it. Everyone sang "Happy Birthday" as Ed, flushed with embarrassment, sat at the table fondling his present. Before sitting down for some cake, Katie walked over to her husband and kissed him on the cheek. It was a moment Jake would remember.[1]

Katie's dream of a new house was about to come true. In September, under Mr. Gingerich's supervision, Ed and Jake began laying foundation block about a hundred yards off Sturgis Road behind and just east of the sawmill. Ed and Jake had been laying block a few days when Mr. Gingerich came on-site to check on their work. He had bad news; nothing was level and they would have to tear down what they had done and start over. Ed, who didn't have his heart in the work, said he wouldn't do that. "Well, you'll just have to," Mr. Gingerich said, "there is no other way."[2]

"If that's the way you want it," Ed replied, "then do it yourself." Ed stomped off and didn't return. Mr. Gingerich and Jake laid the foundation block and Emanuel Hershberger, with the help of Jake and the sawmill crew, built the two-story, four-bedroom, chipboard-sided, Shaker-designed house with the green shingled roof.[3]

Early one frosty mid-October morning, while heading down the hill on Sturgis en route to Ed and Katie's nearly finished house, Jake saw a familiar vehicle coming out of the valley toward him. The occupants of the red Jeep Cherokee, Debbie Williams and Ed, zipped by without a honk, a wave, or, as far as Jake could tell, a look. Since Jake had been busy helping build Ed's house for the past six weeks, he hadn't been seeing much of Ed. He hoped that would change once Ed and his family moved into their new dwelling.[4]

Everyone in Brownhill, including Bishop Shetler, knew that other people were building Ed's house for him. Emanuel Hershberger was telling folks it was a good thing he had blueprints because Eddy was never around.[5] No one had ever heard of an Amish man not having a hand in the construction of his own house.

A few days into November, Jake helped Ed, Katie, and Ed's brothers Atlee and Joe move everything out of the little gray house into the new place. Although the new house wasn't finished inside and there was still a lot of painting to do, Katie wanted to settle in before winter. Jake had never seen her happier. A new house was like a new beginning.

Ed didn't like to paint; he said the fumes gave him a headache, so Katie and Jake did most of the work. One afternoon, about a week after they had moved in, Jake and Katie were working in the front room. Jake was painting the wall while Katie trimmed the baseboard along the floor. She was squatting at the base of the wall with her auburn hair hanging free and her dress gathered up above her knees to keep it clear of the pale blue paint. This was the first time Jake had seen her with her hair down and the first glance he had had of her legs. He didn't stare, sneak peeks, or anything like that (he had too much respect), but he was acutely aware of her presence.

Jake, trying not to be obvious, looked Katie's way only when he could do so naturally, such as when he turned from the wall to dip his brush into the paint can. He had gotten off the ladder and was painting down on the wall close to where she was working when he looked over and saw Ed standing behind her. Jake had no idea Ed was even in the house and didn't know how long he had been in the room watching them. Katie didn't realize Ed was there until he reached down, grabbed her by the hair, and yanked her to her feet. Startled, she dropped her paintbrush and

barked something in German. Ed released her and, without
a word, walked into the kitchen to pump himself a glass
of water. Katie gathered up her brush and went back to
work; Jake continued painting as though nothing had happened and Ed quenched his thirst and left the house. Jake
cleaned up early that day and left without finishing the
room. Just before he went out the door, Katie asked if he
planned to come back tomorrow. Jake said yes, tomorrow
he'd return and complete the job; he'd see her in the morning.[6]

When Jake let himself into the house the next morning,
he found little Danny and Enos playing in the front room.
He heard voices—Ed and Katie's—coming from the bedroom on the first floor. As he played with the children, the
voices in the bedroom grew louder. Ed was shouting something in German and Katie was yelling back in kind. The
kids, paying no mind to the ruckus, continued to romp
around the room. Katie, shouting at the top of her lungs,
suddenly clammed up. Jake was already on his way out of
the house when he heard a loud slapping sound followed
by silence.[7] The next thing he heard were his footsteps on
the porch. He walked straight to his truck, jumped in, and
gunned it down the driveway.

13

Marks of Violence

Jake Powers could not escape the truth; Ed abused his
wife. He yanked her by her hair in a cruel and disre-
spectful way and hit her in the face with force. Jake would
have preferred not to know this; he didn't want the secret

or the burden that came with this knowledge. Men hit women, they did it all the time, but Ed hitting Katie was something Jake would not have believed possible had he not seen it with his eyes and heard it with his ears. He knew the truth and he hated it.

Jake had never thought of Ed as a violent person. Ed didn't pick fights; he was friendly and easygoing; people liked him. From Jake's point of view, everybody liked Ed. He was a popular guy. Jake never saw him drunk, never heard him raise his voice or even say "damn" or "hell." Who would ever believe, for one second, that an Amish man would hit his wife? Who would believe that Ed hit Katie? Everybody thought they were the perfect couple.

Jake didn't know it, but he wasn't the only person who knew that Ed abused Katie physically. Just before Christmas, Katie informed her sister-in-law Annie, Joe Gingerich's wife, that Ed had beaten her. Katie hadn't told this to anyone, including her parents. Levi and Emma had enough to worry about. Annie and Katie had become close after Katie's sister Barbara married Ben Coblentz and moved to Conewango Valley. Breaking her promise to Katie not to tell, Annie told her husband, Joe, and Joe promptly informed Mr. Gingerich that Ed "slapped Katie around pretty good."[1] Appalled and disgusted by this frightening revelation, Mr. Gingerich called Ed, Joe, and Atlee to the house for a secret meeting.[2]

Christmas, in 1991, fell on a Wednesday and on Christmas Day afternoon, Ed, Katie, and the kids climbed into their buggy and rode three miles over snow-covered roads to Levi and Emma Shetler's farm for a big, holiday get-together. The house was packed wall-to-wall with Katie's family—her three brothers and three sisters still living at home, her married siblings and their spouses, and more than a dozen nephews and nieces. Levi, the head of the Shetler clan, was fifty-eight, five years older than his wife, Emma.

Levi, a robust man of great vigor, had, of late, run out of steam. For months he'd been fighting a cold that had settled into his chest and robbed him of his breath. At fifty-eight and two hundred and thirty pounds, his size had become a serious liability, prompting Emma to deny him second helpings at the dinner table, a measure he did not welcome enthusiastically. The fact that he couldn't do his share of work around the farm bothered him more than his diet. Emma and the kids living at home had picked up the slack.[3]

Katie was determined not to let Levi and Emma know of her problems with Ed, but could no longer wear the mask of happiness in their presence. It became obvious that something was wrong and equally apparent that the trouble was Ed. Although worried about Katie, Levi, because he believed that parents should not interfere in their children's marriages, was not about to ask too many questions. Emma agreed that nonintervention was the best policy, but asked questions anyway. What's wrong, she asked Katie, was it Ed?

In response to Emma's concern, Katie blamed her unhappy demeanor on poor health—severe stomach pains that kept her from eating regularly and deprived her of sleep. That's why she had been so lethargic. So everything was okay with Ed? Well, not exactly, Katie replied. They didn't agree on how to discipline the children—Ed liked to spank them or twist their ears when they misbehaved. Katie hadn't been raised that way and didn't believe in hitting or in any way inflicting pain as a form of punishment. Ed accused her of coddling the children, turning them into brats and sissies.[4] They would grow into weak adults; English people would take advantage of them the way they did his father. Amish folks had to learn how to fend for themselves in the English world, how to stand up to English people. Katie didn't see how the English would have anything to do with how she raised her children. Did Ed intend to leave the Amish and take the kids? Was he trying to prepare his children for English life? Is that what this was all about?

The mere thought of Ed leaving the Amish and taking the children with him rocked Emma back on her heels. This could not be true. Ed would never do that. Would he? He says he won't, Katie replied. But we know he lies.

Katie, like her mother, was high-strung, strong-willed, bossy, and stubborn. Recognizing herself in her daughter, Emma offered Katie medication that would calm the anxiety and lift her spirits. Until Katie had a chance to see either Dr. Kanubhai or Dr. Suresh Patel over in New Philadelphia, Ohio (physicians who treated a lot of Amish women for depression), Emma would let Katie take some of her "nerve pills," a central-nervous-system depressant called Xanax. Emma told Katie that without her little pills, she wasn't sure she could manage. As far as she was concerned, they had saved her life. Take the pills, she said. Give yourself a break.[5] Katie, a true believer in Dr. Terrell and his brand of "drugless therapy," declined Emma's offer. She'd try some of Ed's blackstrap molasses.

Katie didn't tell her mother about the hitting; there was nothing she could do about it, so why torture her with the knowledge and make her even more dependent on drugs? Annie Gingerich knew, as did Ed's father, Atlee, and Joe, but the Gingeriches wouldn't tell anyone, including Ed's mother, as long as he kept his promise not to hit her again. Infuriated by Katie's revelations to Annie, Ed had not kept his promise, but no one would know that if Katie didn't tell.

In January, shortly after the New Year, 1992, on a dismal Sunday afternoon in the dead of winter, Katie and her mom were alone in Emma's kitchen while the men were out in the front room and Katie's sisters were cleaning off the big table. The two women were standing side by side at the sink, Katie washing dishes and Emma drying. Katie, thin, pale, and looking haggard around the eyes and mouth, hadn't had much to say. Ed had been quiet as well, which was usual for him. Katie's sleeves were rolled up, exposing her arms to her elbows. Emma was talking then suddenly fell silent in the middle of a sentence. Katie turned to her and asked, "What's wrong?"

"What happened there?" Emma said, pointing to Katie's arms, which were swollen and purple. "What made those bruises?"

Katie issued a derisive, angry laugh, more of a chuckle, then whispered, "Ask Eddie."[6]

14

Two-faced

February, bleak and miserably cold, was a terrible, desperate month for Ed and Katie. Ed became so despondent he simply couldn't manage around her and the kids, spending hour after hour alone in the shed with his beloved diesel machines. Katie, convinced her husband was behaving this way out of spite and to annoy her, kept asking him the same thing: "What am I doing wrong; why are you against me?"—a question Ed couldn't answer even if he wanted to. They were living in a tiny, secret hell they had unwittingly made for themselves and didn't understand.

The one facet of Ed's depression that baffled Katie as much as the reason behind it was his ability to appear perfectly normal—healthy and happy—in the company of everyone but her. Even on his worst days, when he couldn't find the energy to walk over to the sawmill, Ed would immediately perk up and become his old self whenever someone came to the house to say hello. This was particularly true when the visitor was one of his English acquaintances. He had two distinct personalities, one for Katie and the other for the rest of the world.[1] Katie didn't understand why he saved his best for others and wasn't sure which personality, what face, was truly his. Either way she felt betrayed. It was driving her to distraction; was Ed cracking up or was he simply trying to drive *her* crazy? She had never felt so alone, so isolated, so helpless, and, on occasions, so angry.

After Ed said he was too tired to fix the baby's broken high chair, Katie took it to Dave Hochstetter, an Amish man who built and sold furniture out of his barn on Dean Road. When Ed learned that another Amish man had repaired a piece of his furniture, he was embarrassed and enraged. He yelled at Katie for showing him up. She should have thrown the broken chair away and purchased a new one. He would have given her the money. She had gone to Dave Hochstetter out of spite, to make him look foolish.[2]

When winter came, the children's beds were moved into Ed and Katie's room, the only bedroom with a heating stove. Sometimes the children would be awakened by loud voices, Ed and Katie yelling at each other. One night in February, the shouting woke up Enos, who saw his father slap his mother in the face. Katie hit him back and was thrown out of bed onto the floor. In the morning, the children found her sleeping on a cot in the front room.[3]

Except for Jake Powers, Ed's English acquaintances had no idea what was happening in his personal life. He had managed to put up a good front. The crew at the mill didn't see much of him; when he did come to the plant, he wasn't interested as he used to be. The sawmill workers had noticed something else about Ed that was truly out of character: he was losing interest in his English friends. Whenever he saw a car or truck come up the driveway, he'd say, "I don't want to deal with him," and slip into the house.[4]

Ed began criticizing Katie in front of her parents, something he hadn't done before. During a Sunday visit at Levi and Emma's, he complained to everyone in the room that Katie was always nagging him to do this or do that. He accused her of trying to get him to do her chores; he said she was getting lazy. Believe it or not, he had recently made his own breakfast because she refused to get out of bed! If Katie went to bed on time, he wouldn't have to make his own breakfast.

Levi and Emma, struck dumb by Ed's whining, looked on in silent embarrassment as Ed persecuted Katie for being a bad wife. Katie defended herself by pointing out that on the morning of the self-made breakfast, she had been so ill she couldn't get out of bed. This was the first and last time Ed had ever been forced to make his own breakfast. Ed dismissed this as a poor excuse; Katie wasn't sick, she was faking. Not wanting her parents to hear any more of this, Katie didn't respond, giving Ed the last word.[5]

A few days later, shortly after dinner, Katie loaded the kids into the buggy and rode over to her parents' house for a quick visit without Ed, who had gone from the dinner table to the machine shop, where he'd remain until bedtime. An hour after the arrival of his daughter and the grandchildren, Levi, exhausted and ill, put himself to bed, leaving Katie alone with her mother. Taking advantage of the opportunity to speak privately Emma said, "Your father and I have been worried about you. You look tired and you never smile. What's going on with Ed?"

"I don't know why he's so mean to me," Katie replied. "I don't know what I'm doing wrong."

"Is he hitting you?"

"He can't control himself. He's violent."

"Is he hitting the children?" Emma asked.

"No, but I'm worried about the kids in case something happens to me."

"Like what?" Emma asked, frightened and concerned. "What is he doing to you? What could happen?"

"I want you to take the kids if something happens to me. I don't want him getting the children."

"I don't know if we could do that," Emma said. "Levi is sick; I don't know if he could take the kids."

"Then make sure the children go to the Gingeriches. Ed should not raise them."[6]

Emma pressed for details, but that was all she could pry out of Katie. Just before Katie and the kids departed for home that night, Emma begged her to get Ed to a real doctor who treated people with mind problems. She recommended the physicians over in New Philadelphia. If her suggestion took root, Katie gave no sign that it had.

Emma stood at the side door and watched the buggy roll noisily down the driveway. Badly shaken and confused, she wondered if life ever settled down. She had children to raise, a farm to run, and a son-in-law who had become dangerous because he was losing his mind. On top of that, her husband was sick. It was time for a nerve pill, maybe two.

Jake was thinking about turning in when Ed, calling from a pay phone near a sawmill on the other side of Spartansburg, said he needed a lift home. Jake said he was on his way. It was snowing hard and he knew that the back roads would be treacherous. Thirty minutes later, Ed and Jake were in the truck heading back to Brownhill. Ed didn't bother to explain how he had gotten into a situation where, at the last minute, he had to call Jake for a ride. Obviously in no mood to converse, he rode in silence. They were driving along a lonely stretch of Route 6 west of Union City when Ed startled Jake by yelling, "Stop here!" Expecting to hit a deer he didn't see, Jake stood on the brakes. The truck spun around and skidded to a stop in the middle of the highway. "Pull it off over there," Ed said, pointing to the side of the road. Jake eased the truck onto the shoulder and cut the engine. Before he had the chance to ask what it was they had just missed hitting, Ed took off his hat and was out of the truck. As he climbed the barbed-wire fence, Jake wondered why Ed simply announced that he needed to take a leak. Didn't he realize how close they had come to being in a serious wreck? It was a miracle the truck hadn't flipped over!

Jake was thinking about good luck and the fragility of life when Ed, instead of relieving himself, dropped to the ground and started flopping around in the snow. Thinking that his friend was out in that field having some kind of seizure, Jake scrambled out of the cab and was cutting through the headlight beams when Ed jumped to his feet and began walking toward the fence. "Are you okay?" Jake yelled.

Ed didn't respond. He scaled the barbed-wire fence, grabbed his hat off the seat, and climbed into the cab. Jake walked around the front of the truck and slid in behind the wheel. "I was burning up," Ed said. "I feel better now; let's go home."[7]

Katie was still up when the two men walked into the house. She looked at Jake and asked if she could fix him a bite. Jake declined, said he'd already had a big meal with his sister. "I could eat something," Ed said.

"Cook it yourself," she snapped.

"You cook it," Ed growled.

"I better go," Jake said, sensing danger.

"How about some coffee?" Katie asked. The way she said this was almost a plea—she did not want Jake to leave her alone with Ed. "I've got some pie. You don't have to go."

"It's late," Jake said. He was out the door so fast that if Katie spoke to him, he didn't hear her.[8]

A week passed before Jake saw Katie again. He was at the house early in the morning to drive Ed someplace. Jake waited in the kitchen with Katie while Ed finished getting dressed in the bedroom. Katie walked over to Jake and slipped him a twenty-dollar bill. "What's this for?" Jake asked.

"Put it in your pocket," she whispered. "It's for a bottle of Crown Royale. Don't tell Ed and make sure it's a hundred proof."

The next morning Jake bought a fifth of Crown Royale at the State Store in Union City. That afternoon, when he saw Ed disappear into the machine shop, he delivered the whiskey, hidden under his coat, to Katie. She accepted the bottle and the change and seemed quite pleased until she noticed it was eighty-six proof. "I wanted one hundred," she said, sounding almost desperate.

"This was all they had," Jake explained, feeling he had failed her. "I thought it would be okay. I can take it back."

"No," she said. "This will do. Thanks."[9]

Jake returned to the sawmill feeling like he'd gotten away with some kind of crime and worried that if Katie got drunk and got caught, everyone, including Ed, would know who had brought her the booze. In his eagerness to please Katie, he just might have gotten himself into a peck of trouble.

15

The Sermon in the Machine Shop

Never a slave to the clock, Ed had completely fallen out of step with the normal rhythms of daily life. He slept when exhaustion overtook him, skipped meals if he wasn't hungry, and didn't maintain any kind of work schedule or day-to-day routine. Katie was never sure where he was, what he was doing, or how he would behave when she saw him. Most of the time he maintained a brooding and dangerous silence, but occasionally would want to talk, usually about his symptoms—the headaches, dizziness, itchy skin, back pain, and so forth—or about religion. He said Amish ministers and bishops were more interested in telling people how to live than in helping them find Jesus. Amish people worshiped the bishop instead of God and this was bad because the only way to heaven was directly through Jesus; therefore Amish people were all going to hell! Katie didn't argue; this just made him angry and, occasionally, violent.

Katie had ordered, by mail, a small quantity of herbs from an Amish woman named Miller who lived in Crawford County near Guys Mills. These herbs, simply by making the body stronger, were supposed to cure just about everything—and cure it naturally. Katie had purchased the medicine for Ed, but he refused to take it, which infuriated her because she thought he didn't want to get better out of some weird desire to make her miserable. Ed's reason for refusing Katie's herbs, although irrational, had more to do with fear than spite. He suspected she was trying to poison him.[1]

At daybreak on Katie's twenty-eighth birthday, Ed was in the machine shop repairing an engine that had been brought to him by an English customer. He had no idea it was Tuesday, March 17, the day of Katie's birth.

To clean the engine, Ed was using a degreasing solvent Richard Zimmer had told him about. It was called Gunk, and according to warnings on the can and Zimmer's instructions, the solvent had to be significantly diluted and applied in a well-ventilated place to prevent the buildup of toxic fumes that came off the solution. Ignoring these warnings, Ed was applying the solvent full strength in a building closed tight to hold in the heat from the wood-burning stove. Without a breathing mask or gloves, Ed, simply ignoring the fumes, worked all day with the Gunk. At four in the afternoon, when he stepped out of the shed into the cold fresh air, he was overwhelmed by dizziness and almost fell down. He made it to the house, stumbled into the bedroom, and collapsed, fully clothed, onto the bed. He had a terrible pain inside his brain and his hands felt swollen and stiff, and they tingled. He lay in bed a couple of hours, sleeping fitfully, then got up and walked into the kitchen and asked Katie to make him dinner. She and the kids had already eaten. Katie fixed him a meal but he had no appetite; he just picked at his food. When Katie asked him why he wasn't eating, he said the kids were making too much noise. Still dizzy and mentally disoriented, he got up from the table and headed for bed, leaving the dishes for Katie.

The next morning, Ed was a little groggy but felt better. He wasn't dizzy, his hands felt normal, and most of his headache was gone. Katie didn't get up, so he made himself a mug of coffee before heading out to the machine shop to work on an Englishman's motor. The air inside the machine shop was still polluted with vapors coming off the degreased motor and the Gunk-soaked rags. Making no effort to air the place out, Ed went back to work. Initially he was uncomfortable breathing this air, but after a while he got used to it.[2]

Ed worked all morning and into the afternoon without a break. He couldn't remember when the English guy was coming for his motor but felt compelled to work on it until he finished the job. By the time he got the engine assembled, it was three o'clock. He fired it up to see how it would go and it ran like new.

Ed had been breathing Gunk fumes into his lungs for seven hours and was feeling the effects. His headache had returned in the form of a pounding pain behind his eyes; he was so dizzy he thought he might have to crawl out of the shed, and his hands had stiffened up and were tingling as though they weren't receiving any blood.

After a quick stop at the outhouse, Ed stumbled through the back door on his way to his bedroom, where he collapsed without removing the clothes he had been wearing for two days. Katie, having heard him come into the house, covered his body with a quilt. A few minutes later, the entire house smelled of Gunk.

Katie prepared dinner for herself and the children without setting a place for Ed, who was still sprawled out in the bedroom. They were eating their meal when someone knocked at the front of the house. Katie went to the door and was greeted by Dave Lindsey's smiling face; he had stopped by to say hello to Ed and hoped he wasn't interrupting their dinner. Since Dave Lindsey was the last person Katie wanted her husband to see, she was quite forceful in announcing that he was sick in bed, therefore not available for visitors—maybe some other time. Obviously concerned, Dave said he was sorry to hear that Ed wasn't well; he hoped Katie would forgive the intrusion and was halfway off the porch when Ed walked into the front room behind Katie. "I'm okay," he said as he nudged Katie out of the doorway and stepped onto the porch to be with Dave.[3] Fuming, Katie returned to the kitchen to make sure the kids had cleaned their plates. This was exactly the thing she hated most about Ed—he was sick for her but just fine for his English friends. Was Ed pretending to be sick or pretending to be well? Either way, he was a fake, and Katie was getting tired of it.

Dave had stopped by to pick up a saw blade Ed had agreed to sell him. Noah and his crew had gone home for the day, so Ed helped Dave carry the big blade from the sawmill to his truck. Dave didn't have much time to visit; he had to be in Corry by seven for his regular Wednesday-night prayer meeting held at the Bible Believers' Baptist Church. Dave handed Ed the saw blade money and was about to climb into his truck when Ed said he had recently purchased a couple of pigs and wondered if Dave would like to see them. Dave didn't have much interest in pigs, but sensing that Ed didn't want him to leave, said sure, he'd take a look.

The pigs were in a pen behind the house, and as far as Dave could tell, they were nothing out of the ordinary.

The sun had dropped, and as darkness gathered, the wind started to bite. Ed was telling Dave about the motor he had just fixed for the English guy and offered Dave a chance to look it over as well. Eager to get out of the cold and bored by the pigs, Dave readily agreed to accompany Ed over to the machine shop. Dave sneaked a peek at his watch; if he left Brownhill now, he'd make it in time for his prayer meeting. He decided to skip the meeting in favor of his friend, who seemed to be calling out for help. Maybe this was the day Ed would find Jesus and be born again.

Dave followed Ed into the shed and was immediately struck by the overwhelming smell of the degreasing solvent. "What have you been doing in here?" he asked. It was so dark Dave could only make out the bare outlines of the interior—the big engines mounted on the floor, the workbench, some shelving, tools, boxes, and so forth. "What is that odor?"

"I was using Gunk to clean the English feller's motor."

"These fumes aren't good for you; you need ventilation."

"It gave me a headache," Ed replied.

"Katie said you were sick. What's wrong?"

"I don't know."

"You seem a little down," Dave said. "Is everything okay?"

"I wish I knew what I'm doing wrong."

"Who says you're doing something wrong."

"Everybody. I think they're going to boot me out."

"Out of what?"

"Out of the church. Rudy Shetler might kick me out—excommunication."

"What for?"

"I don't know."

"What have you done?"

"You'll have to ask them."

"What about Katie? What does she say?"

"She's with them," Ed replied.

"Ed, you are not free. You don't know it, but you're a member of a cult. You are trapped."

"I think the bishop is out to get me."

"The bishop is not God; it doesn't matter."

"I'll never get right with God," Ed said. "I know that."

"It doesn't matter what the bishop thinks; he can't save you. That's up to *you*. All you need, Ed, is a little faith, a little trust. Trust the Lord as your Savior."

"The bishop—"

"The bishop is only a man, just like you and me. He's a *person*. He can't send you to heaven and he can't send you to hell. Ed, are you listening?" It was so dark in the shed, Dave could barely see Ed, who was just a few feet away leaning against the workbench. Their inability to see each other made it easier for them to talk this way—it was less embarrassing for Ed. They were voices in the dark, voices without bodies.

"I'm listening," Ed said.

"Let Jesus into your heart. You remember, don't you, that verse in John that proves my point: 'that ye may *know* that ye have eternal life, and that ye may believe on the name of the Son of God.' Do you remember that Scripture?"

"Yes."

"Do you remember when I asked your dad about that passage? He had no answer, did he?"

"No."

"There are things they do not want you to know. I told you that. You cannot become a good Christian as long as you are Amish. It gets down to that simple fact."

"I was raised in the church," Ed replied. "My father is a minister."

"You won't get to heaven on your father's coattails. Just because you find a diamond in the garbage doesn't make the trash can a jewelry store."

"What do you mean?"

"The Amish religion is man-made; it is not a true religion. It's the Bible that counts, not what your father says or the bishop. What does the Bible say?"

"What does it say?"

"The second you let Jesus into your heart, you will be saved. You are in bondage, no wonder you are not happy. Accept Jesus as your Lord and Savior and you will be free!"

Ed let that sink in, then said, "I can't talk to my dad about any of this. I never get straight answers."

"And you never will. Not from them. The bishop wants to keep you in bondage. But God, what about God? God doesn't want you to please the bishop; He wants you to have faith in Him! Put your trust in Him!"

"I've been living a lie," Ed said. "My life is a lie."

"Ed, you can be saved. You can be saved right now."

"What about Katie?" Ed asked. "What about her?"

"Will she leave the Amish church?"

"No, never," Ed replied. "Katie would never leave."

"Then she can't be saved," Dave said. "It's up to her to find the Lord. If you stay with the Amish, you'll both go to hell. You save yourself; that's what you do."

"You have overloaded my mind," Ed said, then fell silent.

Dave couldn't see his watch, but knew it was too late for the prayer meeting in Corry. But that didn't matter, because what he was doing here with Ed was much more important. He was on the verge of rescuing a soul from hell. Ed was so close. "Do you have any questions?" he asked.

"It's a lot to think about," Ed replied. "I'm tired."

Dave, feeling a little woozy from the Gunk, said, "Let us pray." Following the prayer, the two men came out of the shed to find the night air cold and intoxicatingly fresh. When Dave started for his truck, he realized he was dizzy from the Gunk and also felt a headache coming on. Physically, he didn't feel very good, but emotionally and spiritually, he was riding high.[4] That evening, amid the foul air of Ed's machine shop, he had made tremendous progress toward the saving of a man's soul. Ed's salvation was no longer a matter of doubt; it was just a matter of time.

16

Ed's Vision

The children were asleep in their beds when Ed stumbled noisily into the house through the back door and met Katie in the kitchen. He reeked of Gunk, had a crooked smile frozen onto his face, and stared at her with eyes that seemed about to pop out of his head.

"Where have you been?" she asked, somewhat startled by his appearance. She was baking bread, which had filled the house with the cozy aroma of yeast. The smell Ed had brought into the house was intrusive and unfriendly.

"In the shop," he replied through a foolish grin.

"What did Dave Lindsey want?"

"Nothing. We talked."

"About what? Did you talk about religion?"

"About everything. He opened my mind."

"You look funny," she said. "What's wrong?"

"I'm going to bed; I'm dizzy and my head hurts."[1] In his stocking feet, Ed quietly floated out of the kitchen like a man walking in his sleep. Katie wanted to remind him of what would be happening in the morning, but he was in no condition to hear or understand. He was somewhere else.

Dave Lindsey's hard-hitting homily in the machine shop, the Gunk fumes, and Ed's melancholy, anger, and guilt, had conspired to weaken his precarious grip on reality. Having lost his sense of time, Ed didn't realize that in the morning, his younger brother Danny and his new wife, Fannie, would be coming from Ontario for a one-week visit. Married six months, the newlyweds would be staying with Ed and Katie. Katie had been looking forward to this day for months, and as Ed tossed and turned and talked in his sleep, she bustled about the house making last-minute preparations for their visit.

Mr. Gingerich had recently purchased seventy-two acres on the south side of Sturgis Road, directly across from the sawmill. In a month, when the weather was suitable, he and his sons would build Dan and his wife a temporary house on this land. A new barn would come, followed by the construction of a permanent house.[2] By the end of the summer, Danny would be farming in Brownhill like his father and his brothers Atlee and Joe. No one was more excited about the homecoming than Katie, who hoped that Danny's presence would raise Ed's spirits and make him the way he used to be. No one had been closer to Ed than Danny.

Arrangements had been made to have George Brown meet Danny and his wife, who was three months pregnant, at the Greyhound bus station in Erie. In the morning, Katie would ask Ed if he'd like to ride up to Erie in the van with Brown to meet his brother and Fannie.[3] Danny had no idea what had been going on with Ed; he didn't know about the hitting or Ed's flirtation with evangelism. Katie hoped that Dan would never have to know of these things, that Ed would come to his senses once his brother was home.

Just before dawn, Ed leaped out of bed like a man who'd discovered a snake crawling up his leg. Having been up past midnight and accustomed to his nocturnal spasms, Katie slept on, undisturbed. Ed frantically felt around the bed for her body and, when he found her, shook her awake. When she came to she heard Ed walking around the room, talking to himself in a strange, high-pitched voice. She sat up in the bed and watched as he paced back and forth at the foot of the bed. There was barely enough light in the room for her to make him out, and she couldn't understand a word he was saying. This added a new wrinkle in Ed's behavior. He had never done anything this bizarre, and it frightened Katie. Trying not to sound fearful, she said, "Ed, what are you doing?"

The sound of his wife's voice stopped Ed in his tracks, and he quit jabbering. He stood silent for a couple of seconds, then lunged toward the bed. "I've had a *vision*," he said in sort of a loud whisper. "A vision from God!"

Katie had no idea what he was talking about. "What do you mean?" she asked.

"I tried to kill the older leader but he wouldn't die. I couldn't conquer him!"

"What leader?"

"Bishop Shetler!"

"You had a dream. It's just a dream—a nightmare."

"No! This is a *vision*—from God! I've got to kill the older leader to make room for the *new* religion. I couldn't do it because he wouldn't die! No matter how hard I tried, I couldn't kill him."

"Come back to bed," Katie coaxed. "Come back to bed."

"The devil wants my soul," Ed said. "He's fighting Jesus for my soul."[4]

George Brown pulled up to the house with his passengers and their luggage at noon. Before he drove away, Katie arranged to have him return at two o'clock for a trip to Cambridge Springs. Ed didn't know it, but he would be seeing Doc Terrell that afternoon. Dan's joyful reunion with Ed and Katie was marred, somewhat, by Ed's shocking appearance: he was ghostly pale and alarmingly thin. Dan had never seen his brother looking so sickly. Ed had changed in other ways, more subtle ways, that Dan couldn't quite put his finger on. He seemed distracted and a little distant. This wasn't the same Ed Gingerich that

Danny had grown up with. Danny asked Ed if he had been sick. Ed said no, he had been fine, except for an occasional headache and bouts of dizziness. Katie took this opportunity to announce that they were all taking a ride to Cambridge Springs with George Brown at two o'clock. She said she wanted Doc Terrell to do something about Ed's headaches. Much to her relief, Ed just shrugged his shoulders and said he had nothing better to do.

At two-thirty, George Brown and his Amish riders—Ed, Katie, Dan, and Fannie—rolled into Doc Terrell's roadside office to find the place as hectic and crowded as ever. Outside on the parking lot, drivers waited in their minibuses, utility vehicles, and cars while their Amish passengers waited inside for the diminutive healer.

When it came Ed's turn to list his symptoms on the scrap of paper destined for Doc's diagnostic machine, he wrote: "no appetite, forgetful" and "can't sleep," which resulted, treatment-wise, in a quickie shoulder rub, a right-foot manipulation, and more molasses.[5]

The Ed Gingerich Danny had known and admired—the rebellious, smooth-talking master mechanic and entrepreneur—had, in his absence, turned into a sickly, disoriented whiner. Katie had changed as well. She had lost her youthful exuberance, she looked edgy, exhausted, and a little desperate. Danny noticed a difference in their marital relationship as well. Although Ed had never been known as a doting husband, he now virtually ignored Katie, and when Katie spoke to him, there was hardness in her voice, a mixture of anger, frustration, and fear. Danny realized he had come home to a situation he knew nothing about and wasn't equipped to understand. Ed seemed to be suffering from a disease that had destroyed his personality, a mysterious malady that lay beyond the curative reach of Doc Terrell and his magic molasses. Something had gone wrong; trouble was afoot.

The most frightening indication that Ed Gingerich's personality had been replaced by someone completely different came at the dinner table that evening when he suddenly began spouting passages from the Bible as he recounted the spiritual vision he said he had experienced the night before. The spectacle of his brother quoting from the Bible and babbling on about having received a message from God about some new religion sent chills up Danny's spine. When Ed started ranting about how, in his dream, he had tried but failed to kill the leader of the old religion, Katie startled her house guests by ordering him to shut up, which he did.[6] The remainder of Katie's earnestly prepared dinner was eaten in silence. This was hardly the time for Danny to talk about something as trivial as his new life as a family man and Brownhill farmer.

After dinner, Ed and Danny climbed into the buggy and rode south a mile and a half down Frisbeetown to brother Joe's. Joe and Danny hadn't seen each other since Danny's wedding up in Norwich. Joe's hopes for a lighthearted reunion with his younger brother were dashed when Ed, wide-eyed and borderline hysterical, blurted out that he had discovered a new religion that was bringing him closer to God. Joe couldn't believe he was hearing this from a man who since early boyhood had been avoiding religion the way an albino hides from the sun. "What's your problem?" he asked in a way that revealed he really didn't want to know.

"The bishop is against me," Ed replied. "What am I doing wrong?"

"Don't ask me," Joe growled.

"Why is everyone against me?"

"Maybe it's because you're too English. Maybe you should pay more attention to your family and start working at the mill."

"I'm sick," Ed said.

"How come you're still mean to Katie?" Joe asked.

"She's against me. We're all going to hell. We haven't been told the truth about Jesus. The Amish leaders don't want us to know."

"Who have you been talking to?" Joe asked.

"I have a spiritual adviser who's helping me find the Lord. It's my only chance."

"Who is this guy, an Englishman? Get away from him."

"I don't know what to do."

Joe Gingerich was in no mood to hear about Ed's problems with the bishop, his spiritual adviser, or his new religion, and he told him so. Joe had his own problems, everybody had problems. Ed was crying like a baby, it was time he grew up and acted like a man, a hardworking family man. It was time the family quit treating Ed like a baby. "Go home," Joe said, "I don't want to listen to this."

"You are out to get me," Ed said. "All of you, and Katie's in it, too."[7]

On Friday, March 20, Ed spent most of the day alone in the bedroom. That evening, when he and Danny were out behind the house checking on the pigs, Danny tried to convince him that nobody was against him. In fact, they were all trying to help him. Danny also begged Ed to stay away from the English man who was trying to change his religion and suggested that all this religious thinking and brooding was making him sick in the head. Ed didn't argue or protest; he just looked Danny in the face and said, "I'm going to do something that will go around the world."[8]

On Saturday, Enos's third birthday, Ed remained in the background as Katie, Dan, Fannie, and the children watched the boy open his presents and blow out his candles. Ed spent the rest of the day out in his machine shop reading his Bible. On Sunday, the twenty-second, they all attended church at Emanuel Hershberger's farm on Old Meadville Road. Emanuel, married to Katie's older sister Mary, had been working two years at the Gingerich sawmill and was the one who had supervised the construction of Ed and Katie's house. Looking pale and expressionless and seemingly unaware of the people around him, Ed plopped down on a chair next to Danny. Ed didn't utter a word until halfway through his father's sermon, when he turned to Dan and, in a loud whisper, asked, "Do you hear those people talking about me?"

"What people? No one is talking about you," Dan replied in Ed's ear.

"I hear them talking; what are they saying?"[9]

At the conclusion of the service, the congregation sat down to a midday meal hosted by the Hershbergers. Katie and Dan stayed close to Ed to make sure he didn't get anywhere near Bishop Rudy Shetler. Later that afternoon, church members who had farm chores that couldn't wait began to leave. Katie and Fannie stuck around to help Mary and the handful of other women clean up the mess. While waiting for Katie, Ed wandered out to the Hershberger barn, where he found Emanuel milking one of his cows. Notwithstanding their mutual association with the sawmill, the two men were not particularly close. Ed's lack of participation in the building of his own house, his absenteeism and avoidance of physical labor at the sawmill, and the fact that he wasn't a farmer made him, in Emanuel's eyes, a slacker. Being married to Katie's older sister, Emanuel had heard rumors that Ed and Katie hadn't been getting along, and based upon what he had seen and heard around the sawmill regarding Debbie Williams, he didn't blame Katie for the problems in their marriage. As far as Ed was concerned, Emanuel Hershberger was just another hand at the mill who owned a small farm and spent a lot of time doing mindless chores like milking cows.

Ed didn't announce his presence in the barn, he just ambled over to where Emanuel was working and leaned against a stall. In the half-light, Ed's face, although partially shaded by his hat, looked porcelain and drawn. Looking up from his milking stool, Emanuel said hello. When Ed didn't respond, he asked, "How's it going, Ed?"

"I'm sure you can tell there is something wrong with me," Ed replied in a slightly jittery voice. "You can probably see that I am different."

"You look the same to me," Emanuel said, stretching the truth. "What's wrong?"

"I'm all mixed up."

"About what?"

"About my soul and Jesus Christ."

Emanuel was shocked to hear words like these come out of Ed's mouth. When did *he* start worrying about his soul and Jesus Christ? Emanuel didn't know what to say. "Is that right?" he muttered, hoping that Ed would change the subject.

"This man I know, my spiritual adviser, told me that just because I'm Amish doesn't mean that I'll go to heaven."

"He's right about that," Emanuel said. "Read your testament, it will tell you that. There is no guarantee."

"I *have* been reading it," Ed replied, with a trace of frustration. "It doesn't make any sense to me. I'm told, by this man, that all I need is faith in Jesus. He says I must commit myself to Jesus. I can't find what I'm looking for in my Bible. I'm confused, and I can't think; do I look funny to you? Can you tell that there is something wrong with me?"

Emanuel Hershberger didn't know what to make of this except that something *was* wrong with Ed, and, yes, he did look a little strange. No one had ever spoken to him about such things before and hearing it from Ed Gingerich added to the strangeness of the conversation. "This man, your spiritual adviser, who is he?" Emanuel asked.

"I better not tell; he is a friend of mine."

"Is he English?"

"Yes. This man has told me things I never knew. He knows all about the Bible and says I'll never be saved as long as I'm Amish. I don't know what to do. What should I do?"

"You should talk to Rudy Shetler," Emanuel said. "Tell Bishop Shetler about this man and what he told you about the Bible and the Amish church."

Ed thought about that for a moment, then said, "Tonight

I'm going to Levi's house. I'll tell Levi that I'm thinking about leaving the church—to save myself."

"If that's what you're thinking," Emanuel said, "you're not getting good advice from the English feller. That is your problem."

"I'm going now," Ed said, then walked, heavy-footed, toward the barn door.[10]

Emanuel returned to his work feeling uneasy and burdened by what he had just heard. He would have to decide whether or not to keep the conversation a secret. He'd have to tell someone; this was too important, too disturbing, to keep to himself. But whom would he tell? The bishop?

That evening, the Shetler family gathered, as they often did on church night, at Levi's house. All of them were present, including Bishop Rudy Shetler and his wife, Fannie. That night, Ed, without warning, horrified Katie by telling Levi, in everyone's presence, that an unnamed English friend and spiritual adviser had opened his eyes to many things about God and Jesus Christ.

"What have you learned from this man?" Levi asked in his unruffled and friendly manner.

"That if I leave the Amish church, I can be saved," Ed replied. "It's the *only* way. That is what he believes."

"Do *you* believe that?" Levi asked. "Did you tell this man he is right?"

"I don't know what is right," Ed replied. "I am confused. We don't have all the answers; I believe that."

"And this man does?"

"He has shown me passages in the Bible—in the Book of John, I can't find it—that says that faith alone is enough."

Bishop Shetler, seated in the rocking chair next to his brother, had been silent. "I know of these men," he said, referring to Evangelists. "They are the devil's soldiers."

"Are you leaving the church?" Levi asked. "What about your family?"

"I don't know," Ed replied.

"I'm not leaving the church," Katie said. "And neither are the children!"

Speaking to Ed, Bishop Shetler asked, "Are you joining with these people?"

"Why are my own people against me?" Ed whined.

"No one is against you!" Katie explained. "Why do you like the English so much?"

Ed, ignoring Katie's question, proclaimed, "I've had a vision . . ."

"Don't tell them about your dream!" Katie snapped. She stood up. "It's time to go!"

"The leader of the new church will conquer the old leader. I tried but I couldn't kill him no matter what I did. I kept trying—for the new religion—but couldn't."

"He just had a dream," Katie said, looking toward Bishop Shetler, who had gotten up from his chair. "It was just a *dream*!"

"No," Ed said, "it's a *vision,* a prophecy!"

That clinched it. Bishop Shetler was on his feet, looking for his wife and his coat. Everyone else in the room, taking their cue from "the old leader," seemed to move toward the exit as though they were part of a slow-motion fire drill. Defeated and humiliated, Katie fought back her tears as Ed looked on in detached amusement. His so-called vision, his dream, had become her worst nightmare.[11]

17

Ed's First Spell

On Monday morning, March 23, Ed was awake, but refused to roll out of bed despite Katie's efforts to get him onto his feet. Standing bedside, she kept saying,

"Ed, please stop doing that and get up!" He was lying on his back and every so often he'd spit up at the ceiling. He'd been doing this for an hour or so and didn't seem to be in the mood to stop. Ed had been doing and saying strange things for some time, but spitting on the ceiling from his bed was a new and disturbing phenomenon, a big step in the wrong direction. He'd clear his throat, spit into the air, then contemplate the phlegm hanging from the ceiling and ask, "What does that say? What is that saying to me? What is it *saying*?"[1]

Ed needed help and so did Katie. She didn't want the children seeing their father acting this way, so she asked Dan to take them to his parents' house and, after that, to fetch her uncle Bishop Rudy Shetler. She would stay with Ed and try to get him to stop that awful spitting. If she couldn't make him stop, maybe the bishop could bring him back to his senses.

Ed was still on his back spitting when Rudy Shetler, accompanied by Dan Gingerich, joined Ed's brothers Atlee and Joe at the foot of Ed's bed. Katie was standing alongside Ed waving a handkerchief over his face, saying, "I have your hankie here."

"What does that say?" Ed said, staring at the ceiling. He seemed to look through Katie; it was as though he didn't see her hovering over him. "What is it saying?"

Katie stepped back from the bed and spoke to Bishop Shetler. "I don't know what to do with him," she said. "Maybe he'll talk to you."

Bishop Shetler planted himself in Ed's view at the side of the bed and said, "Tell us, Ed, why you are spitting? Why would you act this way in your own house in front of your family?"

Ed blurted, "I think my heart is tearing loose. It's coming off, I can feel it!" He rolled off the bed, hitting the floor with a thud at the bishop's feet. The suddenness of the move startled the bishop, who jumped back from the bed.[2] Moments later, Deacon Ben Stutzman, Bible in hand, walked into the bedroom and saw men and women lined against the walls looking on in horror as a man, having some kind of fit, flopped about at their feet like a dying fish. The bishop had dispatched one of his sons to the deacon's house with an urgent message: Ed Gingerich has been seized by the devil. The bishop, Katie, and others needed help in praying against Satan.[3]

Fearing that Ed might injure himself by bumping his head against a piece of furniture as he flailed, kicked, and rolled around the room, Atlee, Joe, and Dan grabbed hold of his arms and legs to hold him down. Ed struggled against his brothers for a minute or so, then went limp. When the men climbed off him, he lay on his back with his eyes open, his hair shooting off in all directions, and his clothing twisted out of shape. Except for his heavy breathing, Ed looked dead, like a corpse that had been dropped out of a window. After all of the noise and excitement, the room was now silent. No one knew what to do or what to say. Slowly, silently, the bedroom onlookers closed in around Ed's body. Ed's parents stepped into the room and saw nothing but people formed into a circle around something on the floor. Mary Gingerich, looking terrified, hung back as Mr. Gingerich knelt alongside his son's head. Ed didn't take his gaze off the ceiling. "Are you sick?" Mr. Gingerich asked in a calm, soothing voice. "Tell us what's wrong."

"Maybe we should take him to a doctor," Mary Gingerich offered.

"This man is not physically sick," Bishop Shetler said. "He has been taken over by Satan. The only thing that can save him is prayer. We will have to pray against Satan!"[4] Bishop Shetler knelt down beside Ed and Mr. Gingerich and, in prayer, asked God to drive the devil out of Ed's soul. Everyone in the circle started saying their own prayers, out loud, attacking the devil in force. In the midst of this cacophony, Ed sat up as though he had come back to life, risen from the dead. The praying stopped. Mr. Gingerich and Bishop Shetler helped him to his feet and walked him out to the front room, to a cot, where he stretched out on his back. Katie came into the room carrying a quilt to cover his feet, legs, and torso. The others had followed her into the room and were clustered into two groups, the men and the women. Several of the women could be heard praying or reading from their Bibles. Ed, the center of attraction, seemed to be sleeping.[5]

Levi and Emma Shetler didn't arrive at the house until shortly before noon. By that time, there were fifteen people standing around the front room watching Ed sleep off the devil or whatever it was that had gotten into him. Bishop Shetler was just about ready to claim God's victory over Satan when Ed woke up with a start, flung himself off the coat, and started crawling around the floor on his hands and knees. The women started praying loudly but were drowned out by Ed's braying, barking, and howling. Amid this racket, they all watched him crawl in circles, like a dog chasing his tail, stopping every so often to spit or rear back his head for a particularly loud, bloodcurdling howl. He had turned into a foam-mouthed, rabid, mad, snapping dog.[6]

Ed had been scooting around on the floor for five minutes when he crawled under the cot and didn't come out. When it seemed safe, Bishop Shetler got down on his knees and ventured a peek under the bed. Ed, curled up like a fetus, was sound asleep.[7]

Emma Shetler believed in God, the devil, and the power of prayer, but she didn't believe that God or the devil had anything to do with Ed crawling around his own living room barking like a dog.[8] Ed had lost his mind, and to get it back, he needed a big dose of heavy medicine like the nerve pills she took whenever she felt the urge to do a little barking herself. Ed needed a handful of those pills, and if that didn't kick the dog out of him, *two* handfuls. There *was* a God, and Emma thanked Him every day for those wonderful little pills.

Emma realized she'd never be able to talk Katie into taking Ed to a physician. Medical doctors prescribed drugs, and to Katie, drugs were the devil. While Ed snoozed like a dog under his cot, Emma approached his brother Joe, a believer in natural cures who was Brownhill's biggest supporter of Doc Terrell. Emma knew that Joe Gingerich was the one who had sold Katie on "the Pennsylvania doctor" and his magical molasses. If she could convince Joe that under the circumstances, Ed would be better served in the hands of a medical doctor, maybe *he* could persuade Katie, just this once, to go modern.

Emma didn't know the older Gingerich boys that well. Danny was the nicest, Atlee the shyest, and Joe the toughest. A little on the wild-and-woolly side, Joe had a fierce stare, a booming laugh, and a backslap that could knock you down the stairs. He meant well, worked hard, looked after his family, and, as far as Emma knew, was on good terms with the bishop.

Emma wasn't in the habit of walking up to Amish men she barely knew and initiating conversations, but this was an emergency. Overcoming her nervousness, she got right to the point: Ed was suffering from some kind of mental illness that could only be cured with special medicine the English called tranquilizers. She held up her bottle of Xanax and said, "These work!"—shaking the pills for emphasis.

"Where do you buy them?" Joe asked.

"You get them from a doctor. My doctors in New Philadelphia have these pills. Let's ask George Brown to drive Ed over this afternoon. My doctors can help him."

"With drugs?" Joe asked.

"Yes. Ed needs medicine to call him down."

"Ed has a doctor and he don't allow drugs," Joe said.

"He's no good!" Emma blurted.

Joe looked surprised. "You don't like Doc Terrell?"

"He doesn't treat mind problems," Emma replied. "He's

just a chiropractor; he can't do anything for Ed. Ed is insane!"

"He ain't insane!" Joe replied.

"Then what's wrong with him?" Emma asked, thinking that Joe might be a little thick in the head. "Why is he acting like a dog?"

"He's tired," Joe answered, shrugging his shoulders in resignation. "His nerves are bad."

"He's out of his mind," Emma said, sensing that she was making progress. "If we don't do something now, Ed could hurt himself."

"I don't know about *that,*" Joe replied.

"Let's call Dr. Caldwell up in Waterford," Emma said. "He treats Amish people and he makes house calls. Ed won't have to go anywhere."[9]

Joe relented and said he would send Danny over to George Brown's house to make the call. In a few days, when Ed was well enough to travel, they'd take a trip down to Cambridge Springs to see Doc Terrell, for a permanent cure.

Danny arrived at George Brown's house at two in the afternoon. To Dr. Caldwell's receptionist, he identified himself as a Brownhill Amish man named Danny Gingerich whose brother Ed was "having trouble with his nerves." Could Dr. Caldwell come to the house next to the sawmill on Sturgis Road? At the moment the doctor had a waiting room full of patients, the receptionist told him. Was this an emergency? Should an ambulance be dispatched? Was the patient on Sturgis Road ill enough for the emergency room? No, he wasn't that sick; he was just having problems with his nerves. Well, then, Dr. Caldwell would stop by the house after office hours, around six o'clock.[10] Would that be all right? Danny said it would be fine.

At three o'clock, Mr. Gingerich and the other men, including Danny, left the house to tend to chores, leaving Ed, now sleeping *on* his cot, alone with the six women.

Mary Gingerich, Ed's mother, didn't want all of the men to leave. "I'm afraid of him," she said. "What will we do if he acts up again?"

"He'll be fine," Mr. Gingerich replied. "He's sleeping and we'll be back before he wakes up."

"One of the men should stay with us," Mary insisted. "We can't handle him."

"Don't worry," Mr. Gingerich said. "Ed wouldn't hurt anyone."

"Well, I don't like it," Mrs. Gingerich said as the men filed out of the house.[11]

The men had been gone an hour, and as Ed snored on the cot, the women worked in the kitchen preparing dinner. Mary Gingerich, at the table worrying over a cup of tea, said to Katie, "How can you live this way? I'm scared to death! How can you be so brave?"

"I love him," Katie replied. "He's my husband."[12]

At five, with the men still out doing chores, the women decided to serve themselves dinner and feed the fellows when they returned. Katie walked out to the front room to check on Ed and found him lying on his back with his eyes open, staring at the ceiling. "Come to the table and have something to eat," she said.

"I can't," he replied without shifting his gaze.

"Yes, you can," she said.

"I can't; my arms hurt, my legs hurt, and my back is sore. I can't move."

"You'll be all right," she said, pulling him to his feet. With her help, he shuffled into the kitchen and plopped down at the table.

"This chair is too hard," he complained in a high-pitched, tentative voice. Katie walked into the front room and returned carrying his rocking chair. She placed the rocker up to the table and helped him into it. "I don't think I can eat," he said.

"I know you can," Katie said. "You can eat." Ed stuffed a forkful of mashed potatoes into his mouth and swallowed hard. "What do you want to drink?" Katie asked.

"Oh, my God!" Ed shouted, startling everyone in the kitchen. Mary Gingerich jumped up from the table and headed for the living room.

"What's wrong?" Katie asked, trying to sound calm.

"My heart just jumped from one side of my chest to the other! Get me back to bed!"

Katie helped Ed back into the front room, where he collapsed with a groan onto the cot. She picked the quilt off the floor and covered him. "Close your eyes so you can go to sleep," she said.

"I'm hot," he snapped. "Take off the blanket." Katie pulled the quilt away and hung it over the back of a chair. "I'm afraid to sleep," he said. "I'm afraid to close my eyes; I'm afraid of what I'll see."

With the other women clustered in the background, Katie pulled a chair next to Ed's pillow and sat down. Every so often Ed would mutter something in his sleep and Katie would say, "What?" He never answered. It became quiet as the room gradually lost its light. Someone in the room was praying, softly.[13]

Ed slept, but it was not a restful, healthy sleep. His hands and feet twitched, and Katie noticed that beneath his closed eyelids, his eyeballs were constantly moving—frantically darting about. Ed slept in this fashion for fifteen minutes then suddenly, without warning, sat up and screamed. It startled Mary Gingerich so badly she almost fainted. Katie reached for Ed, to settle him down, but couldn't stop him from rolling off the cot onto the floor. He gathered himself up onto his hands and knees and scrambled across the floor toward the women, who scattered like hens being chased by a fox. As though he were the one being pursued, Ed took refuge under the desk that sat against the front wall beneath one of the windows.

Katie followed her husband across the room, got down on her knees, stuck her head under the desk, and said, "What are you doing under there? Come out!"

Following a few moments of silence, Ed said, "Leave me alone."

A voice, Mary Gingerich's, came out of the dark: "Maybe you should leave him in there until the men come back."

Ignoring the advice, Katie said, "Ed, come out. Please."

"I am afraid," he replied from the safety of the desk.

"What will your father think when he sees you like this? Come out of there before your father comes back."

"Is Dad here?" Ed asked.

"No. Come out. I want you to come out now. Hurry. Let's get some light in here. Get some light in here," Katie said to the women, who scattered about in the darkness. Someone lit a kerosene lamp and the room suddenly broke into shadows.

"I'm dizzy," Ed said as he crawled out from under the desk. Katie helped him to his feet and held him around the waist as he made his way to the cot. "I don't want to lay down," he said, carefully lowering himself on to the edge of the bed, where he sat with his elbows on his knees, his hands supporting his head.[14]

Emma approached the cot, carrying her bottle of Xanax tablets. "Take these," she said. "They'll help you sleep."

Ed grabbed the bottle and squinted at the label. "What are these?" he asked.

"They're nerve pills," Emma said. "They'll help you relax."

Ed twisted the cap off the bottle and dumped the contents, about fifteen pills, into his mouth. He handed the empty container back to Emma. "We'll see," he said, falling back on the cot.

"I didn't think he'd take them all!" Emma said to Katie. "He was supposed to take *two*."[15]

"I wish I knew what's wrong with him," Katie said.

"He's having a nervous breakdown," Emma replied.

"What have I done wrong?"

"Nothing. It's not your fault."

"Then whose fault is it?"

"It's no one's fault."

"Why is he so nervous, then? What's wrong with his nerves?"

"The doctor will know," Emma said.[16]

Ed's eyes were closed and were no longer darting about on the other side of his eyelids. The Xanax had also put a stop to the twitching in his hands and feet. The room was quiet except for the rhythmic sounds of his breathing and his mother's praying.

Emma was thinking that her pills had knocked Ed out so cold the doctor wouldn't be able to wake him up when she heard the sounds of horses and buggies coming up the driveway. The men had returned. Emma's concerns over Ed's ability to regain consciousness were suddenly swept aside. The ruckus out front had jolted Ed awake: his eyes snapped open and he virtually exploded off the cot. Screaming, "Dad! Dad!" he flew across the room, pulled open the front door, and stumbled, barefoot, out into the yard, where he collapsed in the snow as if he'd been shot in the back with a tranquilizer dart loaded for rhino. Katie and Emma, having bolted out the door behind him, looked on as Mr. Gingerich, holding Ed by the ankles, and Danny, on the other end, carried Ed's limp frame back into the house.

"I can't move," Ed groaned as they lowered him onto the cot.

Covering Ed with the quilt, Emma bent close to his face and whispered, "It's the pills; you took too many." Ed gave her a blank look, managed a blink, then shut his eyes.[17]

Ed snored as Bishop Shetler, Levi Shetler, his brothers Atlee and Joe, and Deacon Ben Stutzman filed into the house, wet from the late March snow. They shook the snow off their hats before they entered the front room. "Has the doctor been here?" Levi asked.

"We're still waiting," Emma replied. She was now trying to decide whether or not to mention the Xanax pills to Dr. Caldwell.

The doctor arrived at quarter after seven. Handing his overcoat to Katie, he apologized for being so late. The snowstorm and his unfamiliarity with Rockdale Township had caused him to get lost. In the flickering light of kerosene lamps, Dr. Caldwell saw, in one part of the room, a half-dozen Amish men standing around a small bed. On the other side of the shadowy room, he noticed a clump of Amish women, Bibles in their hands, chanting some kind of prayer. He felt like he'd been called to deliver Rosemary's baby.[18]

"My husband has been acting wild," Katie said to the doctor as he walked across the room to the cot. Ed was sitting with his feet on the floor, looking better than he had in days. Katie couldn't help feeling frustrated: bring an English man into the room and Ed immediately perks up.

"How are we doing?" the doctor asked.

"Check and see if my heart is still there," Ed replied, otherwise sounding normal. "I think it jumped to the right side."

"All right," the doctor said. "Unbutton your shirt and we'll take a listen." He examined Ed with the stethoscope and, apparently satisfied that everything was where it should be, stuffed the instrument into his bag. "What brought this on?" he asked.

"I don't know," Ed replied. "I don't know why I feel so strange."

"When you say *strange,* what do you mean?"

"Confused. Did I act weird?"

"Yes," Katie said. "You were wild."

"I don't remember a thing," Ed said. "I do remember talking to an English man."

"When?" asked the doctor.

"I can't remember exactly," Ed replied. "But I remember the conversation."

"What were you talking about?" Dr. Caldwell asked.

"Religion. We had a big talk on religion."

"What religion?"

"A new one," Ed said. "It's where everyone goes to heaven, not just some people."

"Did you and this man argue?"

"No, he just told me things I didn't know before."

"Like what?"

"Amish people think they're going to heaven—but they're not! They haven't accepted Jesus Christ into their hearts. They worship the bishop instead of Jesus and have the wrong Bible!"

"Do *you* believe those things?" asked the doctor.

"I don't know; I'm confused."[19]

Katie had left the room, and when she returned, she had a bottle of blackstrap molasses she had purchased the last time she and Ed had visited Doc Terrell. She handed the bottle to Dr. Caldwell and asked, "Would this be helpful?"

The doctor carried the molasses to a kerosene lamp and read the label. "I don't think so," he replied. "I'll write you a prescription for some tranquilizers."[20] He walked over to the desk Ed had recently crawled under and wrote out the prescription. When finished, he handed it to Katie and said, "Tomorrow, if he isn't feeling better, give me a call. He looks tired. Do you have any idea what brought this on?"

"No," Katie replied.

"Has he acted strange before?"

"No."

"The pills I prescribed will help him sleep," the doctor said, slipping into his coat. "Don't you hate this weather?" Katie opened the door for the doctor and thanked him for coming out to see Ed on such a bad night. "Call me tomorrow if Ed isn't feeling better," he said, just before disappearing into the night.[21]

Emma hadn't mentioned the Xanax pills. As it turned out, tranquilizers were just what the doctor had ordered.

In the morning, after Ed had a good night's sleep, Katie would be able to buy him nerve pills of his own. He'd have to learn, however, just to take a couple at a time. Maybe this would be the end of Doc Terrell and his blackstrap-molasses nostrum.

Following Dr. Caldwell's departure, Katie and the women returned to the kitchen. The men hadn't eaten and were expecting dinner. At Katie's urging, Ed joined the other men at the dinner table. He didn't eat much and halfway through the meal stood up and said he was turning in for the night. Katie followed him into the bedroom to help him out of his clothes. He climbed into bed and immediately fell asleep.

It was late, the roads were snowy, and no one was in the mood for socializing, so, once the dishes were washed and the uneaten food put away, the time had come for everyone to go home. Katie, badly shaken by the day's events, asked her mother to spend the night. Emma said she would and sent Levi home in the buggy without her. She would sleep in the children's room.

Deacon Ben Stutzman said good-bye, as did Rudy Shetler, who, just before departing, pulled Katie aside to remind her how important it was to keep Ed away from the English man trying to convert him into an evangelist. Ed was a troubled man, an easy target for Satan, who was a powerful foe. Dr. Caldwell's pills might help Ed sleep, but only prayer could drive the devil away. It would take a lot of prayer.[22]

Mr. and Mrs. Gingerich were the next to leave. Mary Gingerich, a nervous wreck, looked like she could use a little tranquilizing herself. Emma felt sorry that Ed had hogged her Xanax. It was a shame he hadn't left a couple of pills for his mother.

Katie walked down the hallway and stuck her head into the bedroom to check on Ed. She found him sleeping soundly. Joe and Annie left, and Katie, feeling a little more optimistic about her husband, told Emma that she wouldn't have to spend the night. It wasn't necessary. Ed was sound asleep, and if something did happen, Danny and his wife would be there to help. Emma could catch a ride with Atlee and Susie, who lived out her way. Having agreed to the change of plans reluctantly, Emma went out the door with Atlee and his wife. Before leaving, she promised to return in the morning.

With the visitors out of the house, Danny and his wife went upstairs to bed. Katie, fully dressed, climbed into bed next to Ed. Several times during the night, he cried out in his sleep, waking her up with a start. Whenever he made a sudden move, she tensed up, not knowing what to expect. Just before dawn, she got up and made her way to the kitchen to make herself a cup of hot tea. A new day was about to begin and she didn't know what to do.

18

"The English Have Ed"

Danny, following a quick, snowy trek to the outhouse in the sunless morning light, took a place at the kitchen table as his wife and Katie prepared a breakfast of eggs, sausage, pancakes, and mashed potatoes. "How is Ed doing?" he asked.

"He's still sleeping," Katie replied.

"Did he have a good night?"

"Yes, he slept well."

"I bet it was them nerve pills your mom gave him."

"Drugs aren't good for you," Katie said. "I don't want Eddie on drugs."

"Do you think he's better now?" Danny asked. "I never seen him like that before."[1]

"I don't know; I better check on him." The moment Katie walked into the bedroom, she knew Ed was in trouble. On his back staring at the ceiling, he ignored her invitation to join his brother at the breakfast table. She was about to help him out of bed but drew back in terror when he regarded her with a pair of bulging, bloodshot eyes that dominated the room. "Ed, what's wrong with you?" she managed.

In a whining voice that seemed to be coming out of his nose, Ed spoke: "I saw Danny, Atlee, and Joe flying with angels and they were joking about my illness!"

"It was a dream," Katie said. "You had a nightmare; come and have some breakfast."

"I know what you're trying to do," Ed said. "You and them are trying to poison me." He turned his gaze to the ceiling and spit into the air. It was happening again.

Katie backed out of the room. "He's spitting again," she said to Danny when she walked into the kitchen.

"Should I get the bishop?" Danny asked.

"No. Ed's going to the hospital," Katie said. "He can't stay here. He thinks we're trying to poison him!"

"Did you tell him he's going to the hospital?"

"No; he's not going to like it."

"What should I do?" Danny asked, getting up from the table.

"Run over to your dad's; have someone call for an ambulance; then come back here with Atlee and Joe."[2]

Mr. and Mrs. Gingerich and their younger children were in the kitchen having breakfast with Ed and Katie's kids when Danny came into the house out of breath, carrying snow on his boots. In the living room, where the little ones couldn't overhear, Danny informed his parents that Katie had decided to put Ed into the hospital. "What happened?" Mr. Gingerich asked.

"He's having another spell."

"Oh, my God!" Mary Gingerich exclaimed. "Where is he?"

"At home."

"Who's with him?"

"Katie and Fannie."

"They are there alone?" Mary asked, obviously alarmed.

"Ed wouldn't hurt anyone," Danny replied, trying to calm his mother. "They'll be okay."

"What's he doing?" Mary asked.

"He's spitting on the ceiling again."

"I'm going to George Brown's to call nine-one-one," Mary said. "I'm going right now!"

"Me and Danny will round up Atlee and Joe and stop by and tell Levi and Emma," Mr. Gingerich said.[3]

Joe Gingerich, the first to arrive at Ed's, found his younger brother in the front room sitting on the edge of the cot staring into space. Katie and Fannie, standing together a few feet away, seemed relieved that someone had arrived. Joe greeted Ed but got nothing back, not even a look. Atlee rolled in next, followed by Danny and his father.

Mr. Gingerich didn't like what he saw in Ed. Sitting on the cot with his bare feet planted firmly on the floor, his hair in disarray, his skin white, fists clenched, and the muscles in his neck pulsating, he had the posture of a man about to attack or to run. Right now he was in a holding position.[4] Mr. Gingerich stepped closer to Ed, who didn't look up. "You're going to the hospital," Mr. Gingerich said. "There's nothing to be afraid of."

Ed raised his head but didn't look at his father. "Why is everybody against me?" he cried.

"You have a serious illness," Mr. Gingerich replied. "You have to be treated in a hospital. Your mother has called the ambulance to take you there. We're trying to help you."[5]

Ed looked at Katie. "Why are you doing this to me?" he screamed. Before she could open her mouth, Ed sprang to his feet and started toward the door. Before he hit full stride, he was grabbed by Atlee and Joe, who wrestled him to the floor. Ed fought wildly, throwing off his brothers, and was about to climb back onto his feet when Danny jumped on his back, collapsing him to the floor. As the two men rolled across the room, Katie and Fannie pressed themselves against the wall to avoid being rolled over. After Atlee and Joe piled on, Ed started losing steam and the struggle ground to a stop.[6]

"Be careful; don't hurt him!" Mr. Gingerich yelled.

The brothers had grown up wrestling each other, so it was no secret that Ed, although the strongest by far, had the least stamina, physically. Fighting Ed until he was completely out of gas was the only way to defeat him, and to achieve this feat required two of them, at least. Otherwise, Ed wouldn't stop fighting until he had won; he had to win. Weakened by his illness, exhausted and outnumbered, Ed was carried to a wooden chair, where he would sit, with Atlee holding one arm and Joe the other, until the ambulance arrived. Danny took up a position behind the chair so he could wrap an arm around Ed's neck if he tried to run.

The sound of a vehicle pulling up the driveway brought Katie to the door expecting to greet the ambulance. Instead, it was George Brown with Mary Gingerich and the Shetlers in his van. George didn't come into the house; he'd wait outside until the ambulance came and then haul everyone to the hospital.

Ed, surrounded by his guards and looking like a man about to be fried in the electric chair, looked on blankly as his and Katie's parents spoke to each other in hushed tones the way people converse at funerals.

Noon was approaching, it had stopped snowing and what had fallen was melting, making mud on the roads and dripping sounds off the roof. At the sound of another vehicle coming toward the house, everyone stopped talking. Joe and Atlee felt Ed stiffen. Katie went to the door and stepped outside as the orange-and-white Mill Village Volunteer Fire Department ambulance came to a stop in front of the house. Doug Peters climbed out of the emergency vehicle as Assistant Fire Chief Andy McLaughlin pulled up his black Chevy Blazer ahead of a car driven by Dave Dowler, another volunteer firefighter. Counting George Brown's GMC Suburban, there were now four vehicles in front of the house. Having no idea what they would encounter inside the Amish house, the three volunteers approached Katie carrying a medical kit, a body board, and an ambulance cot equipped with drop legs and wheels.

"My husband, Edward Gingerich, has had a nervous breakdown," Katie said.

"According to the dispatcher," one of the men said, "he's going to the Hamot Medical Center in Erie."

"We'll follow you in our van," Katie replied.

"Where is the patient?" asked one of the volunteers.

"He's inside the house. Be careful; he's been acting wild."[7]

The emergency men and their equipment had just gotten inside when Ed rose off his chair and screamed, "Don't kill me!" Atlee and Joe tried to hold on to his arms but were flung off. Ed stumbled toward the door with Danny, his arms around Ed's neck, hanging on his back. After he had taken a couple of steps, Ed and Danny went sprawling across the floor from the force of a block Atlee threw into their legs from behind. The Mill Village volunteers looked on in disbelief as Ed started crawling around in circles, chomping his teeth, barking, and occasionally spitting.[8]

Katie yelled, "Ed, stop it!" She caught up to Ed, reached down and grabbed him by the back of his collar, and tried to pull him to his feet. "Get into the ambulance!" she shouted as he pulled her around the room like a dog on a leash. Ed finally stopped crawling, got to his feet, looked at Katie, then broke into a crazy, mocking smile. Katie stepped up to him and, without warning, shocked everyone by throwing a looping right-hand punch that landed flush on the left side of his jaw, knocking him clean off his feet and onto his back. He hit the floor with a thud, shaking the house.[9] As Ed lay blinking at the ceiling, his mother, sobbing loudly, ran into the kitchen. The firefighters look at each other as if to say, "Did I see what I think I just saw? Did an Amish woman just punch the lights out of an Amish man?" Ed rolled onto his stomach, got up on his hands and knees, and started crawling and barking again.

Frustrated and out of patience, Katie, speaking loud enough to be heard over Ed's animal sounds, asked, "Why do you act this way? Do you want the hospital men to hurt you? They'll *make* you get into the ambulance!"[10]

Mr. Gingerich, not wanting Ed fighting with the medical volunteers, instructed Atlee, Joe, and Danny to wrestle their brother down and, if they had to, carry him out to the ambulance. As it turned out, restraining Ed was a bigger job than Mr. Gingerich imagined. Instead of being subdued, Ed and his three brothers rolled about the floor in a frenzied ball of torsos, legs, arms, hands, feet, and hair-tousled heads. Ed kicked, thrashed, squirmed, crawled, and slid while his brothers ate elbows, shoes, and knees and were repeatedly tossed into furniture and thrown against walls. Realizing that Ed had the strength of the devil, Mr. Gingerich jumped on the rolling pile, to no avail. Ed was a force that could not be stopped. The Mill Village firefighters decided if they didn't weigh in, someone was going to get hurt.

Unable to manage seven opponents, Ed was brought under control, quickly and completely. He offered no resistance as they rolled him onto the body board and strapped him down. Ed was carried that way out of the house then loaded onto the ambulance cot and wheeled to the emergency vehicle. As the emergency men slid into the back of the ambulance, Mr. Gingerich walked into the kitchen to fetch his wife. "We're going to the hospital," he said. "The English have Ed."[11]

Waking Up in a Mental Ward

Doug Peters radioed Hamot Medical Center that he and two other Mill Village firefighters were en route with a twenty-seven-year-old Amish man, a mental patient named Edward Gingerich, who was being hauled to the hospital in restraints. Because the patient had put up a fight and was at the moment talking to himself, Peters suggested they be met at the emergency-room entrance by security personnel. Members of the Amish man's family, including his wife, who was having him committed, were on their way as well.[1]

Andy McLaughlin and Dave Dowler alighted from the vehicle and were met by a doctor and two security men—an off-duty Erie police officer in his city uniform and an unarmed contract guard assigned to the hospital by the Wackenhut Security Agency. The firefighters pulled Ed out the back of the ambulance and were about to roll him through the emergency-room doors when the doctor, a psychiatrist, asked why the Amish man was strapped to the board. While one of the Mill Village emergency men tried to explain the restraints, the doctor said something to Ed that provoked what sounded like a rational response. Fifteen minutes earlier, while being hauled up Route 19, Ed was telling his captors that his heart had torn loose and he was drowning in his own blood.

"Can you walk on your own?" the doctor asked.

"Sure," Ed replied.

"Untie the patient," the doctor said. "Let him walk into the hospital."

The Mill Village emergency men removed the straps and helped Ed off the gurney.[2] As Ed, the psychiatrist, the two security men, and eight members of Ed's family paraded through the emergency-room doors, the volunteer firefighters climbed into the ambulance for the trip back to Mill Village. Ed was out of their hands.

The doctor and the guards escorted Ed directly to the emergency-room treatment area and sat him on a bed in one of the examination cubicles encircled by a draw curtain. Katie and Mr. Gingerich headed for the registration/check-in counter while the others took seats in the vacant waiting room. Emergency-wise, eleven o'clock on a Tuesday morning was not a busy time. On the hospital admissions form, under "Patient's Occupation," Katie wrote: "farmer and sawmill operator." In the space regarding why the patient was being admitted, she put "trouble with his nerves," and scribbled "cash" where it called for insurance data. Once Katie completed the paperwork, Mr. Gingerich joined the others in the waiting room while she was escorted by a nurse or some kind of aide to Ed's examination cubicle. She found him looking and sounding like his old self, talking calmly with the doctor. The physician introduced himself as a psychiatrist and asked if he might speak to Katie in private. He closed the curtain around Ed's bed and let Katie to a nurses' station where Ed wouldn't be able to hear what they were saying.

"Your husband seems fine," the doctor said. "Why did they bring him here strapped to a body board? Was he violent?"

"Yes," Katie replied. "He went haywire. That's why we called the ambulance."

"That's not what the patient is telling me," the doctor said. "He doesn't know why you called the ambulance or why they tied him down. He seems perfectly normal, lucid. Does you husband have a history of mental illness?"

"No."

"Exactly what did he do that made you call the ambulance?"

"He was acting strange, crawling around on the floor like a dog."

"Anything else?"

Katie was flustered and getting angry. As usual, when Ed turned on his Amish-boy charm, the English fell under the spell. It was obvious the doctor believed Ed and not her. "He was acting wild," she said.

"Could he have been joking, you know, fooling around?"

"He was not joking," Katie replied. My God, she thought, they're going to send him home!

"Perhaps you people overreacted," the doctor said. "Putting a man into a mental ward is a big decision. Maybe your husband was angry, emotionally upset. Did you have an argument?"

"He spit on the ceiling," Katie said, her eyes filling up with tears.

"I'm trying to picture what happened," the doctor said. "We don't want a misunderstanding." Katie and the doctor returned to Ed's bed. "I have other patients to see," he said. "I'll leave you now but will come back and give Ed a more thorough examination."

"How long will you be gone?" Katie asked.

"Not long," the doctor said. He parted the curtains and was gone, leaving Katie alone with her husband.[3]

"What are you trying to do, kill me?" Ed growled the moment the doctor was out of earshot. Ed's rage had bubbled up into his eyes; they looked small, piercing, and threatening. It was as though the psychiatrist had taken Ed's good personality with him, leaving behind all that was bitter, fearful, dangerous, and dark. "You are trying to get rid of me," Ed said. "I know why."

"Why?" Katie asked.

"So you can marry Danny."

"Where do you get these ideas?" Katie asked.

"You and my brother are against me," Ed said. "I know about you and my brother."

"Why do you do this? Why didn't you act up this way in front of the doctor?"[4]

Ed didn't answer. His eyes glazed over and he was somewhere else.

Atlee, Joe, Danny, and his wife, and Mary Gingerich were driven back to Brownhill by George Brown, who had agreed to haul them up to Erie later in the afternoon after they had seen to their chores. Emma and Mr. Gingerich did not leave the hospital and were sitting quietly in the waiting room when Katie, obviously distressed, approached from the examination area. "Where are the guards?" she asked, looking about the room. "I need the guards. Ed is starting to act like he did at home! Where is the doctor? He never came back! Why did they leave? Ed is about to have a spell!"

"I'll get help," Emma said. "Go to Ed." Katie headed back to Ed's cubicle as Emma got up and started for the glass-enclosed security station at the far end of the waiting room. She could see the in-house Hamot guard, the man in charge of the shift, sitting behind a desk inside the tiny enclosure.

Katie returned to the examination area to find Ed lying on his back talking to himself. Katie spoke to him but he didn't acknowledge her presence. The doctor was nowhere in sight and there were no nurses or other patients around. Katie ran back to the waiting room. "Where are the guards?" she asked Emma, who had returned to her chair. "Ed is acting up!"[5]

Emma jumped to her feet and ran to the security post. "We need help!" she said to the guard on duty. "He could get violent!"

"They're coming," the guard replied. "I called them."

Katie returned to the cubicle hoping to find the doctor talking to Ed. Instead, she found Ed, wild-eyed and pallid, spitting into the air. He was about to blow. "Get help!" she screamed as she burst back into the waiting room. As Emma got to her feet, the double doors next to the security post flew open and into the waiting room ran the psychiatrist, a nurse, two Wackenhut guards, and the off-duty cop. Katie and Emma followed the hospital crew into the examination area.

Ed greeted his visitors by sitting up in bed looking like a man who had just been jolted out of a deep sleep. Much to Katie's relief, he was no longer putting on a good show for the English doctor. Clearly out of his mind, he ranted and raved about angels in the sky, Katie's attempt to poison him, and his heart, which had torn loose and was flopping around inside his chest.

The nurses stepped up to the bed and handed Ed a clipboard containing a paper he'd have to sign before they could commit him to the mental ward. "What is this?" he asked.

"A voluntary commitment form," the nurse replied. "If you don't sign it, we can't take you."

"Why not?" Katie asked. "Look how sick he is."

"If he doesn't sign it," the nurse replied, "you'll have to go to court. We can't commit him against his will."

"But he's crazy!" Emma blurted.

"That's not for you to decide," the doctor said.

The nurse offered Ed a ballpoint pen, which he took with his left hand. "I can't make a signature," he said, "because I have no feeling in my right hand."

Katie was not amused. "Sign the form," she snapped.

"I can't!" Ed replied.

"Yes, you can."

"I don't want to."

"Sign the paper."

"My hand, I—"

"Quit lying; sign the form," Katie said, her voice quaking in frustration.

"No," Ed quipped. "I won't."

He handed the pen back to the nurse, who took it with a shrug.

Emma moved closer to Ed and, in German, said, "If you don't sign the paper, the guards can do to you whatever they want."

A queer, puzzled expression crossed Ed's face. "What?" he mumbled.

Emma went in for the kill: "They can hurt you."

Ed stuck his left hand out for the pen, the nurse gave it to him, and with that hand he awkwardly scribbled his name across the bottom of the form.

The nurse took the clipboard, flipped a page, and handed it back to Ed. "Sign this one, too," she said.

Ed balked. He looked at Katie and whined, "What are they going to do to me?"

"Sign the form," she replied, making no effort to conceal her impatience. "Just sign the paper."

Ed turned to the doctor and said, "They're against me!"

Emma spoke up, again in German: "You better sign. If you don't, the guards won't like you. You better cooperate."

Ed hesitated for a couple of seconds then signed the form with his left hand. He handed the clipboard back to the nurse and asked, "Now what?"[6]

"We'll get you settled into a room," the doctor said. "Give you some medication to help you rest."

The nurse had left carrying the clipboard and a few minutes later returned pushing a wheelchair. "Here we go," she said.

"What's that for?" Ed said, clearly alarmed.

"Get in," the nurse replied. "We're giving you a ride."

"Where to?" Ed asked.

"To another part of the building. Come on, get in."

"I can walk."

"Look, it's a rule," the nurse said, becoming stern. "Let's go."

Ed swung his legs off the bed onto the floor and stood

up. The nurse positioned the chair behind him and ordered
him to sit down, which he did. She snapped his foot sup-
ports into place, backed him away from the bed, and
pushed him toward the door that led to the tunnel that
connected the main part of the hospital to the mental ward.
The doctor, the security man, Katie, and Emma fell in
behind. Katie, having never been inside a hospital, had no
idea where they were going or what to expect. This was
Ed's first time, as well.

When Ed and his entourage reached the entrance to the
mental-ward section of the hospital, the doctor explained
they were taking Ed to a place that was off-limits to visitors, even family.

"You mean we can't visit him?" Katie asked.

"You can see him when he gets his room," the doctor
said. "First, he'll be isolated, sedated, and observed. He'll
be assigned a room later."

"How long before I can see him?" Katie asked.

"We'll let you know."

"When will he get better?"

"We won't know that," the doctor said, "until we find
out what's wrong with him. Then we can begin his treatment."

"Can we stay in the waiting room?" Katie asked.

"Sure, but there's no point in that. Go home. At the desk
leave a phone number where you can be reached. We'll
call you when Mr. Gingerich can have visitors."[7]

At the end of the hallway, Ed disappeared through a set
of double doors that closed behind the nurse, the wheelchair, and the three security officers. The doctor said good-
bye to Katie and Emma and walked off in that direction.

"He thinks we've abandoned him," Katie, with tears in
her eyes, said to her mother. "He's all alone."

"There is no other way," Emma replied as they headed
back to the waiting room and Mr. Gingerich.[8]

"How's he doing?" Mr. Gingerich asked when Katie and
Emma joined him in the waiting room.

"We can't even stay with him," Katie said. "He thinks I don't love him. He blames me for everything."

"He's not in his right mind," Emma said. "He'll get medicine."

"I'm staying all night."

"Why do that?" Emma asked.

"I want to show Ed that I love him. I'm not leaving until I see him again."[9]

One of the women who worked behind the registration desk approached Katie. "Your husband is having some trouble," she said. "The nurse wants to know if you can come back and help calm him down."

Katie, Emma, and Mr. Gingerich got to their feet. "When he's having a spell," Katie said, "he doesn't always listen to me. I'll try to settle him down."

"Please follow me," the woman said.

"Can we come, too?" Emma asked.

"Who are you?" the woman asked.

"She's my mother," Katie said. "And that's Mr. Gingerich, Ed's father."

"Let's go," the woman replied, "all of you."[10]

They passed through the big double doors that had swallowed Ed and his wheelchair and entered the mouth of a long corridor, obviously a tunnel of some sort that led to a place different from anything Katie had ever seen. Having passed through a second set of doors at the end of the tunnel, the registration lady led her Amish followers past a nurses' station into another hallway lined with little, brightly lit, windowless rooms with white, plastic-covered mattresses on the floors and against the walls. The doors to these rooms, also white and made of metal, featured little windows with chicken wire inside the glass. As they entered this hallway, Katie spotted, about twenty yards down the corridor, the nurse who had pushed Ed in the wheelchair. Next to her, holding a huge syringe with an incredibly long needle, was the psychiatrist. They were standing in the opened doorway to one of the funny-looking little rooms. Katie approached the doctor and the nurse, followed their gaze into the room, and saw a bizarre but familiar sight—Ed on the floor being chased and wrestled down by three men. And, yes, he was barking.

"They are trying not to hurt him," the doctor said. "But he's a handful."

"Ed, stop it!" Katie yelled, knowing full well that Ed was beyond her control.

Mr. Gingerich, his gray hair and beard looking very white under the intense light, stepped into the padded chamber and dove into the pile of arms and legs. He and the guards quickly got the best of Ed and were able to hold him down long enough for the doctor to pull up his shirttail and plunge the needle into his back. The drug took effect in a matter of seconds and Ed went limp. The guards climbed to their feet and, perhaps out of habit, backed out of the room. When Mr. Gingerich, breathing heavily, came out of the cell into the hallway, the doctor slammed the door with a bang. Katie peeked through the chicken glass and saw Ed, in the midst of all that white, sprawled out like he'd been shot—a wild animal brought down and caged.[11]

20

An English Visitor

On the morning after Ed's hospitalization, every Amish person in Brownhill knew that Ed Gingerich, one of their own, would be starting his day in a mental ward. The Amish are not strangers to mental illness or to mental-health institutions—most have a friend, neighbor, or relative who has been treated for depression or some other kind of nervous or emotional disorder. Ordinarily, the news that someone in the Amish community had been signed into a mental ward, albeit tragic, was not particularly shocking or startling. The way Ed had ended up in the hospital—going berserk in the presence of his family, his in-laws, and the bishop, being strapped against his will on a plank, then carried off by the English—had the Brownhill Amish talking about nothing else. Stories of Ed's shenanigans in the emergency room and the mental ward—his attempts to escape, the padded cell, and so forth—were being told and retold that morning throughout the settlement. The only Brownhill people who didn't know of these details, and would never know, were the English. Ed's closest English friends—Jake Powers, Richard Zimmer, and Debbie Williams—were baffled by the news. If Ed had developed some kind of mental illness, it certainly had come on suddenly. It seemed more likely that Ed had done or said something that had been grossly misinterpreted. Ed *was* a bit of a rebel, but that didn't make him *nuts*.

No one in the Amish community doubted for one second that Ed Gingerich had lost his mind. What they didn't know, or couldn't agree upon, was *why* he had flipped out. Bishop Shetler and Deacon Stutzman suspected that Ed's involvement with his English friend, the evangelist, had opened the door for the devil. Of course, if Ed had been a better Amish man, he wouldn't have been talking religion with an evangelist in the first place. The solution was direct and simple: once the hospital medicine brought Ed back to solid ground, he would have to separate himself from evangelists bearing false passes to heaven, settle into the daily routines of Amish life, and return to the church. There was nothing wrong with him that God, family, and hard physical labor wouldn't cure.

Others in the Amish community, those who had never liked or trusted Ed (people such as Dan Stutzman), believed that he had simply cracked under the strain of being Amish, a way of life he couldn't abide. Levi and Emma Shetler subscribed to this theory but would never admit it to others. They had known Ed nine years; he had lived in their house and they knew that on the outside he looked like an Amish man, particularly to the English, but inside he was something else—a person they didn't understand. If the Shetlers and Dan Stutzman were correct, medicine and prayer, although good things, would not, in the end, deliver Ed from his sickness. As far as they knew, modern science had not produced a drug that made a person love farming and hate pickup trucks. For Ed to be cured, he'd have to leave the Amish, and that included Katie and the children. Levi and Emma hoped they were wrong, but deep in their hearts, they knew they were right—God help them; God help them all.

The sawmill, on that Wednesday morning following Ed's hospital admission, opened for business as usual. Katie's brother Emanuel couldn't find a tool he needed to make an adjustment on the sawing assembly and walked over to Ed's machine shop to look for it there. While rooting around Ed's workbench, he came across an item he rarely saw, something that didn't fit among an Amish man's belongings. It was a shiny, black credit card. He picked it up and saw that it was a department-store card from Kaufmann's—issued to a Delberta Williams. How did Debbie Williams's credit card get into Ed's machine shop? Realizing that the subject of Debbie Williams was at best a touchy one with Katie, Emanuel decided to leave the card where he had found it—to let this sleeping dog lie. It was none of his business. He found the tool he needed and returned to the sawmill.[1]

At eleven o'clock Wednesday morning, twenty-four hours after Ed's admission to the hospital, he was moved to a private room where he could receive visitors as soon as the antipsychotic, antidepressant, and side-effects drugs took hold. Although it was obviously too early to make a full diagnosis, all the signs—the visual and auditory hallucinations and the fear that Katie and his brothers were out to get him—pointed to paranoid schizophrenia. The psychiatrists looked in on the patient at one o'clock and found him listless from the tranquilizers but lucid enough to entertain a visit from Katie, Emma, and Mr. Gingerich, who had been at the hospital since early morning waiting for the opportunity to see him.

Notwithstanding the doctor's assurances that Ed was no longer out of his mind or violent, Katie was nervous about how he was reacting to the knowledge that because of her he was doped to his eyeballs and stuck in a mental ward. When the doctor gave Katie the green light to visit, she asked Emma and Mr. Gingerich to enter the room with her. Even if Ed was angry, it was less likely he'd attack her in the presence of Emma and his father. But with Ed, she could never tell. Where were the security men?

Looking cozy in his hospital pajamas and blue terrycloth robe, and seated casually on the edge of his bed, Ed greeted his visitors with a wide, sleepy smile. Katie instantly realized she was not in danger. This was not the man who had spit on the ceiling and turned into a dog. Overcome with relief and happy to the point of delirium, she asked Ed how he felt. Other than feeling a little drowsy, he reported that he felt great. He had even gotten his appetite back; it was just too bad the food was so lousy. Everybody laughed. Did he have any memory of what he had done to get himself hospitalized? No, not really, Ed said. He did recall working in the machine shop with the Gunk fumes and then feeling kind of weird. The other stuff—all the crazy things the doctor told him he did—he couldn't remember. You don't recall anything? Emma asked in a voice that revealed her skepticism. What about the ambulance trip and all that business in the emergency room? Nothing, Ed said, not a particle. Wait a minute, he did remember wrestling a male nurse—a little guy who came into the room to give him the needle. "He tackled me," Ed said with a smile. "You should have seen how little he was."

"Do you remember talking about religion?" Katie asked.

"No."

"About a new religion?"

"No."

"You told everybody about your spiritual adviser. You said you were thinking about leaving the church."

"I don't remember that," Ed replied.[2]

Obeying the doctor's instructions to keep their first visit with the patient brief, Katie, Emma, and Mr. Gingerich, at two in the afternoon, were in George Brown's van, on their way back to Brownhill and the chores that awaited them. They were amazed at how quickly and completely Ed had recovered. According to the psychiatrists, he very possibly suffered from a serious mental disease, but it was an affliction that could be controlled by the proper use of the right mix of drugs. No one knew for sure how people like Ed contracted this disease, but in most cases it could be managed. Katie had to admit that the medicine the doctors had given Ed at Hamot seemed to have done a lot more for him than four years of Doc Terrell's blackstrap molasses. Perhaps Doc Terrell's healing powers didn't extend to problems of the mind. Maybe Emma had been right. As for Ed, he spent the rest of the day sleeping.

Word of Ed's hospitalization had not reached Dave Lindsey, who happened to stop by the sawmill about the time Ed was being visited by Katie, Ed's father, and Katie's mother. Noah Stutzman gave Dave the news: "Ed is in the hospital for a nervous breakdown. The ambulance came for him yesterday," he said.[3] At first Dave thought this was a joke, some kind of weird, Amish-style humor. But Noah wasn't kidding; Ed *was* in the hospital, Hamot Hospital in Erie. Dave couldn't imagine his friend having a "nervous breakdown," that was impossible. He pressed for details but got nowhere. Getting a Mafia hit man to spill the beans was a lot easier than pulling this kind of information out of an Amish man.

That evening, Dave telephoned the Hamot Medical Center and was informed that an Edward D. Gingerich had been admitted to the hospital and could be visited. The following morning, Thursday, March 26, he drove to Erie to determine what had happened to his friend and Christian protégé. Dave didn't know that Ed had alerted Bishop Shetler and others to the fact that he was receiving religious counseling from an outsider. He had no idea that, as Ed's unidentified English spiritual adviser, he was, even as a hospital visitor, *persona non grata*.

Because Dave had hoped for a private visit, he thanked God when he walked into the room and found Ed alone. Except for looking a little groggy and out of uniform in his hospital garb, Ed seemed perfectly normal. He recognized Dave immediately and virtually jumped off the bed to greet him. Ed asked how Dave had found out about his being in the hospital and Dave explained that Noah down at the mill had told him something about Ed having a nervous breakdown. Dave said that he didn't believe it then, and now, seeing Ed in the flesh, he knew that it must be wrong. What was going on? Why *was* he in the hospital? What was he doing in a *mental ward*?

Ed replied that he wasn't quite sure himself how he had ended up in a mental facility. He didn't remember doing any of the crazy things they said he had done and he couldn't even recall being delivered to the hospital in an ambulance. He must have blacked out, and when he came around, he found himself in Erie, Pennsylvania, drugged up and confused.

Dave was eager to know what, if anything, Ed remembered about the long session they had in the machine shop when they had spoken of the Bible and being born again through Jesus Christ. Dave was afraid that whatever it was that had caused Ed temporarily to slip out of gear had also wiped out his memory of what he considered a big step

toward Ed's salvation, significantly setting back their progress. On that account, Ed had good news—not only did
he remember that marathon discussion, he had since, except for his blackout period, thought of little else. In fact,
after Dave went home that evening, Ed, feeling strange
after working two days with the degreasing solvent, had
gone to bed and dreamed all night about starting a new
religion in which everyone went to heaven.

The mention of the degreasing solvent sharpened Dave's
own recollection of those hours with Ed inside the machine
shop, the air almost unbreathable because of the solvent
fumes. Dave recalled how the solvent fumes had affected
him and suddenly the mystery of Ed's so-called nervous
breakdown was solved. Ed wasn't crazy; he had simply
experienced a violent reaction to the Gunk he was using,
improperly, to clean an engine. It all made perfect sense.

Dave carefully explained his theory to Ed, who was less
interested in the Gunk explanation than he was in deter-
mining from Dave where in the Bible he could find the
passage that promised guaranteed salvation. Ed said he'd
been trying to remember the exact words to that verse but
because of the drugs and so forth hadn't been able to get
a handle on it. He was worried that he had remembered it
wrong. Was there such a passage and, if so, where was it?

Dave was thrilled and humbled by his friend's courage
and spiritual devotion. Despite his illness and the fact that
he had been obviously misdiagnosed as insane, Ed was
seeking out the Lord. All of Dave's efforts, and Lazar's,
too, had not been in vain. Ed was on the road to being
reborn in the name of Jesus Christ.

21

Drug-Addled

On Friday, April 3, 1992, with Pamelor and Navane in his blood, big words like paranoid schizophrenia in his head, and $8,000 no longer in his bank account, Ed went home.[1] He no longer listened to voices no one else heard, imagined angels fluttering above his bed, or feared being poisoned by his wife. He wasn't cured, he wasn't well, but he wasn't sick enough to be left in the hospital. After ten days in the mental ward, it was up to Katie to see that Ed kept taking his medicine and traveled up to Erie once a week to be seen by the psychiatrist who'd be monitoring his progress. Ed had complained to his doctors and their helpers that the drugs they prescribed made him tired and feel kind of stupid. How long would he have to take this medicine? Was he going to feel this way the rest of his life? His doctors had to admit there was a lot they didn't know about his disease or exactly how the medicine he was taking would affect him, but they did know this: It would be much worse if he quit the drugs. Without the medicine, he would surely relapse and end up back in the padded room rolling around with the security men. Therefore, he could not, under any circumstances, go off his medicine. Ever.

Ed had his first outpatient session with the psychiatrist on April 7, just four days after his release from the medical center. George Brown drove him and Katie to the doctor's office in downtown Erie not far from the hospital. To the psychiatrist's question regarding how he was making it on the outside, Ed complained bitterly about the effects of the medicine. He was constantly drowsy, even in the morning, after a long night in bed. He was slurring his words and every so often his hands would tremble. He felt, looked, and sounded like an eighty-year-old drunk. But that wasn't the worst part. What really drove him to distraction were the open sores in his mouth, which was always dry regardless of how much water he drank. Could the doctor do anything for the sores and his parched mouth?[2] The doctor took a look and said the problem was a yeast infection. They had a drug for that.

Ed suffered through another week, then another, and on his third visit to the psychiatrist in Erie, he threatened to take himself off the medicine if something couldn't be done to diminish the side effects. Sympathetic to Ed's suffering and worried that his patient would do the unthinkable if the side effects weren't at least ameliorated, the doctor prescribed Symmetrel and Pestoril in place of the Pamelor and Navane. The doctor explained that it sometimes took a month or longer of trial and error to figure out the correct "recipe" and dosage. Every patient was different; there was no such thing as a standard fix. Ed warned the doctor that he might not be able to wait several months while they played around with various combinations and amounts of drugs. As it stood now, he couldn't work more than a few hours in his machine shop without having to go into the house and take a nap. He had felt better before he went to the hospital. Katie was losing patience as well. She was starting to wonder if Doc Terrell had been right after all.

Lazar LeMajic didn't know that Ed was a mental patient until he was out of the hospital and home. The vision of Ed going haywire was so foreign to Lazar's image of him, he simply refused to believe it until Dave Lindsey explained that Ed *had* acted strange but was merely reacting to the Gunk fumes in his machine shop. Ed's stay in the mental ward was a big mistake, an overreaction by his wife. Ed was the sanest person Lazar knew and the good news was this: According to Dave Lindsey, he was still reaching out for Jesus!

Lazar drove out to the sawmill to touch base with his Amish buddy and was told that Ed hadn't been around all day. He was probably in the machine shop or, if not there, at the house. Lazar knocked at Ed's door expecting to meet the Ed Gingerich he knew—an outgoing and energetic young Amish man with a head full of ideas and plans for his machine shop. Instead, what he saw was a pallid, glassy-eyed stick of a man with pillow-matted hair, a thick tongue, and trembling hands. Lazar made an effort to hide his shock as Ed stepped outside to talk. "I guess you heard I was in the hospital," he said.

"Yes, Dave told me. What happened?"

"They say I did crazy things, but I don't remember any of it."

"Dave says it was fumes from the Gunk. You gotta be careful with that stuff."

"Yeah. Dave and me were talking in the shop and after that I felt weird. Next thing, I'm up in Erie."

"Why did they put you in the mental ward?"

"There's something wrong with my brain—the chemicals aren't right. The bishop came to see me 'cause I was talking about leaving the church. I'm trying to straighten myself out, but the medicine I got don't suit me."

"There's nothing wrong with you, Ed; you're not crazy. If anyone is nuts, it's the bishop."

"I hope they find a better medicine," Ed slurred. "I'm really tired; I was taking a nap. All I do is sleep."

"Ed, before I go, I want to leave you with a verse that will help you through this: 'For God so loved the world, that he gave his only begotten Son, that whosoever believeth in Him, should not perish, but have everlasting life.' "[3]

Looking drug-addled and weary, Ed mumbled good-bye and shuffled back into the house. Lazar drove out of

Brownhill that day wondering what in God's name they were doing to his friend.

The day after it happened, Jake Powers heard that Ed had some kind of fit and was taken away in an ambulance. Jake had not seen this coming, and as far as he knew, no one at the sawmill had either. He tried to get the details from the boys at the mill but didn't come away with much information. They either didn't know or weren't talking. He asked about Katie and the kids and was told they were fine. Jake could have driven up to Erie to visit Ed but chose not to. He didn't feel comfortable in hospitals and couldn't stand the thought of seeing Ed in a mental ward. He'd wait until Ed got well enough to come home and visit him there. In the meantime, he checked in at the sawmill every day in the event that someone had news of Ed's progress. That's how he found out that Ed was back in Brownhill. Ed had been home a couple of days.

Jake decided to give Ed some time to recover at home before he paid him a visit. Ed had been out of the hospital about two weeks when Jake, at nine in the morning, knocked on his door. He was greeted by Katie, who looked tired and depressed. Without much to say, she led Jake into the front room, where Ed, fully clothed except for shoes and socks, lay stretched out on the cot with his bare feet hanging off the end of the bed. Katie then disappeared into the kitchen. Without making the effort to sit up, Ed said hello.

Jake had been nervous about visiting Ed because he had no idea what he would find. No one he talked to seemed to know how Ed was progressing. From what Jake saw before him, it was obvious that Ed wasn't doing well at all. His colorless face seemed frozen into an expression of absentminded bewilderment. He looked drugged and sickly, and he sounded pathetic when he lowered his voice and said, "She makes me take naps in the afternoon. She won't let me go anywhere in a truck."

Having no idea what had happened to his best friend, Jake sensed that the Ed Gingerich he had spent so much time with during the past two years was gone and wouldn't be coming back. Jake wasn't even sure that Ed would remember this visit. Following a few minutes of small talk, he said, "I better be going."

"From now on," Ed said, "Katie comes first, then the kids."[4]

Two days later, Richard Zimmer came to the house to say hello and, like Jake Powers, was stunned by what was left of his neighbor. Richard had no idea Ed was so ill. Instead of talking about his machine shop, Ed, obviously focused on Katie, told Zimmer that from now on he was putting her first. When he got better, he'd think about having more babies, something that would make his father very happy. But he'd have to get better; otherwise, no more kids. In the nine years Zimmer had known Ed, he had never seen him like this. The poor guy looked and acted like a dope addict.[5]

Ed didn't show up for his fourth appointment with the psychiatrist in Erie. The doctor hadn't done a thing for him and the pills he was taking had turned him into a zombie. He talked it over with Katie and they agreed that he would be better off without the medicine, so, on April 28, the day he was scheduled to see the psychiatrist, Ed quit his drugs.[6] His experience with the hospital medicine had convinced Katie that Doc Terrell's drugless therapy was the way to go. In the future, when Ed wasn't feeling well, she'd let Doc Terrell handle the problem. She'd put her trust in the "Pennsylvania doctor."

Katie hoped that Ed would bounce back once the hospital medicine had worn off. Three days after stopping the drugs, he did perk up, but it was a nervous energy tinged with hostility. His English pals—Jake Powers, Dave Lindsey, and Lazar LeMajic—thinking that he needed his rest, didn't come around anymore. Dan and his wife, Fannie, were back in Ontario winding up their affairs before moving back to Brownhill. Ed didn't have any projects going in the machine shop and at the sawmill; he just got in the way. He couldn't stand being around his parents; his dad wanted to preach to him and his mother wanted him to leave so she could stop trying not to look frightened. His parents, his brothers, his sisters, Katie—they were always watching him, looking for the slightest sign that he was slipping, waiting for him to blow up. When he walked out of the room, he knew they were talking about him. He couldn't stand the scrutiny. He didn't feel comfortable around his family but had nowhere else to go. He felt trapped and began to suspect they were plotting against him. The headaches came back with a vengeance. The pain became so intense Ed thought his head had swelled up to the point that it would actually explode, scattering his brains in every direction. Katie frequently found him standing in the middle of the room pulling out his hair. "It's on fire!" he'd scream.[7]

In Brownhill, the first day of May brought signs of spring. In a few days, the hardwood forest would begin to take on color—a delicate, mintlike shade of green—proof that winter wasn't coming back soon. Children came out of their houses, men and horses took to the fields, and freshly washed shirts, pants, sheets, and diapers flapped on backyard clotheslines like so many flags. This was Katie's favorite time, but this year she wasn't enjoying the routines of spring. She and Ed were cut off, in self-imposed isolation from the world. Convinced that his brothers were out to kill him, Ed didn't feel safe leaving the house. Some of his English acquaintances came to the door, but Katie, per her husband's instructions, turned them away. Ed would hide in the bedroom until he heard their vehicles pull away from the house. The couple stopped going to church because Katie couldn't be sure how Ed would behave and she didn't want her mother seeing him in his current condition. If Emma laid eyes on Ed, she'd, one, be worried about Katie, and, two, try to get Ed back on drugs and into a mental ward. Katie was avoiding her parents because she didn't want to get drawn into another argument about Doc Terrell versus the so-called real doctors.[8]

Katie didn't know what to do with Ed. When he was on his drugs he slept all day; off the medicine he became nervous, frightened, and preoccupied with God and the devil. His head was full of crazy ideas: God and the devil were locked in combat, fighting for his soul; all of his internal organs had mysteriously disappeared; people were listening in on his thoughts; and Katie and his brothers were still trying to kill him by making him eat poisoned herbs. No matter how hard she tried, Katie could not convince Ed that none of these things were true. Where did he get these crazy ideas?

It got worse. Ed started hearing things—God speaking to him in his brother Dan's voice, and Satan, speaking as a female, telling him that Katie was blocking his path to salvation. "Kill her," Satan said. "Kill her to save yourself!" Ed had visions as well: a man surrounded by angels, all purely white, hovering overhead. The man, wearing a blinding white suit, was God, and when God spoke, in Danny's voice, he warned Ed against listening to the devil.[9] Ed couldn't sleep for more than a couple of hours at a stretch. At night, he'd prowl the house talking to himself, God, and the devil, singing gospel songs and trying to read and make sense out of his Bible. In bed next to Katie, he'd scratch at his dry skin until he bled. Ed was lost, wandering about in a private inferno only he could sense, creating for Katie a hell of her own.

On May 2, a Saturday, Ed, after a long, torturous night of visions and bizarre conversations with himself, announced to Katie that he had decided to shoot himself.[10] He just couldn't stand it any longer. His anger and violence had always been directed at his wife; it never crossed her mind that he might harm himself. She gathered up Ed's .22 rifle, his .410 and twelve-gauge shotguns, wrapped them in an old blanket, and hid them in the buggy shed among her garden tools.[11]

That evening, Ed ignored Katie's pleas to come to bed and spent the night roaming the house in the company of his white-suited God figure, floating angels, and devil's voice. Katie, in and out of bed all night checking on Ed, was, at daybreak, almost as strung out as he. It was Sunday but neither one of them was in shape for church. In addition to her regular chores, Katie would spend the day keeping the kids away from Ed and trying to talk him into taking his blackstrap molasses.[12]

Emma Shetler hadn't seen her daughter for several days and when she and Ed missed another church service, the older couple decided to ride over to Ed and Kate's house to make sure they were all right. The moment they turned into the driveway and their daughter's home came into view, they knew there was trouble and it was all about Ed. Ed was leaning halfway out of one of the front-room windows, waving his arms and talking gibberish in that squeaky voice he had when he was having one of his spells. Atlee and Joe were standing in the yard pleading with him to withdraw from the window and get back into the house. They were working their arms as well. Had a passing motorist on Sturgis Road caught this scene, he might have concluded that the Gingerich boys were at it again—blowing off a little steam after church. Who would have guessed that Ed Gingerich was blowing his top? Inside the house, behind Ed, stood Katie, his parents, and his uncle Mose, visiting from Conewango Valley, New York. Ed was out of control again and nobody knew what to do with him.[13]

Just before noon, he had started pulling at his hair and was complaining that he was burning up inside. Although it was forty degrees and windy outside and only sixty in the house, Ed had opened all the windows on the first floor. It grew so chilly that Katie, worried about the children, started closing the windows. This angered Ed, who followed her around the house opening them back up. Katie wanted the children out of harm's way, so she told the oldest boy, Danny, to walk Enos and little Mary to Grandpa Gingerich's house. She instructed her son to tell his grandfather that Daddy wasn't feeling well. When Mr. Gingerich received the message, he suspected the devil had reentered Ed and was making trouble. That's when he sent for Atlee and Joe.

Ed was still halfway out the window when Levi and Emma entered the front room. "Close the window!" Katie shouted above Ed's babbling. "It's freezing in here!"

"Leave me alone!" Ed screamed.

"Why are you doing this?" Katie bellowed. "What is wrong with you?"

"Go away," Ed shouted. "If you don't leave me alone, I'll hit you!"

"Oh, my God!" Mary Gingerich cried. "Katie, be careful!"[14]

Ignoring her mother-in-law's warning, Katie walked up behind Ed and reached around his waist and tried to pull him back into the house. He held his ground by grabbing onto both sides of the window frame. Realizing that wouldn't work, Katie squeezed her body between Ed and the window and tried to pry his fingers off the frame while pushing back against his body with one of her feet against the wall for leverage. It was a pretty good technique and was beginning to work when Ed suddenly let go—causing both of them to fall on their backs with Katie on top. Katie scrambled to her feet before Ed, ran to the window, and pulled it down with a bang. She turned and started to say something to Ed, who came up to her and threw a punch that missed her face but got the window, spraying shards of glass down on his brothers standing outside. Ed withdrew his fist and seemed surprised to find it bloody. "Look what you made me do!" he screamed. "I cut my hand!" He held it out for Katie to examine.

Katie took Ed's hand and examined it. "It's just a small cut," she said. "You need a bandage."

Ed pulled his hand away and brushed it against his shirt, leaving a stain. "You are out to get me," he said.

"Why did you break the window?" Katie asked. She was angry and didn't care who knew it. "That was stupid!"

Ed stepped back and pointed a bloody finger at her face. "I know what you want," he said.

"I want you to stop acting stupid!" Katie shot back.[15]

Looking stunned by her remark, Ed fell silent and regarded her with a pair of bulging, panicked eyes. "The devil has him!" his father whispered. Ed's eyes, showing a lot of white underneath, seemed ready to roll up completely into his head. His face glistened with sweat and he was breathing heavily through his mouth. He stood there looking like the farmer in one of those old monster movies who'd just came face-to-face with the beast. To his mother, Ed *was* the beast; fearing the worse, she ran out of the house.[16] Katie, still disgusted that Ed had broken a window, walked into the kitchen to get a broom to sweep up the glass. Ed spun around and, without a word, scrambled up the steps to the second floor. Katie returned with the broom and a dustpan and started sweeping up the debris.

Upstairs, Ed opened a window facing Sturgis Road and climbed out onto the roof over the front porch. Atlee and Joe were standing in the front yard consoling their mother when Joe looked up and saw Ed. Mrs. Gingerich followed his gaze and screamed, "He's going to kill himself!"— which brought everyone out of the house. If it was Ed's intention to kill himself by jumping off the roof, he had his work cut out for him because he was only ten feet off the ground. Ed leaped off the house and landed on a pile of dirt about four feet below the edge of the roof. He stood on top of the mound and threw his arms skyward into a V the way Richard Nixon used to do it. "Ed, get down from there!" Katie yelled from below.

Ed dropped his arms and looked down at her. "Who do

you think you are—Jesus?" he said.[17] He dropped into a sitting position and slid off the pile on the seat of his pants, hitting the ground running. As he sprinted toward Sturgis Road, Atlee, Joe, and Uncle Mose climbed into a buggy and rolled down the driveway after him.

The women—Katie, Emma, and Mrs. Gingerich—went back into the house, where Levi fetched some wood for the heating stove. Mr. Gingerich said he'd nail some boards over the broken window to keep out the cold. Katie walked upstairs and shut the window Ed had opened to climb onto the roof. She returned to the first floor to find Emma and Mary sitting at the kitchen table. "He hasn't gotten any better," Emma said, expressing the obvious. "Is Ed still taking the medicine they gave him at the hospital?"

"No," Katie replied. "He doesn't like the way it makes him feel."

"He's got to take that medicine," Emma said. "This is what happens when he doesn't."

"He won't even take his herbs," Katie said. "He thinks I'm trying to poison him."

"I don't see how you can live with him," Mary Gingerich said. "He's dangerous!"

"Why does he hate me?" Katie asked. "What have I done?"

"I'm afraid he'll hurt the children," Mary said. "Don't have any knives in the house, take away all the knives!"

"I couldn't do that," Katie said. "If something happens, it happens. It's in God's hands."

"Ed doesn't know what he's doing," Mary continued. "I'm afraid of him. He scares me to death."

"I've hidden his guns," Katie said. "He doesn't have his guns."

"Get the knives—his hunting knives—he loves his knives," Mrs. Gingerich said.

"If he doesn't get better," said Katie, "I'm taking him back to Doc Terrell."

"Terrell is no good," Emma blurted. "Ed needs a regular doctor."

"I think the devil has got Ed," ventured Mary. "Get rid of his knives! Do it for the children!"[18]

Out on Sturgis Road, the men in the carriage were moving west toward the Frisbeetown intersection. They didn't know which way Ed had turned at the foot of the driveway but figured he'd be heading for his father's house. The moment they cleared the rise in the road a hundred yards west of the driveway, they spotted him. He was sprawled facedown in the middle of Sturgis just beyond the intersection. At first they thought he'd been run over by a truck. When they got to him, they realized he had just run out of gas and collapsed on the road. He wasn't hurt, just exhausted from his quarter-mile sprint. Uncle Mose pulled the buggy off to the side as Atlee and Joe tried to help Ed onto his feet in order to get him off the road before a car or truck came barreling over the rise. Ed wasn't helping a bit. His body was so limp, his brothers had to carry his deadweight to the buggy. Getting him into the rig was not easy and it wasn't pretty. Eventually, they managed to stuff his body—flopping arms, legs, and head—into the cargo space behind the bench. With Uncle Mose at the reins, Joe sitting beside him, Ed crumpled in the back, and Atlee walking alongside the buggy, they turned onto Frisbeetown Road and rolled north to the Gingerich house. Suddenly, without warning, Ed awoke from his stupor with a bang and the single-minded desire to *immediately* get out of the carriage. Joe climbed into the back to wrestle him down while Uncle Mose shifted the horse into a gallop. Atlee, whose job it was to nab Ed if he got out of the buggy, had to run to keep up.

Buggies aren't constructed to contain wrestling men. From his position outside the rig, as he ran helplessly alongside the rocking carriage, Atlee heard canvas tearing then saw arms and feet exploding out of the top and sides of the rig. The poor horse, pulling three men in a bucking, rocking, bouncing buggy, staggered up the driveway to the Gingerich house. The moment Uncle Mose pulled the exhausted animal to a halt, Ed quit fighting and fell limp. The buggy—torn, tattered, and without much of its roof— looked like it had been swept up by a twister and dropped in another country. Joe, looking a lot like the buggy and breathing like the horse, helped Atlee and Uncle Mose carry Ed into the house. They dumped him on the floor in the middle of the front room, then stood back and waited for him to go off like a firecracker. This time, though, there was no explosion. Ed curled up like a baby and went to sleep.

22

Another Spell, Another Stint

Ed slept three hours on his father's floor. He looked awful, was too weak to walk, but otherwise seemed normal. He was sorry about the buggy and said he'd pay to have it fixed. He wanted to go home.

Atlee and Joe helped him to the battered buggy and drove him back to Katie, who was alone at the house. The kids were staying another night with their grandparents and Levi and Emma had gone home. Emma had offered to stay the night with her daughter, but Katie thought it unnecessary. Ed's brothers half carried him into the bedroom, where he collapsed onto his bed and immediately fell asleep. Katie covered him with a quilt. "He doesn't eat," she said to the brothers, "he won't eat anything I give him because he thinks it's poison."[1] Atlee and Joe said they were willing to stick around to keep an eye on their brother but were sent home to their wives. Katie assured them that everything would be fine. What Ed needed was a long, deep sleep.

Just after dark, while she was sitting at the kitchen table over a cup of tea, Katie heard screams coming from the bedroom. Thinking that Ed was having another nightmare, she decided not to disturb him. The screaming stopped. Katie got up from the table and was about to sneak into the bedroom to make sure Ed wasn't sleeping under the bed when she heard him making his way toward the kitchen, singing, in German, a gospel song called "O God, Our Father." Ed moseyed into the kitchen and, taking no notice of Katie, drifted into the front room, all the while singing in a high-pitched childlike voice. Katie watched him settle into a rocking chair. A few minutes later, he stopped singing and began talking to himself and his demons. Katie tried to make sense of what he was saying until she realized it was his religious gibberish. He carried on that way for hours. At dawn, she found him curled up under the desk, sound asleep. Not wanting his relatives to find him under the furniture when they came to see how he was doing, Katie poked him awake and coaxed him onto the front-room cot.[2]

Levi and Emma returned to the house at ten o'clock that morning to find Katie, Mary Gingerich, Joe Gingerich, and Joe's wife, Annie, clustered around Ed. He was stretched out on the cot in the front room looking pale, skeletal, and unkempt, and although his eyes were closed, Emma thought he was just pretending to be asleep. "How's he doing?" she asked.

"He had a bad night," Katie replied.

"What did he do?" asked Mary Gingerich. "You shouldn't have been with him alone."

"He had bad dreams," Katie said. "I think it was the drugs he took."

"No," Emma said, a little too loudly. "He *needs* the medicine."

"We're taking him to Doc Terrell," Joe said. "George Brown is riding us down today."

"Terrell can't fix Ed," Emma said. "Take him to my doctor."

"We like Terrell," Katie replied.

"We trust him," Joe said, ending the debate.[3]

An hour after Levi and Emma had arrived at Ed's house, Ed, Katie, Emma, Joe, and Annie were sitting in George Brown's red GMC Suburban van on their way to Cambridge Springs. Ed sat stiffly and blank-faced in the backseat between Katie and the window, showing no interest in the passing countryside or what was being said around him. When Katie tried to engage him in conversation, he turned to the window and didn't respond. By the time George Brown pulled off Route 19 onto Doc Terrell's parking lot, no one was speaking. Terrell had been open for business for less than one hour and already there were six vehicles in the lot dwarfing his tiny building.

The mood in the van going back to Brownhill was much brighter than it had been on the way down to Cambridge Springs. That was because Ed's three-minute visit with Doc Terrell had made Katie and Joe feel much better. Unfortunately, it was Ed who was sick, and as far as Emma could tell, he looked as bad coming home as he had going.[4]

Tuesday at dawn, May 5, Ed walked into the kitchen humming a tune unfamiliar to Katie. She was working at the sink with her back to him, but knew, without looking at his face, that he was out of control. The weird, high-pitched voice that crawled out of his mouth when he was having a spell gave him away. She turned and there he was, standing perfectly erect, his feet close together, arms hanging stiffly at his sides, and his eyes rolled up into his head. He shuddered, let out a piglike squeal, awkwardly spun about, then ran screaming into the front room. Afraid that he would charge out of the house and disappear into the woods or get run over by a car, Katie ran after him, fully prepared to tackle him at the door. But Ed didn't go for the door; instead, he charged toward one of the unbroken front-room windows and, when he couldn't get it open, smashed his fist through the glass. He cut himself again and the sight of his own blood seemed to calm him down. He stood quietly in front of the broken window as Katie fetched a towel and wrapped it around his hand.

Emma showed up just before noon and found another front window out, Ed lying on the cot talking vigorously to the ceiling and Katie sitting at the kitchen table with her face in her hands. "He won't take his herbs," Katie said.

"He belongs in the hospital," Emma replied. "He needs something stronger than herbs. He's going to kill himself."

"I'm not sending him back to Hamot. He hates me for that. That medicine they gave him made him worse."[5]

Emma said she'd been thinking about another hospital—the one in Jamestown, New York, the Jones Memorial Health Center. A year earlier, Katie's aunt Ella, Mose Shetler's wife, had a nervous breakdown up in Conewango Valley. They took her to the Jamestown Hospital and two weeks later she was home, good as new. Jamestown, by car, was just ninety minutes away. Emma would make the arrangements. She'd gather up the family and get in touch with George Brown, who'd drive them all to New York with Ed. They'd do it today before Ed did something they'd all regret. Life was full of tough decisions and the burden of this one fell squarely on Katie because Ed was obviously incapable of thinking for himself. So, what would it be? Did Katie want more broken windows, second-story jumps, or did she want another chance for a cure?

Katie dreaded the thought of sticking Ed back into a mental ward. He would not go peacefully. If he had only given Doc Terrell's blackstrap molasses a chance, she might not be faced with this terrible dilemma. Katie knew that her mother wasn't the only one who wanted Ed under lock and key. His parents, Atlee, and her uncle Rudy, the bishop, had all recommended hospitalization following Ed's latest rampage.

She also realized that Ed's strange moods and unpredictable behavior had the entire family on edge and on hold, and that wasn't fair to any of them. And she never knew what to do with the children when it looked like Ed was about to explode. Emma *was* right, something had to be done. Okay, she said, why not give Jamestown a try? Except for another big medical bill and the possibility that Ed would not get better and hate her even more, she had nothing to lose.

At four o'clock, everyone in the room—Katie, Emma, Levi, Mr. and Mrs. Gingerich, Atlee, Joe, and Annie— knew that in one hour, George Brown would be pulling up to the house for Ed. The only person who didn't know that Ed was about to be hauled to the hospital in Jamestown, New York, was Ed. It had been decided that the one to break the news would be his father—a task Mr. Gingerich was not looking forward to. George Brown had said he would arrive at five. At a quarter to, when Mr. Gingerich approached the cot to speak to his son, he found him sleeping soundly. Mr. Gingerich put a finger to his lips and waved Atlee and Joe, both carrying several lengths of rope, to the bed. Carefully, Mr. Gingerich tied Ed's legs together just above the knees and at his ankles, while Atlee worked a rope around his chest, binding his arms tightly against his torso. Ed awoke with a start, screamed, and fought against the restraints, but could manage only to roll off of the cot onto the floor, where he remained under the weight of his brothers, who were sitting on his chest and legs.[6]

Soon, George Brown parked his van at the top of the driveway and tapped his horn. A few seconds later, Mr. Gingerich, Atlee, and Joe staggered out of the house carrying a screaming, wiggling, hog-tied Amish man. They were followed to the van by the women and Levi Shetler.

Once the vehicle got rolling, Ed, laid out across the rear seat, settled down and eventually drifted off to sleep. An hour and a half later, George pulled to a stop in front of the hospital's emergency-room entrance. Mr. Gingerich and Katie climbed out of the van and walked into the building to arrange for Ed's admittance. No one had called ahead; therefore, no one at the facility knew they were coming. While they were inside, Atlee and Joe maneuvered Ed, still tied up but no longer resisting, out of the van. Twenty minutes later, Katie and Mr. Gingerich walked out of the building accompanied by a pair of burly young hospital men wearing white shirts, white coats, white trousers, white socks, and black shoes. They found Ed lying barefoot on the pavement next to the right front wheel of the van and humming a gospel tune. He was the only one smiling. "How come you got him tied up?" one of the hospital men asked.

"He can get wild," Mr. Gingerich replied.

"What's wrong with him?"

"He's had a nervous breakdown," Mr. Gingerich said.

"How do you know that?"

"It's happened before. He was in Hamot."

"In Erie?"

"Yes. Ed didn't want to come, so we had to tie him."

"You can untie him," said one of the men in white.

"Are you sure?"

"Yes. He's in our custody now. Please take the ropes off."[7]

Atlee and Joe undid their knots, unwound the rope, and helped Ed to his feet. Except for a slight stiffness in his walk and his ruffled hair, he looked perfectly normal. Flanked by the men in white and followed by his entourage in brown, purple, and blue, Ed strolled into the hospital through the entrance with the fancy glass doors that saw you coming and opened wide. As they proceeded through the waiting area, past the reception counter, en route to the examination cubicles, Katie and the Brownhill contingency started to relax. Perhaps having gone through this routine before had made it a little less frightening for Ed.

The sight of this unusual procession—a tall, barefoot, crazy-haired Amish fellow followed by three Dutchmen and four Amish ladies in their brown bonnets, blue ankle-length dresses, purple shawls, and clunky black shoes—brought the place to a standstill. Hospital employees, patients, and visitors stopped what they were doing to gawk. What was going on? Nobody in the group looked sick or hurt. Which one was the patient? Was it the tall guy between the white coats? At that moment, the tall guy between the men in white coats answered the question as to who was sick. He made it quite clear. Emma saw the whole thing coming the moment Ed stopped in his tracks as though someone had called out his name. He stiffened, rolled back his eyes, dropped to all fours, and started crawling across the floor as fast as he could, his hands slapping loudly against the tile. As Ed knocked over an IV stand, a couple of chairs, a small table containing glass jars, a chrome pan, and a handful of utensils of some kind, Katie, with her hands balled into fists at her sides, yelled, "Why does he do this?" Ed, too busy barking and crawling to consider the rhetorical question, crawled straight for the underside of a hospital bed, perhaps looking for a good place to hide. He didn't make it to the bed, though, because the men in white flattened him to the floor then grabbed him by the arms and dragged him into a place they called the "seclusion room." With impressive ease, Ed's captors lifted him onto the examining table and told him to lie back and relax. Ed immediately complied and, after a couple of minutes, seemed to have fallen asleep. Katie took this opportunity to go to the desk and complete some papers while the others found seats in the waiting area.[8]

Ed had been sleeping about twenty minutes when his eyes popped open. He sat up, looked around, and, because the hospital attendants couldn't get to him in time, climbed off the examination table. With amazing speed and preternatural strength, he began ripping supply cabinets and medical appliances off the wall. Before the hospital men had him pinned flat to the floor, he had done a thorough job of stripping the place down. The room was littered with pill bottles, cotton balls, Q-Tips, tongue depressors, bandages, gauze, a blood-pressure cuff, and a lot of broken glass. The yellow-painted walls bore holes where the supply cabinets had been. Dangling from these walls were loose wires that had once supplied power to electrical fixtures and miscellaneous medical devices. Following the surprise room trashing, Ed, back on the examination table, was being held down by the hospital guys, who were no longer in a good mood. Although there was nothing left in the room to destroy, Ed wasn't getting off that table again.[9]

Shortly after the melee, the psychiatrist walked into the room armed with a syringe containing two hundred milligrams of the antipsychotic drug Mellaril. The doctor administered the shot and then asked, "What seems to be the problem here?"

"What?" Ed asked.

"How are you feeling?" the doctor asked.

"I've got a bad case of liver cancer," Ed said. "I saw a light so bright I thought I was in hell. Do you know my brother Danny?"

"No," the doctor replied.

"When Danny blew into Katie's cunt, I saw an angel fly out of her mouth."[10]

There wasn't much the doctor could say to that. "Someone will talk to you in the morning," he said on his way out of the room.

After receiving a second injection—two milligrams of Ativan, a tranquilizer—Ed spent his first night at the Jamestown Hospital in a tiny room not unlike his padded, wire-windowed accommodations at Hamot. The drugs kept him under throughout the night and in the morning he said he felt extremely tired and weak.

Denied visitors during his first week, Ed settled into the standard mental patient's routine of drugs—in Ed's case lithium, Mellaril, and Cogentin—one-on-one talks with mental-health professionals, group-therapy sessions, and simple crafts, referred to as recreational therapy, to keep him busy.[11] On his eighth day, George Brown delivered his first visitors—Katie, his three children, and Emma. The visit, which Katie had been looking forward to with high hopes and nervous anticipation, took place around a circular table in the visitors' lounge. The children, meant to be a delightful surprise, found their father unenthusiastic and cool. Katie and Emma were also denied a warm greeting, which caused Katie's heart to sink. Denied their father's attention, the kids quickly became bored and turned into an annoyance. Bringing them had been a mistake. Ed didn't look well. He was pathetically thin and pale, his voice was squeaky and weak, and patches of flaky, dry skin marred his forehead, nose, and cheeks. He showed no interest whatsoever in the children, didn't ask one question about how Katie was getting along without him, and completely ignored Emma. Katie didn't volunteer any information regarding the events that had led up to his hospitalization, apparently a subject of little interest to Ed, who never inquired about any of it. Assuming that Ed didn't remember anything, his lack of curiosity puzzled Emma. How could someone wake up one morning in a mental ward and not want to know exactly how he had gotten there? As far as Emma knew, none of Ed's doctors had spoken to Katie or anyone else in Brownhill about these events. If Ed didn't know what he had done or didn't want to say, his doctors wouldn't know how violent he could be toward Katie.

As they sat around the visitors' table, Ed talked about his doctors, the nurses, the food, when he got up in the morning, when he went to bed at night, and how the medicine made him feel he wanted to sleep all the time. The conversation never went beyond Ed—what Ed was doing, how Ed was feeling, what would happen to Ed? It was always Ed.

For Katie, the low point in the visit came when Ed's uncles from Conewango Valley, Noah and Rudy Gingerich, walked into the lounge. Ed was so happy to see them! His eyes brightened, he flashed a big smile and sprang to his feet. All of a sudden it was a party, with Katie, the kids, and Emma watching from the sidelines as Ed and his uncles enjoyed each other's company without them. "When are you going home?" one of the uncles asked.

"The day after tomorrow," Ed said, shocking Emma and infuriating Katie, who had to discover this vital piece of information by overhearing Ed's conversation with a relative he saw three times a year.[12] Once again, Emma was mystified. Why in God's name hadn't Ed revealed this information directly to his wife, the one most affected by the news? Was he *trying* to hurt her? And that wasn't all. If Ed *was* being released in two days, he was getting out of the hospital after ten days; was that enough? Was he ready to go home?

23

Saved from the Bishop

On Saturday, May 15, with George Brown and Emma waiting outside in the GMC van, Katie wrote the hospital a check for $2,600 then followed the aide as he pushed Ed out the door in a wheelchair. Too drugged to be depressed or psychotic, Ed rolled to freedom thinking that his illness had been caused by a chemical imbalance in his brain. He left Jamestown, New York, with bottles of pills, prescriptions for more pills, and the name and address of a local shrink in Union City. He had everything he needed except the foggiest idea as to why he was so angry, down in the mouth, and scared to death he was going to hell. He had medicine for his spells but no idea who he was or why he acted the way he did toward Katie. His doctors and nurses, friendly and helpful in their white-clad, sterile sort of way, people who had known him as well as Doc Terrell knew his patients, had provided him drugs, bedrest, and the promise that all would be well if he kept on his pills. That's what he had gotten for his $2,600—drug-induced sleep, an encouraging word, and a slap on the back as he rolled out the door.

Following ten days of bland food, hospital boredom, meaningless chats with the mind doctors, and all those woeful talk-therapy tales, Ed was eager to get back to the grimy, dark, oily-aired interior of his machine shed, where he could be alone with his motors. There, among his mechanical friends, he was in control; he was the doctor.

During Ed's hospitalization in New York, none of the Brownhill Gingerichs made the ninety-minute trip to visit him. This didn't mean they were unconcerned or fed up with Ed and his mental illness, he had simply picked an inconvenient time to have his breakdown. The day after he had been tied up and hauled off to Jamestown, his brother Danny and his wife had arrived from Canada to make Brownhill their new home. Danny had problems of his own. A week earlier, the house near Norwich he and Fannie had been renting burned to the ground. No one was hurt but much was lost.

Back home in Brownhill, surrounded by his family, Danny would get the help he needed to start his farm on the seventy-two-acre plot across the road from the sawmill. There was a lot to do, including raising a barn, constructing a temporary dwelling, and planting the corn. No one had time to ride up to Jamestown to visit with Ed. Mr. Gingerich hoped that when his son got well and came home, he'd pitch in, help his brother start his farm, and get his mind off himself and those weird religious ideas Dave Lindsey had drilled into his head. What could be better for his physical health and state of mind than returning to his wife and children and laboring shoulder to shoulder with his brothers to help Danny start his farm in Brownhill. As Mr. Gingerich saw it, there was no better way for Ed to get back into God's good graces.

Ed returned to Brownhill too drug-addled and preoccupied with his own misery to pay any attention to his brother Danny and the flurry of activity associated with setting up the new homestead. Once Mr. Gingerich laid eyes on his pale, listless son, he realized that Ed was in no condition to participate in farmwork, carpentry, or anything else that required energy and physical strength.

Ed had been out of the hospital four days when he decided to stop taking his medicine.[1] He never had any intention of talking to the psychiatrist in Union City. He hadn't left the house since coming home, hadn't spoken more than a few words to Katie, and showed no interest in the children. He had spent most of his time in bed drifting in and out of a drug-induced stupor. He hadn't even managed to work up an enthusiasm for his beloved machine shop. He didn't want to spend the rest of his life in his bedroom, so he decided to clear his mind by quitting the drugs. Katie supported this decision fully.[2] Ed had given the medicine a chance to work and it had failed him. And so had his doctors at the hospital. It was obvious that modern medicine had no cure for what was happening to him.

On Friday, May 21, two days after Ed took himself off the drugs, Katie arranged to have George Brown drive them down to Cambridge Springs to see Doc Terrell. Joe Gingerich went along to keep his brother company and to assure him that Doc Terrell had the power to cure his ills. Ed didn't believe that for one second, but he went along

with the joke to please Joe and to keep Katie off his back
while he tried to find his own way to health and happiness.

Katie had been avoiding her parents. Ed was in no condition to socialize and she didn't want Emma and Levi to
know that he had quit his hospital medicine and had returned to Doc Terrell, a man the Shetlers disapproved of.[3]
Emma came to the house a few days after Ed had been
treated by Doc Terrell to see if he had improved and to
check on Katie. Katie was working in her garden and Ed,
although it was almost noon, was still in bed. Knowing
that she couldn't lie or hide the truth from her mother, but
in no mood to argue her case, Katie told Emma that Ed's
drugs hadn't worked, so he was back with Doc Terrell. "Is
he any better under Terrell?" Emma asked.

"No," Katie replied. "All he does is sleep. He doesn't
like to talk, and when he does, I don't like what he says."

"What does he say?"

"He says it wouldn't be wrong if we got divorced—if
we did it the right way."

"What is the right way?"

"The Christian way."

"What is that?"

"I don't know. I told him we're not getting divorced."

"Is Ed in trouble with an English woman?"

"I asked him that and he said no. He's too sick. I think
he's been talking to his evangelist friend. He says he isn't,
but I don't believe him."

"You have to keep him away from those Satan wor-
shipers," Emma said. "They put weird ideas into his head."

"I just want him to get better," Katie said. "How long
can I live like this?"[4]

When Dave Lindsey heard that Ed was back in the hospital
for mental illness, he asked around but was unable to determine exactly what Ed had done to get himself committed. Someone said he was being punished because he'd

gotten mad at his wife and had broken some furniture. Dave couldn't imagine Ed, under any circumstances, losing control of himself. As far as he was concerned, there had to be more to the story than Ed flipping out and ending up in the mental ward. Dave felt that he knew Ed Gingerich as well as anyone and better than most, and this was not a man who was crazy. Perhaps the Amish didn't know the difference between a man with a mind of his own and a man out of his mind. In totalitarian nations, dissidents were often branded as crazy and sent away. Dave wondered if Bishop Rudy Shetler, a dictator in his own right, was somehow behind Ed's hospitalizations.

Dave didn't get up to Jamestown to visit Ed, but in mid-June, about a month after Ed's discharge, he stopped by the sawmill and was told he'd find Ed in the machine shop. Except for looking a bit small for his clothes and a little pale for June, Ed looked and acted the way he always did when Dave stopped by to visit. And as always, he was eager to talk religion. He said he had been reading his Bible and was trying to believe that regardless of who you were or what you have done, salvation was yours the moment you accepted Jesus Christ as your Lord and Savior. Dave took this opportunity to preach evangelical redemption, assuring Ed that everybody had lapses in morality, but unlike the Amish, who shunned its sinners, Jesus forgave. Once Ed freed himself of the bishop and turned to Jesus, he would be saved.[5]

Out of Step

Living the murky, uncertain half-life of an untreated half-sick schizophrenic, Ed Gingerich had nothing useful to do and nowhere to go. He was adrift without a role to play in a culture that rigidly defined roles. He was unhappy and ill at ease at home, too exhausted to accomplish anything meaningful in his machine shop, too disoriented to carry on business at the sawmill, and too jittery and unpredictable to socialize with family and friends. In his more lucid moments, he felt like the village idiot and the town drunk all rolled into one. When he wasn't sleeping, he killed time by hanging around the sawmill, where he got in the way of a thriving business and became an embarrassing annoyance to Noah Stutzman and the other workers.[1] If Ed was in need of vocational therapy, the sawmill, as far as Noah Stutzman was concerned, was not the place for him to get it.

On the twenty-fifth of June, in 1992, a Thursday, Ed and Katie, at three in the afternoon, were in George Brown's GMC van heading south toward Cambridge Springs and another session with Doc Terrell. Ed had not been sleeping well or eating as he should and complained of pains in his lower back. At Katie's insistence, he was about to visit Doc Terrell for the second time since his release from the Jamestown hospital. He was no more enthused about seeing Terrell on this day than he had been on any other, and given the doctor's obvious inability over the past four years to influence the status of his mental health, he had no cause to be optimistic.

In the tiny room surrounding the monstrous examination chair, Doc Terrell reappeared from behind the flimsy curtain hiding his mysterious diagnostic machine and zeroed in on Ed's right foot and ankle. He gave the ankle a good twist, pulled one of Ed's toes, rose to his feet, and scribbled what he had done on a sheet of typing paper that passed for Ed's medical record.[2] On the trip back to Brownhill, Ed did something he had trouble doing in bed; he fell asleep while Katie, to keep her spirits up, made small talk with George Brown.

Katie's continued reliance upon Doc Terrell in favor of a more conventional medical practitioner had created a sore spot in her relationship with her parents. Emma Shetler was particularly distressed over her daughter's stubborn refusal to put Ed back on his hospital medicine and into the professional care of a medical mind doctor. She blamed Joe Gingerich more than anyone for steering Katie in the wrong direction. To avoid the inevitable argument that would erupt over Doc Terrell, Katie had discontinued the weekly visits to her parents' house.[3]

The family divisiveness over Doc Terrell was especially hard on Katie's father, Levi. Although Levi had always preached that a parent should never interfere in a child's marriage, he agreed with Emma that in Ed and Katie's case, something had to be done. His worries about Ed's mental health, the welfare of his grandchildren, his daughter's safety, and the effect of Ed's sickness on Katie's relationship with her mother had come at a time when the fifty-nine-year-old farmer had serious medical problems of his own.

Three months earlier, Levi had come down with a bad cold that found its way into his lungs. In May, a week before they hauled Ed to Jamestown, Levi, still coughing and short of breath, was examined by a physician in Union

City. X rays revealed pulmonary edema—fluid in the lungs—so the doctor prescribed pills to drain the excess water out of his system. The medicine seemed to work, and although Levi still couldn't get in a full day of physical labor, he felt much better. By July, however, he was coughing again and at times had great difficulty catching his breath. He couldn't work at all and spent a good deal of time in bed gasping for air. It was during this period that Ed wasn't getting any better either, and Katie and Emma were at odds over Doc Terrell.

In mid-July, with Levi flat on his back and suffering terribly, Emma decided he needed medical treatment much more ambitious than merely "doctoring for his liquids." She had recently heard of a doctor in Conneaut Lake, Pennsylvania, who had a good reputation among the Amish of that region. On July 20, a neighbor drove Emma and Levi to Conneaut Lake, a tiny lakeside resort village thirty miles west of Brownhill, where Levi was examined by the physician. The news was not good. His blood pressure was extremely high; he was dangerously overweight; and his lungs were so congested he could barely breathe. Believing that Levi was on the verge of a heart attack, the doctor in Conneaut Lake recommended immediate hospitalization. That night, Levi was admitted into the Meadville Medical Center and placed under the care of a heart specialist named Dr. Arno, who informed Emma that her husband, suffering from a serious heart condition, would have to lose a lot of weight, get his cholesterol down, and take pills to lower his blood pressure. After five days at the hospital, Levi came home minus the five quarts of liquid that had been drained from his lungs. He felt much better, but with a seriously damaged heart, would have to slow down, eat less, take his blood-pressure pills, and avoid stressful situations. If he didn't do these things, it was very likely he'd have a heart attack.[4] If he didn't follow his doctor's orders, it could cost him his life. It was as simple as that.

• • •

July had been warm and dry, but August was hot and drier. It hadn't rained in weeks, road surfaces had turned into a fine powder, and everything was covered in dust. Since Ed didn't work and slept a good part of the day, he sat out on the porch all night to escape the heat and brood. In the morning, when everyone else rose to face another day, he would go to bed, alone and apart, the only man on earth.

On Thursday, August 13, in the midst of the heat spell, Ed—lost, depressed, and without hope—sat stone-faced next to Katie in the back of George Brown's van en route to Cambridge Springs for yet another session with Merritt Terrell. When the Pennsylvania Doctor asked him what was bothering him this time, the best Ed could manage was, "Pimples."[5]

25

Punxsutawney Healer

Summer had turned to fall, which had led to a long, harsh winter. The weekend of March 13 and 14, heavy snow and single-digit temperatures had kept Ed, Katie, and the kids cooped up in the house. Ed's health had not improved. In February, he had seen a giant rabbit peering into the house through a window, and he was still obsessed with heaven and hell. Exhausted and in despair, Katie was losing hope. Ed spent most of the weekend closed off in the bedroom, where he napped fitfully between bouts of frantic Bible reading.[1] Katie, taking breaks from the children, her household chores, and the plain, peach-colored quilt she was sewing, periodically offered him a dose of blackstrap molasses or invited him to the kitchen table for a bite to eat. Ed would have no part of the blackstrap but could be coaxed to eat a little. His refusal to take Doc Terrell's elixir angered Katie; she suspected he did this out of spite, to get her goat. If, at the wrong moment, she pushed too hard, tried to insist, his eyes would bug out, he'd stiffen, and in that funny voice he used just before having one of his spells, he would accuse her of trying to kill him with poison.[2] When he got like that, wild-eyed and coiled for action, thoughts of her safety and the children's outweighed concerns for his health. Knowing firsthand how violent he could be, she would back off. Sensing that Ed was on the verge of a spell, she and the children moved out of the bedroom that weekend and slept by the stove in the front room.[3]

On Monday morning, Mr. Gingerich and Ed's brother Dan came to the house to help Katie paint one of the upstairs bedrooms. Ed pitched in that afternoon, but after an hour said he couldn't continue because the paint fumes had given him a terrible headache. He went to bed. They finished the job around five, and before going home for dinner, Mr. Gingerich, concerned that his son didn't seem to be improving, stopped by his bedroom to say good-bye. He caught Ed reading the Bible, and the moment he stepped into the room, Ed launched into one of his disjointed evangelistic homilies. Mr. Gingerich didn't like what he saw or heard. It was obvious the chiropractor in Cambridge Springs hadn't done Ed any good at all; he was clearly losing ground and on the verge of completely losing his mind. Mr. Gingerich, hardly one to run to the doctor every time someone sprained an ankle, came down with a fever, or even broke an arm, realized that Ed had a mental problem that could only be cured by modern medicine. Before departing, he asked Ed if he had any objection to being examined by a medical doctor. Ed said that he didn't, as long as they didn't try to put him back in the hospital.[4] Nobody was going to dope him up and stick him into the nuthouse again.

That evening, Mr. Gingerich called Atlee, Joe, and Dan to his house to discuss what should be done about their brother. It was obvious Ed was not himself; he had filled his head with crazy religious ideas, had accused his wife of having an affair with Dan, and was convinced she and his brothers were trying to poison him. Mr. Gingerich was worried that Ed might be turning dangerous. He was concerned about Katie and the children. Perhaps it was time to think seriously about putting him into some kind of institution where they could keep him until he was better, regardless of how long it took.

Joe Gingerich, the second-oldest son and an enthusiastic believer in herbal remedies and the healing magic of Doc Terrell, had a better idea. He had just heard about a special healer, an Amish man named Jacob Troyer, who ran a sawmill in the Smicksburg settlement near Punxsutawney and could tell what was wrong with people simply by looking at their eyes. He then prescribed the right herbs that would take care of the problem. It was all natural, no drugs, and from what Joe had heard, Troyer was good with people like Ed who had trouble with their nerves. Joe's plan was this: find out how to get to Troyer's house in Smicksburg, run the idea past Katie, and, if she approved of Troyer, line up a driver to taxi Ed, Katie, and members of the family a hundred miles south to the Smicksburg settlement. Joe assured his father that Jacob Troyer had the reputation of being one of the best herb doctors around. They owed it to Ed.

Mr. Gingerich's plan for Ed was more drastic, decisive, and conventional than Joe's. But Joe would get his way. Mr. Gingerich was not a forceful man; he hated confrontation and he didn't know how to respond to Joe's argument that the so-called real doctors and their hospitals had had two shots at Ed and had failed. Mr. Gingerich could have pointed out that it was Ed who had decided not to follow the doctors' orders, that if he hadn't quit his drugs, he' might not have gotten sick again. The hospitals *had* failed by discharging him too soon, before he got used to his drugs or before the doctors found the dosage and combination of chemicals that might have minimized the side effects. But there was no point in arguing with Joe; in the end, his youth, exuberance, and enthusiasm for his own ideas would overwhelm his father. Moreover, Joe's scheme offered a path of least resistance. It would be a lot easier taking Ed to Troyer than getting him back into the hospital. While Mr. Gingerich didn't believe that another Amish man could cure Ed with special herbs, he saw no harm in giving it a try. Joe Gingerich was so sure of Jacob Troyer, maybe he was right.

At ten the following morning, Atlee, with Dan at his side, rolled up the driveway behind Atlee's mud-splattered horse on their way to check on Ed. Before they reached the house, they realized, from the smoke rising out of the chimney, that he was in his machine shop. They pulled up to the shed and walked in, expecting to catch Ed diligently at work on one of his motors, a good sign that maybe he wasn't as sick as their father had thought.

They found Ed in the smoky, half-lit, foul-smelling shack sitting on a crate reading his Bible in the yellow glow of a kerosene lamp. He looked up but didn't lay down his Bible when his brothers entered the shop, giving the impression he considered their presence an intrusion. Following an awkward silence, Atlee asked Ed why he was reading his Bible in the machine shop. Had he been working on a motor? No, Ed replied, he was in the machine shop to get away from Katie and her constant nagging and the children and their nerve-racking noise. He needed the peace and quiet to do some serious thinking about how, as a repugnant sinner, he could get back into God's good graces. Ed solemnly informed his brothers that although it had him exhausted and depressed, he at least had come to realize that his terrible illness was simply God's way of forcing him to choose between a life in Jesus or an eternity in hell. He was part of a divine plan. But before he could ask for salvation, he had to humble himself before God by confessing his sins to anyone who would listen. This kind of talk, especially from someone like Ed, made Atlee and Dan extremely uncomfortable. A man's relationship with God was a highly personal matter, something he didn't talk about with others, not even family. The last thing they wanted to hear was another man's confession, and they said so, bluntly. Ed was not deterred. Since they had interrupted his meditation, they might as well know that their own souls were very likely in jeopardy. Just because they were obedient Amish men on good terms with the bishop was no guarantee they were en route to heaven. No. It took more than that. They had to establish a relationship with God through Jesus Christ; merely being faithful followers of Rudy Shetler was not the way to eternal life. Bishop Shetler was no match for the devil.[5]

Atlee and Dan, deciding it was time to leave, said good-bye. They weren't sure if Ed's illness caused him to talk this way or if having his head full of these crazy obsessions was making him ill. Any hope that he was at least not getting worse were dashed when Ed announced that he knew what they were up to, and he knew who was behind their plan. It was no use denying it. Deny what? the brothers asked. The attempt, he said, to poison him to death with Doc Terrell's blackstrap molasses. Katie had spiked the medicine and they were trying to get him to take it. "Someone in the family," Ed said, "is going to die."[6]

Greatly disturbed by what they had just seen and heard, Atlee and Dan drove straight to their father's house. Following a lengthy discussion about Ed, the consensus was this: If they didn't get help for him soon, chances were he'd kill himself.

The next afternoon, at one o'clock, Atlee and Dan, at their father's request, went back to check on Ed. They found

him in the machine shop holed up with his Bible, looking
dazed and confused. It was Wednesday, March 17, Katie's
twenty-ninth birthday, and the brothers wanted to know
why Ed wasn't in the house with his wife and the children
celebrating the occasion. What was he doing, in the middle
of a snowstorm, sitting by himself in a freezing machine
shop reading a Bible? In answering this question, Ed, not
altogether coherent, repeated what he had said the previous
day, and by the time he finished his sermon, lecture, or
whatever it was, he was alone again in the shed. Atlee and
Dan were trudging through the snow toward the house to
consult with Katie about what to do with Ed. They found
her in the kitchen cleaning up after the midday meal. A
year before, one week before Ed was hauled off to Hamot
Hospital on a Mill Village body board, a time when everyone was focused on Ed, Katie's birthday would have slid
by without notice had Emma not stopped by to wish her
well. Ed's stint in Hamot was followed by the one in
Jamestown and a series of fruitless trips to Merritt Terrell
in Cambridge Springs. On this Saint Patrick's Day, 1993,
Katie, a year older and still no closer to a cure for Ed, was
showing the effects of a marriage that had given her nothing but misery.

Sitting around the kitchen table that day, with the snow
coming down and Ed off by himself in the machine shop
searching his Bible for answers to questions that were driving him crazy, Katie, Atlee, and Dan decided to try Jacob
Troyer, the Amish herb healer down near Punxsutawney
who could diagnose a person's disease by peering into his
eyes. God only knew what Troyer would see when he
came eyeball to eyeball with Edward Gingerich.

Atlee returned to the machine shop to propose the idea of
Jacob Troyer to Ed. He'd go slow and emphasize the fact
that Troyer was an Old-Order Amish man. Dan, in the
meantime, rode south on Frisbeetown Road to George
Brown's house, where he hoped to arrange transportation

for the two hundred-mile round trip to Troyer's house and sawmill in the Amish enclave surrounding the village of Smicksburg. George Brown said he was sorry he couldn't make the run; he was booked that night to drive an Amish couple to the doctor's office in Meadville. Using George's telephone, Dan called a backup driver but struck out there as well. It wasn't going to be easy finding someone, without notice, to drive that night, all the way to Punxy in the middle of a snowstorm. In desperation, Dan called Sid Workman, a sawmill customer who, during the past three years, had been friendly with Ed. Sid, a fifty-year-old electronics salesman, lived a few miles south of Brownhill in subdivision called Rockdale Acres. When Dan ran into him at the mill several months after Ed had been discharged from the hospital in Jamestown, he had offered to help Ed in any way he could. Ed needed help now, so Dan, taking Sid at his word, gave him a call, and got his answering machine. After the beep, Dan, intimidated by the technology and a little tongue-tied, said this into the machine: "Eddy is bad again."[7] Following that rather abbreviated message, he hung up and headed back to Ed's place.

Dan walked into the machine shop just as Ed, sounding fairly normal, was telling Atlee that he wouldn't mind being hauled down to Punxy to see the herb feller as long as they didn't come back without him. He would go if Atlee promised that the trip was not a trick to stick him into another nuthouse. He knew that Katie and her parents had been plotting to do just that, and he was having no part of it. Atlee assured Ed that Katie had no such plans and promised that the trip to Troyer's place was on the level. Dan reported that the best he had done was to leave a short message on Sid Workman's phone gizmo. As it stood at the moment, they had no transportation.

Atlee suggested they join Katie in the house, but Ed said he wanted to remain in the shop and talk. He said he was feeling so low he was willing to try anything as long as it didn't involve drugs. If he didn't get better soon, he'd put a gun to his head and end the suffering. Why make the devil wait? Ed was talking like this—about suicide, the devil, and being abandoned by God—when they heard a car pull up to the sawmill. Dan stepped outside just as Sid Workman climbed out of his green Chevy Corsica. It was four in the afternoon; Sid must have gotten the message and come straight to the shop. He was a sight for sore eyes.

It was the urgent tone in Dan's voice rather than his message—"Eddy is bad"—that had brought Sid directly to Ed's place. One look at his friend made Sid glad he had responded so quickly. Physically, Ed looked like a prisoner of war, right down to the hollow look and the blank stare. Sid was shocked; he had no idea his Amish pal had deteriorated so badly. Hearing him ramble on about God and the devil, waving his Bible to emphasize his points, left no doubt in Sid's mind that Ed was on the verge of a complete mental breakdown. Realizing he had been called to drive Ed to the hospital or to some kind of mental-health facility, Sid said, "I'll take Ed anywhere you want. Just tell me where."[8] This was an emergency. When Atlee said they were thinking about taking Ed to a man near Punxsutawney, a long way off, on a very bad night, Sid was not deterred. "I'll take Ed anywhere," he said, figuring that Ed's family had found a good treatment center in the Punxsutawney area.[9] The fact that they were taking Ed to a facility so far away suggested to Sid it was a special place; therefore, he wasn't going to let a spot of bad weather stand in his way. Ed was fortunate to have a family that recognized how sick he was and was willing to do whatever it took to get him well.

Atlee, Dan, Sid, and Ed walked to the house, where the final decision about Ed would be made by Katie. She served the men coffee then joined them at the kitchen table. The name of Jacob Troyer came up several times in the ensuing discussion as the healer they were thinking about taking Ed to see. No one bothered to tell Sid Workman that Jacob Troyer was an Old-Order Amish man who treated his patients out of a house next to a sawmill. Katie brought the powwow to a close by announcing that they would go to Troyer's that night if Sid was willing to take them there under such bad conditions. She said Joe Gingerich had given her directions to Troyer's place. She said she was willing to start the trip right away but suggested they wait until everyone had a chance to eat dinner. Sid left the Gingerich house that afternoon promising to return at seven-thirty to pick up Ed and anyone else who wanted to go.[10] It was snowing heavily and about to get dark and they had a two-hundred-mile road trip ahead of them, but everybody was excited over getting Ed the treatment he needed. That is, everyone but Ed, who was too sick at the moment to be excited about everything.

26

"I Am a Quack"

At seven-thirty, Sid Workman's headlights lit up the wall behind Katie, Ed, and the three children, who were waiting in the front room with their coats on. As Sid drew the Chevy Corsica up to the house, they stepped off the porch to meet him. Sid dropped the Gingerich children—Danny, Mary, and Enos—at their grandparents' house on Frisbeetown and picked up Lizzie, Ed's twenty-two-year-old sister, who squeezed into the backseat next to Ed and Katie.

Before getting under way, Sid, at Katie's behest, drove the little Chevy down the long driveway back to Danny's house to pick up Ed's brother, his wife, Fannie, and their two-year-old son, Johnnie. With Danny and his family pressed into the front seat, the compact car, loaded with six adults and one child, headed out of Brownhill en route to Punxsutawney, a long, dark, and snowy trek.

Sid picked up Route 8 in Union City and bore south through Titusville, Oil City, and Franklin, where, thirty miles into the trip, he found Route 322 and followed it twenty-five miles south and east to Clarion. Crossing under I-80, he pushed through the driving snow to Brookville, where the narrow, two-lane highway began to rise and fall and twist and turn through the Appalachian foothills. Stuffed into the backseat with Katie and his sister, Ed, while the others talked, carried on a conversation with himself. Whenever someone asked how he felt, he would groan, "This disease is very bad."[1] Conversation halted as they approached their destination. Ed was now grabbing his head and crying out as though he was in terrible pain. A few miles below DuBois, Sid, wondering why these people hadn't found a doctor closer to Brownhill, turned south onto Route 199 and passed through a village called Sykesville that showed no signs of life. Once out of Sykesville, about two miles west of Punxsutawney, the home of the mythical groundhog, he asked Katie for final directions to the doctor's office. A mile later, when they came to Route 210, she told him to turn right, which took them south to a wide spot in the highway called Trade City. Sid, relying completely on Katie's directions, had no idea where they were or where they were going. They were absolutely in the middle of nowhere, causing Sid to worry that Katie was lost. At the Trade City traffic signal, barely visible through the flying snow and hanging above an intersection without any traffic to direct, Katie told him to turn right, heading them west toward Smicksburg on a road without a number or, as far as Sid could tell, a name. They had to be lost. Five miles down the unmarked highway, they rolled up to and stopped at another lonely traffic light, this one over the deserted intersection of Routes 210 and

954. It was nine-fifty and they were in downtown Smicksburg, a Christmas-card scene of historic stone houses, a country store, a steepled church, and a post office about the size of a one-room schoolhouse. They had found the center of an Amish enclave populated by more than three hundred families organized into twelve church districts, one of the largest settlements in the state.

"Is the doctor in Smicksburg?" Sid asked.

"Take that road there," Katie said, pointing to the sign that read 954 SOUTH.

"Where does it go?"

"To the doctor's house; we're almost there."[2]

They motored south on Route 954, a rolling one-and-a-half lane farm road, past dormant tourist attractions—gift shops, Yoder's Quilt Outlet, places that sold homemade Amish furniture, and a country store that advertised, on a massive white sign with large, black letters, CHEESE, BUTTER, GIFTS, BLOCK CHOCOLATE, SMOKED MEATS, BULK FOODS, CANDY, SPECIALTY FOODS, ICE AND CUBES. On this black, snowy night, these tourist spots had the appearance of abandoned movie sets. Sid's headlights lit up a cluster of headstones perched on a patch of land that rose gracefully from the road, a cemetery without a fence, an office, an entrance gate, or a sign announcing its name. "Slow down," Katie said, "we're almost there."

Sid looked about and saw nothing that even hinted at being a hospital, clinic, or doctor's office. The only sign of civilization, if not life, was the spartan graveyard with its rows of uniformly shaped and sized snowcapped headstones. "Where are we?" he asked.

"There!" Katie snapped. "Turn right here," she said, referring to a driveway beyond the cemetery on the eastern side of the road that ran alongside a square, two-story, white clapboard house topped by a green-shingled roof and fronted by a wide porch accessed by a steep, fifteen-step flight of stairs. The rather large dwelling, which looked new but not modern, featured a yellow brick chimney built into its front. The odd, unattractive placement of the chimney, the white linen window curtains pulled to one side, and the mellow glow of gaslit lamps, suggested that this was an Amish home, which begged one question: what were they doing calling on an Amish family with Ed in the backseat of the car losing his mind? As Sid rolled onto the driveway and pulled alongside the house, he saw several large piles of logs, mounds of sawdust, high stacks of lumber, and a cluster of unpainted buildings and sheds made of wood. The Amish man who lived in this house owned an impressive-looking sawmill.

"Why did you bring us here?" Sid asked. "Are we lost?"

"This is the place," Katie replied. "This is where the doctor lives."

"This doesn't look like a doctor's office," Sid observed. "This is an Amish house."

"That's right," Danny said. "This must be where Jacob Troyer lives. Joe said he had a sawmill. We have found it."

"We have found what?" Sid asked.[3]

Katie had delivered Sid and the others to the home of Jacob Troyer, a forty-six-year-old Amish man, folk healer, and sawmill operator who practiced a little-known brand of alternative medicine called "iridology," based on the idea that a person's iris, if carefully examined, reveals past injuries, sickness, and inherited proclivities for specific diseases. Troyer and his family were about to turn in when someone knocked loudly on their front door. It was almost ten o'clock, much too late for patients, and on a night like this, who would be out and about? The pounding continued. Startled and not sure he wanted to open the door, Troyer yelled, "Who is it?"

A woman replied, "Is this the Troyer house? My husband is sick!" Jacob Troyer opened his door, and there, on his front porch, stood three Amish women, a pair of Amish men—one of whom carried a sleeping child—and the English driver who had apparently brought them to the house. "Come in," he said.

"My husband is sick," the shortest woman said as she stepped into the house. The others followed.

"It's kind of late," Troyer muttered.

"This is an emergency," Katie said. "Are you Dr. Troyer?"

"Jacob Troyer," he replied. "Who are you?"

"Katie Gingerich, and this is my husband, Ed. We came down from Rockdale Township. This is Danny, Ed's brother, and Fannie, his wife. And this is Sid Workman, our driver."[4] Workman, exhausted from the difficult drive and still trying to figure out what was happening, shook hands with the doctor. Troyer introduced his wife and their fifteen-year-old son, Mose, to the snowy strangers from Rockdale Township. His daughters had already gone upstairs to prepare for bed. If there was any question in Troyer's mind which Amish man was Ed Gingerich or why his wife considered him an emergency case, Ed erased any doubt when he dropped to his knees and began crawling in circles at their feet. Mrs. Troyer took this opportunity to join her daughters on the second floor. Ed stopped crawling and ran his fingers over the surface of the hardwood floor. "This is nice," he said.[5]

The Troyer boy, Mose, decided to join his mother and sisters. "Good night," he said to his father. "I'll see you in the morning."

Ed jumped to his feet, ran to the boy, and yelled, "Morning? There will be no morning! Do you think morning will ever come?" Terrified, the youngster backpedaled toward the stairs. Ed followed. "Do I look normal?" he screamed into the boy's face. "Can you tell there is something wrong with me?"[6] The boy turned and ran up the stairs. Ed turned to Troyer: "Do I look normal?" He seemed to have calmed down.

"You need a *real* doctor," Troyer replied. "I'm a quack."[7] He turned to Katie and said, "Take this man to a hospital; he needs to be put into a mental ward. I can't help him."

Danny spoke up: "We can't afford hospitals. Eddie has been going to Dr. Merritt Terrell. Can Doc Terrell help him?"

Troyer laughed. "There's nothing that man can do for your brother; he has a serious mental problem. Can't you see that? You shouldn't have brought him here. Why isn't he in a hospital? I think he could be dangerous!"

"Eddie wouldn't hurt anyone," Danny replied. "He has a problem with his nerves and he doesn't like drugs. Check into his eyes and tell us what herbs to give him. He won't take his blackstrap molasses."

"Blackstrap molasses?" Troyer blurted. "Is Terrell still selling blackstrap molasses? That stuff won't do him any good!"

"We've come a long way," Katie said. "Since we're here, look at all of us. We have money; we can pay."

"I can't do much for your husband; he's already sick. I don't cure illness."

"That's not what we heard," Danny said.

"I find tissue and organ weaknesses," Troyer replied. "I can strengthen these weaknesses with the proper herbs. If you have the right nutrition, you don't get sick. That is how it works."[8]

Troyer's disclaimer and the irony of an overweight smoker lecturing a physically fit farmer on preventive health care didn't attenuate Troyer's image as a great healer. Such is the power of reputation and positive testimony. While Sid Workman sat at the kitchen table trying to figure out why Katie and Danny had hauled Ed all the way to Smicksburg to see a cigarette-smoking Amish man, Ed and the others were in an adjacent room being examined by this healer, a man who referred to himself as a quack. Sid sat in Troyer's kitchen an hour, during which time he heard, from the other side of the wall, snatches of conversation in German. Fannie and the toddler came out

of the examination room first, followed by Danny and
Lizzie. They joined Sid at the table. Danny, his wife, and
Ed's sister each carried a white piece of cardboard the size
of a large index card. Sid got a look at Danny's when he
laid it on the table. The card featured a pair of lidless eyes
sectioned off into dozens of pie-shaped, dartboard-looking
zones labeled kidney, heart, lung, liver, spleen, and so
forth. According to the trademark and manufacturer's information beneath the bizarre, phrenology-like eye maps,
the card had been issued by:

IRIDOLOGISTS INTERNATIONAL
Bernard Jensen Enterprises
Escondido, California

Katie walked out of the examination room carrying a
diagnostic eye card and three bottles of herbs. When she
set the tiny brown bottles on the table, Sid caught a
glimpse of the labels and noticed they came from the same
outfit that produced the charts with the weird-looking
eyes.[9] Pie-eyed and pale, Ed soon wobbled out of the examination room in front of Troyer looking like he had just
lost six pints of blood. He stood stiffly next to the doctor
as Katie, seated at the table, wrote a check for $340.[10]

Sid climbed out of his chair; it was past midnight and
time to go. Ed was turning into a zombie, drifting snow
was closing roads, and Sid, still trying to cope with the
shock and disappointment of having brought Ed one hundred miles to the home of a quack, was tired. Jacob Troyer,
weary himself and afraid of Ed, wanted these people out
of his house. He led them from the kitchen to his front
door and held it open as they filed out of the dwelling.
Katie, the last to hit the door, asked a parting question
before being ushered into the night. "What can I do to
make him take his medicine?" she asked.

Troyer, making it clear he wasn't thrilled about seeing
Ed and didn't want him back, said, "Your husband has a

mental problem. Take him to a hospital. I'm afraid of suicide. There is nothing I can do for him. Good-bye and
good luck."[11]

With these uninspiring words ringing in her ears, Katie,
clutching her eye chart and Ed's little brown bottles, followed the footpath through the snow to Sid's Chevy, then
climbed into the backseat between Ed and his brother. Sid
rolled down Troyer's driveway onto the road back to
Smicksburg and the long, treacherous ride home.

Slumped in the middle of the backseat, Ed drifted in and
out of sleep as Sid inched his way north through that winter's most severe snowstorm. About halfway home, Ed
jerked awake with a yelp, grabbed his head with both
hands, and groaned, "Oh, my God, my brain is boiling
over!"[12] In an effort to relieve his brother's pain, Danny
pulled off his shoes and began hand-rubbing his feet. Ed
dozed off and didn't wake up until Sid stopped the car in
Mr. Gingerich's driveway to drop off Lizzie. It was two-
thirty in the morning. A few minutes later, Danny and his
family were out of the car heading for their front door. As
Sid plowed up Ed's driveway past the sawmill, Katie
thanked him for the ride and offered a twenty-dollar bill.
Careful not to reveal his belief that the entire trip was a
dangerous and exhausting waste of precious time, Sid refused the money, stating that he was glad to help in any
way he could. Ed was a good friend and that's what friends
were for. "I'll bake you some bread," Katie said as she
and Sid helped Ed to the house.[13]

The unrelenting wind continued to drive the snow into
white, sculptured waves that seemed to be crashing against
the sawmill, the log piles, and the outbuildings. It was
Thursday, March 18, the last day of Katie's life.

Liver Pills

A lthough she was physically and emotionally exhausted from the Punxsutawney trip, before turning in, Katie tried to persuade Ed to drink the mix of ginseng powder she had purchased from Jacob Troyer. Agitated and at loose ends, Ed, in a shrill voice, declared that he wasn't going to be poisoned and wasn't coming to bed. Stating that he had an urgent need to speak to his father, he bolted out of the house and was swallowed up by the storm. It was three in the morning.[1]

Danny Gingerich, although worn-out from the long, torturous Punxsutawney trip, hadn't been able to sleep, so at five in the morning he hitched up the buggy and rode over to Ed's to see if Jacob Troyer's medicine had made him any better. Apparently it hadn't. Danny found Katie distraught and by herself, drinking tea at the kitchen table, and Ed, back from his father's house and still wearing his shoes, sleeping under his bed.[2] The children, spending the night with their grandparents, were out of the house.

Katie, obviously at her wits' end, informed Danny that Ed had run off in the middle of the night to seek spiritual advice from his father. She woke up to find him sleeping on the floor *under* the bed. This was a bad sign. It was happening again; Ed was acting weird—on the verge of another one of his spells. It was the devil, Danny said. For some reason, Satan had his eyes on Ed and wouldn't let him alone. It wasn't Ed's fault; he was being stalked by the devil.[3]

Katie said she was out of ideas. She had tried everything—drugs, psychiatrists, hospitals, prayer, tender loving care, herbs, Doc Terrell, Jacob Troyer—and nothing worked. "What am I supposed to do with him?" she asked.[4]

Dan didn't have an answer. Instead, he reminded her that it was Thursday, March 18—the day of the big wedding. In a few hours, Noah Stutzman, the head man at the sawmill, was marrying Lovina Hertzler at Amos and Rebecca Hertzler's house on Smith Road. Following the marriage ceremony, there would be an all-day reception at Dan Stutzman's place on Dean Road. Dan and Mary Stutzman were the groom's parents. Everyone in Brownhill would be attending the party, the first big social event of the year. Guests were being bused in from Ontario, eastern Pennsylvania, Ohio, and New York. The only adult Amish person in Brownhill who wouldn't be attending this important shindig was Mr. Gingerich. He was leaving that morning for his brother-in-law's funeral in Indiana. Mr. Gingerich would be making the trip alone because his wife, Mary, didn't want to miss the Stutzman-Hertzler wedding. What, Danny wanted to know, was Katie going to do about Ed? Would he be attending the festivities?

Katie said she had given that question a lot of thought and had decided, given Ed's apparent mental situation, not to include him in the celebration. He was simply too unstable and too sick to enjoy it anyway. As much as she wanted to attend the marriage ceremony, she planned to haul Ed back to Doc Terrell that morning. The "Pennsylvania Doctor" had office hours on Thursdays and would be open for business at eleven o'clock. Later in the day, if someone else in the family was willing to stay with Ed for a while, Katie and the children could spend a few hours at the reception. She realized that the trip to Punxsutawney had been a mistake; if anyone could cure Ed, it was Doc Terrell.[5]

Danny approved of the plan and said he would leave at

once for his brother Joe's and give him the news. Maybe Joe would accompany Ed and Katie that morning to Cambridge Springs. In the meantime, Katie would try to line up transportation for the trip.

At eight o'clock, ten minutes after Danny had gone out the door, his sister Lizzie walked into the house with the Gingerich children. It had stopped snowing, and although the sun was still obscured by clouds, small sections of blue were opening up. It looked as though the storm had either moved on or died. Worried that the kids would wake up their father, Katie asked them to play outside in the snow. Katie and Lizzie were talking at the kitchen table when someone knocked at the front door. It was Richard Zimmer. He had been driving by and thought he'd stop to check on Ed. At the moment, Katie said, Ed was asleep, but she was glad Richard had called. Was there any chance he could drive her and Ed to Cambridge Springs later in the morning? Ed's doctor, a chiropractor named Merritt Terrell, had an office a couple of miles south of town along Route 19. He opened his doors at eleven, and if possible, Katie would like Ed to be Doc Terrell's first patient. Zimmer said he'd be glad to give them a lift. He'd come back to the house around ten-thirty with his girlfriend, Kim. Zimmer said that his neck had been bothering him lately, an old injury; maybe this guy Terrell would give it a good crack.[6]

Ed rolled out from beneath his bed at nine o'clock. Katie was in the backyard tending the chickens and the goats and Lizzie was out front keeping an eye on the children. Looking like a wino who'd been living ten years in a cardboard box, Ed left the house and slogged down the driveway en route to his father's place. The children saw him and paid him no mind, but Lizzie, when she caught sight of her brother high-stepping it toward Sturgis Road through the knee-deep snow, called out to him. If Ed heard her, he didn't let on. He kept walking, eyes straight ahead, like a man on an important mission with a lot on his mind.

Mr. Gingerich, dressed in his Sunday best, was sitting in his favorite rocking chair with a battered suitcase at his feet when he heard someone approach the front door. Thinking it was the English neighbor who would be driving him to the Greyhound bus station in Union City, he was surprised to see Ed barge into the room. The last person he expected to see that morning was his troubled son. How could Ed have forgotten that his father was about to depart for Simon's funeral in Indiana? This was no time for one of those long, religious discussions.

Unconcerned or unaware that his father was about to begin a journey, Ed pulled up a chair and exclaimed that everybody was out to get him. "She's trying to poison me!" he cried.[7]

Although there was nothing Mr. Gingerich could do or say that would calm his son, he said, "Everybody loves you."

"Even God hates me," Ed replied.

"Don't say that. You are not well, God can make you better."

"It's my chemicals; they are out of balance," Ed blurted. "What about my chemicals?"

"When I return from Indiana," Mr. Gingerich said, "I'm taking you to a medical doctor. Until then, the best thing is to ask God to forgive you."

"God won't because I am possessed by the devil. I can hear the devil's voice, not God's. It's the voice of a woman. I don't hear God!"

"You will," Mr. Gingerich replied, "if you listen for it."

"I am listening, but all I hear is the devil!"[8]

Upon his return home, Ed wandered into the kitchen and caught his wife, his brother Joe, and his sister Lizzie sitting around the table talking about him. The talking stopped the moment his presence became known. Given his paranoia, he assumed, at once, they were conspiring to kill him. Katie, seeing him stiffen, tried to put him at ease by announcing that Richard Zimmer was coming by shortly to drive them all down to Cambridge Springs to see Doc Terrell. What did he think of that?

"I guess it's all right," Ed said, to everyone's relief.

"Lizzie is taking the kids to Danny's. We'll pick them up later," Katie said. "Do you want to wash up, put on fresh clothes?"

Ed turned and, without responding, walked into the front room and stretched himself out on the cot. A trip to Doc Terrell's was hardly a surprise. Already that year he'd been to Cambridge Springs four times. Since 1988, Ed had made sixteen trips to the little yellow house. As long as they didn't try to force him to take the blackstrap molasses they had spiked with poison, he had no problem with Doc Terrell.

At ten-thirty, Richard Zimmer, accompanied by Kim Kerstetter, a blond woman in her forties who had known Ed and Katie for years, pulled up to the house in a pickup truck. Ed, Katie, and Joe climbed into the backseat of Zimmer's club cab.

Richard Zimmer noticed that Ed didn't look well and, on the way to the doctor's office, didn't have anything to say. Richard asked Ed why he was going to a chiropractor, had he twisted an ankle, did he have a sore back, or what? Making it obvious that he was in no mood to talk, Ed mumbled something about his chemicals, then lapsed into silence. Zimmer, confused by the reference to chemicals, didn't push for an explanation.

As they passed through the heart of Cambridge Springs, Ed said to Zimmer, "I'm sorry I'm causing you this trouble."

"No trouble," Zimmer replied.

"If Terrell can't cure me, I'm gonna kill myself. I can't stand it anymore."[9]

Zimmer, finding Ed's reflection in the rearview mirror, said, "That's the coward's way out." He and Kim exchanged glances; they couldn't believe Ed was talking suicide. Katie said nothing, which struck Zimmer and Kim as odd. What was going on here? Why were they taking a suicidal man to a chiropractor's office? "Is this guy any good?" Zimmer, referring to Doc Terrell, asked as they pulled off Route 19 into the Pennsylvania Doctor's already crowded parking lot. "I've heard of the guy, but I've never been here."

"He's very good," Joe replied. "He's worked on a lot of our people. He's drugless. People come from all over."

"I can see that," Zimmer said. "That van over there is from Indiana. Maybe I'll let him look at my neck; it's been bothering me for years."

"He can fix your neck," Joe replied. "Doc Terrell can fix anything. Just tell him your problem."[10]

If Terrell considered Ed's symptoms—"can't sleep," "sweats," and "temper"—rather vague and inappropriate for an emergency case, he didn't make note of it. Moreover, the doctor didn't ask his patient what he meant by "temper," and exactly how that emotion applied to his not feeling well. If Doc Terrell had any idea what he was treating Ed for, he didn't write it in Ed's medical file, and didn't reveal this information directly to the patient.[11]

Doc treated Ed that day by manipulating one of his toes then finishing off with something he hadn't done before; he placed his hands on Ed's scalp and cracked his knuckles. Not sure how the cracking of Doc's knuckles would accrue to his benefit, Ed wondered if it was done purely for effect. Was Ed supposed to think that the cracking sound came from his own head?[12] Could Doc Terrell actually believe that Amish people were that stupid? Perhaps the good doctor had confused Amish good manners and timidity with stupidity.

As Ed was being ushered out of the examination room, feeling desperately ill and frustrated by Terrell's outlandish doctoring techniques, he said, "If you can't cure me, just say so."

"I'm giving you liver pills," Terrell replied. "Take the liver pills."

"I don't want liver pills," Ed said. "Give me something stronger for my headaches; I can't go on like this."

"Drugs are not the answer," Terrell scolded. "No drugs."[13]

Having treated Ed, the doctor agreed, for Ed and Katie's convenience, to examine their English friend and driver Richard Zimmer. Seated in the big chair, Richard carefully explained that twenty years ago he had been thrown off a horse and landed on his head. Since that accident, he had been troubled by his neck. "Take off your left shoe," Terrell ordered.

"The problem is in my neck," Zimmer replied.

"No, the problem is you have an infection. Let me see your foot."

Richard removed his shoe and looked on in amazement as Terrell grabbed his big toe and gave it a yank. "That will do it," the doctor said matter-of-factly. "Pick up your blackstrap molasses from the woman at the desk."

"That's it?"

"It's taken care of," Doc replied.

"You've fixed the infection?"

"Yes."

"My big toe is infected?"

"It's your blood. Your blood is impure. The blackstrap molasses will take care of that. It cleans the blood."[14]

28

The Work of the Devil

Richard Zimmer, still complaining about paying fifty dollars for a jar of blackstrap molasses, stopped in Cambridge Springs at the Golden Dawn grocery store so the women could do a little shopping. Joe said he would wait in the truck with Richard. He'd keep an eye on his brother, who, at the moment, was asleep in the backseat. Katie and Kim had been in the market about five minutes when Ed awoke with a start. "Where are we?" he asked.

"Cambridge Springs," Zimmer replied. "The girls are picking up some groceries."

"I better help Katie," Ed said, climbing out of the truck onto the freshly plowed parking lot.[1] He adjusted his hat and with a slight wobble, walked into the squat, sign-cluttered building.

"Is he gonna be okay in there?" Zimmer asked.

"Oh, yeah, Eddie's fine," Joe replied.[2]

Katie emerged from the store fifteen minutes later carrying a full bag of groceries. Behind her, Kim held the door open for Ed, who had his arms around a cardboard box filled with fifteen one-gallon jugs of springwater. Katie had purchased the bottled water for Ed's sister Lizzie.

"What's with the water?" Zimmer asked as they drove out of Cambridge Springs.

Before Katie could answer, Ed said, "I know why she bought it."

"Why?" Katie asked. It was more of a challenge than a question.

"So you can poison it, then trick me into drinking some. You can't fool me; I know what you're trying to do."

A moment passed without anyone speaking, then Richard said, "Ed, I hope you're kidding."

"He's not," Katie replied, her voice laced with bitterness and resignation. "He believes it."[3]

Joe decided to change the subject. Speaking to Richard and Kim, he asked, "Did you know that Noah Stutzman got married this morning?"

"Is that why the mill is down?" Zimmer responded.

"Yeah. It'll be open tomorrow, but Noah won't be there." Joe chuckled.

"I didn't know he was getting hitched," Zimmer said. "Who did he marry?"

"You know Amos Hertzler?"

"Yeah, up on Smith Road."

"His daughter Lovina."

"Who married them?"

"Rudy Shetler."

"Where are they throwing the reception?" Kim asked.

"Dan Stutzman's farm. You know him?"

"Sure," Zimmer said.[4]

Talk of the wedding made Katie uneasy. She glanced at Ed to determine if he had been following the conversation. She wasn't sure how he would react when he learned that he wouldn't be attending any of the marriage festivities. To her relief, Ed seemed lost in his own world, oblivious to what was being said around him.

Ed never showed much interest in weddings and the like, and although Noah Stutzman and his brother Henry worked at the sawmill, Ed had never been close to either man. His relationship with their father, Dan Stutzman, had been strained and cool. These factors, and Ed's preoccupation with his illness, allowed Katie to hope that being excluded from the big party wouldn't bother him a bit, cause any fuss at all. But with Ed, she could never be sure of anything.

Katie had worked out a plan for the rest of the day. Later that afternoon, she and the children would attend the reception, without Ed. Atlee, who had attended the wedding ceremony at the Hertzlers' that morning and would be at the Stutzman reception early in the afternoon, would come to the house and stay with Ed until Katie and the children came home later that evening. Danny and Joe and their wives would spend the evening at the Stutzmans', and would be joined by Atlee later that night once he had been relieved by Katie.[5] Everyone had agreed to the plan but Ed, who wasn't going to be enlightened until the very last minute. Worry about Ed had everyone on edge. Atlee,

Joe, and Danny would have felt a lot better had their father not been attending that funeral in Indiana. If Ed listened to anyone, it was Mr. Gingerich.

Arriving in Brownhill, Richard drove to Danny's house, where Ed and Katie's children were being watched. Richard and Kim, having accepted Katie's invitation to join the family at lunch, a midday meal of chicken, potatoes, and applesauce prepared by Fannie Gingerich, piled out of the truck and followed their Amish neighbors into the house.

Ed took a seat at the kitchen table with his two brothers, wife, sister-in-law, Richard Zimmer, and Kim, but didn't eat anything or join in the conversation. He just sat there, occasionally mumbling to himself, with a slightly goofy, faraway look on his face. Except for Katie, who watched him closely, no one paid him any attention. Fannie, obviously looking forward to that afternoon's festivities at the Stutzmans', was telling Kim about the wedding. Everyone suddenly became aware of Ed when he said to Katie, "I'm coming with you tonight."

"You can't go," she replied. "You're too sick."

"I have to come," Ed said.

"Why is that?" Katie asked. "You don't like these things."

"It's the only way I can be saved."

Holding firm, Katie said, "No, we've talked about this and you are not going. You're staying home with Atlee. You won't be alone. You need your sleep."

"I know who you are," Ed said.

"Ed, stop it. Richard and Kim don't want to hear this."

"You are the devil."

"I don't know why you talk like that. That's why you shouldn't go to the Stutzmans'; you say weird things. What's wrong with you?"

"Can't you tell?" Ed replied. "God has forsaken me."

"God wants you to get better," Katie said. "Doc Terrell wants you to get better; we all do."

"Are the children going to the wedding party?"

"Yes."

"I don't want them to go."

"Ed . . ."

"I want them to stay home with me. If I can't go, they shouldn't either."

"I'm taking the children. I've decided."

"Please let them stay home with me. I want them."

"No," Katie snapped, revealing some of her anger and frustration. With Ed, nothing was easy. He was embarrassing Richard and Kim.

No one spoke for a minute or two. Ed seemed to have drifted off somewhere, then he said, "I'm so sick."

Richard and Kim had never seen him this way. They didn't know what to do. It was so pathetic. What could they say?

"You don't take your medicine," Katie said.[6]

Appearing dazed and confused, Ed acted as though he hadn't heard her. His eyes glazed over and he was gone. Looking like a man who had just been told something unbearably awful, he sat motionless in the chair staring blankly through a pair of holes cut into his face. That's why when he spoke, he startled everyone; it was like a corpse climbing off the autopsy table. He muttered, "There goes the moon—right into the sea."[7] That's all he said, but it was enough to convince Richard Zimmer it was time to leave. He stood up and so did Kim.

Before they walked out of the kitchen, Katie offered to pay Richard gas money for the trip to Cambridge Springs and back. Richard refused the ten-dollar bill and, trying to conceal his concern for Ed and her, expressed hope that Ed would be feeling better after he got a little sleep. "Enjoy the big shindig over at the Stutzmans'," he said as he followed Kim out the door.

Katie helped Fannie clear the table, spoke to Danny about that day's strategy with Ed, then bundled up the children for the short ride home in Dan's buggy. It was a little after one when Katie, Ed, Dan, and the children rolled away from the house down the long snow-covered drive-way. Ed hadn't spoken to anyone but himself since arguing with Katie about attending the wedding party. He ignored everyone in the buggy as they rode quietly along the edge of Sturgis Road, leaving behind the skinny, treadless tracks that steel-rimmed carriage wheels press into the snow.

Danny Gingerich didn't think that Doc Terrell, Jacob Troyer, or English mind doctors who had drugs for every-thing could cure Ed of his spells. That was because Ed's problem had nothing to do with his health or disease. Ed had fallen prey to Satan, who was fighting God for control of his soul. Only the devil would make Ed think that Katie and his brothers were trying to kill him. The ridiculous notion that Danny and Katie were having an affair had to have been planted in Ed's mind by Satan. He had told Danny many times that God and the devil were fighting over his soul and Danny believed him. That's why Ed was praying all the time and trying hard to be religious. When-ever Ed had one of his spells, he was no longer Ed; he was the devil. You don't battle the devil with drugs, black-strap molasses, or even Rudy Shetler; you fight Satan with the Bible, faith, and prayer. The only protection one has is God. Danny had faith that in the end, the Lord would prevail and Ed would emerge a new man, a better and stronger husband, father, brother, and son. He just had to weather the storm, hold tight to his belief in God.

Danny followed Ed and the family into the house. He'd stay awhile, keep an eye on his brother, who, at the mo-ment, didn't look like he had snapped out of his stupor. If Ed's God-fearing loved ones stayed at his side, the devil might keep his distance, then eventually give up. It was like holding off beasts with campfires, making it through the night.

Danny positioned himself next to Ed at the kitchen table as Katie made tea and the children, playing in the front room, made noise. Ed was quiet, but he didn't look re-laxed. When Katie put a mug of steaming tea in front of him, he regarded the ginseng-laced drink wearily. Danny sipped his and tried to draw Ed into conversation. It was like talking to a fence post. Katie joined them at the table. "Drink your tea," she said. Ed gave no sign that he heard her. He just sat there, blank-faced, staring into space. "I don't know why he acts this way," Katie said to Danny. "He won't take his medicine."

"How do you feel?" Danny asked, trying to make eye contact with his brother. "I hope you're not having one of your spells."

Ed didn't respond or move even slightly.

"Ed?"

"I'd like to do something," Ed said, his voice high-pitched and tinny.

"What?" Danny asked, suddenly encouraged.

"I can't do it," Ed replied.

"Can't do what?" Danny prodded.

"I really couldn't."

"Do what?"

"No, I don't want to," Ed said, as though arguing with himself.

"What are you talking about?" Katie asked.

Ed laughed, derisively.

Speaking to Danny, Katie said, "He does this all the time. It doesn't make any sense."

"I don't want to hurt anybody," Ed said in his false voice. "I love everybody."

"Why would you hurt someone?" Danny asked. "Why would you do that?"

Ed pushed his chair away from the table and got to his feet. "I'm going to bed now," he said as he walked out of the kitchen.

Katie got up from the kitchen table and carried Ed's full cup of tea to the sink. "Is he all right?" Danny asked.

"I don't know," she said. "He's tired."

"What was he talking about? What did he mean?"

"That's the way he talks when he's like this," Katie said. "He says weird things."

"How long will he sleep?"

"Sometimes he sleeps all day. You don't have to stay. Go home and get ready for the wedding."

Danny stood up. "I've got chores," he said. "I can stay her if you want, until Atlee comes."

"Go home. I'll see you later."[8]

Danny left the house.

Katie walked into the front room to quiet the children. She asked the oldest, Danny, who was going on six, to be in charge of Enos and Mary while she checked on their father, who wasn't feeling well. Shoeless, she tiptoed into the bedroom and, without removing her dress or her stockings, climbed into bed with Ed. She could tell from the sound of his breathing that he was asleep. Too wound up to sleep herself, she lay next to him for about twenty minutes then, being careful not to disturb him, slipped out of bed. Out in the front room, the children were making a racket; she was afraid they would wake up their dad.[9]

At three-thirty, Atlee, on his way home from the Stutz-man shindig, decided to stop by Ed's to see how his brother was feeling following that morning's treatment at the hands of Doc Terrell. Atlee's tour of duty with Ed didn't start until five, but having things to do on his farm, he had left the party early. After a word with Ed, he'd take care of the chores, then come back to the house so his sister-in-law could take her turn at the party.

Atlee found Katie in the kitchen, fussing with the children so they'd be ready for the party. "How is he doing?" he asked.

"He's sleeping now," she replied.

"Did Terrell do him any good?"

"He won't take his medicine and he doesn't eat. I can't make him."

"I'll try to get him to take his herbs," Atlee said.

Katie asked Atlee to tell her about the party and he was

describing the affair when they heard loud sobs coming from the bedroom. Katie was about to investigate when Ed, looking as though he had come face-to-face with the devil, staggered into the kitchen. "I have to go to the wedding," he cried. "It's the only way I can save my soul."

Fed up with his bizarre talk and his irrational, unreasonable demands, Katie stood firm. "No," she shouted. "You're too sick. You won't even take your medicine."

"Because you're trying to poison me!" Ed yelled.

"You *know* that's not true," Katie said, her voice weary with frustration.

"Why would we want to do that?" Atlee asked.

"Because I have the devil in me; you're trying to kill the *devil*!"

"How can you say that?" Atlee replied, keeping his tone moderate in an effort to calm things down, lower the intensity. "We're trying to help you."

"You always take her side," Ed said as he turned and walked into the front room, where the children were playing, oblivious to what was going on.

"He's not getting better," Atlee whispered to Katie. "I wish Dad were here."

"He can't go to the party," Katie said. "I won't let him."[10]

Atlee promised to return after his chores, then walked out of the kitchen. He spoke briefly to Ed, who was sitting on the cot in the front room, then Katie heard the front door close behind him. Atlee was gone, leaving Katie and the children under the same roof with Ed, alone.

Atlee had been out of the house five minutes when Katie threw on a shawl and, using the back door, stepped outside to check on the chickens, goats, and pigs. When she returned, Ed was in the front room stretched out on the cot. He didn't seem bothered by the children, who, anticipating a party, were excited and loud. Katie walked into the bedroom and slipped into a freshly pressed, plum-colored dress. She put on her shoes and came back into the kitchen. She was standing at the sink washing dishes when she heard Ed crying again. The deep-throated sobbing came from the front room, where she thought he had been sleeping. Suddenly the crying stopped and the house grew quiet, even the children were still. The next thing she heard was the muffled sounds of a person walking on stocking feet. Ed was coming into the kitchen. Katie turned to face him and there he was, towering over her. "What's wrong?" she asked.

Ed stepped back and, without uttering a word, slammed a huge fist straight into the middle of her face, smashing her mouth and nose and knocking her prayer cap into the sink. Her legs gave way and she collapsed to the floor. Sprawled at his feet and bleeding from the face, but still conscious, she managed to say, "Why do you do this?"[11]

"Is this the way you want it to be?" he asked.

"Why?" Katie sobbed.

"I am the devil!" Ed screamed.[12]

Little Mary, standing in the kitchen behind her father, began to cry. "Danny," Katie said, "get Uncle Dan; tell him Daddy is sick. Hurry!"[13]

Having just witnessed his father punch his mother in the face, Danny tore out of the house to fetch his uncle. Coatless and barefoot, he ran as fast as he could in the places where the snow wasn't knee-deep. He left his mother in her purple dress, bleeding at his father's feet. He also fled the little ones, Mary and Enos. Too small and too frightened to run, they were left behind to witness what their uncle Dan would call the work of the devil.

"You Wouldn't Understand"

Silhouetted against the slate gray horizon, a barefoot boy, his trousers bouncing at the end of his suspenders, streaked across the vast, white landscape. He stopped to catch his breath at the foot of his uncle's driveway, then ran the remaining quarter mile to the unpainted, clapboard house. The boy fumbled with the door, burst into the front room, and in the presence of his uncle gasped, "Daddy isn't feeling good."[1]

The boy said nothing more and his uncle didn't ask for details. The fact that he had run a half mile through the snow for help suggested the seriousness of the situation. This wasn't the first time this had happened. Ed was apparently in the throes of another spell and Katie needed help bringing him under control. The last time Ed had broken some windows, jumped off the front porch roof, and sprinted down Sturgis Road until he collapsed from exhaustion. Dan realized that when Ed flipped out he could be violent and that anything was possible, but the thought that his brother had assaulted Katie didn't cross his mind. If anybody was going to be hurt as a result of these spells, Danny figured it would be Ed.

Danny didn't bother hitching up a buggy or throwing on a saddle, he just led the bay mare out of the barn, climbed on, and rode her down the driveway toward Sturgis. As the horse galloped toward the house past the sawmill, he saw no evidence that anyone was home or on the property. The place looked abandoned. Wondering if perhaps Ed had run to his father's place with Katie chasing him, Danny dismounted, lodged the animal in Ed's horse shed, then headed for the house. Maybe Ed had blown his top because Katie wouldn't let him go to Stutzmans' wedding party. As Danny approached the front porch, four-year-old Enos came out of the house. His face was red and he was crying. Danny walked up to him and asked, "What's wrong?"

"Mommy is bleeding," he managed, between sobs.[2]

Dan ran into the house with Enos walking in behind him. As Dan's eyes adjusted to the darkening interior, he saw, in the kitchen, something that nearly overwhelmed him with horror. Katie, stretched out on her back between Ed's knees as he straddled her chest, was being frantically pounded in the face and head by a pair of blood-covered, blood-spraying fists. Her face was battered beyond recognition; she issued no sound, and made no effort to protect herself.

"What are you doing?" Dan screamed. "Get off her!"

Ed rose and, with Katie's still body lying between his feet, calmly said, "This is what she deserves."[3] Then, as if to underline his point, he lifted his right foot as high as he could and, as though stomping a bug, brought it down into her face, causing a sickening thud and splattering more of her blood. He looked down at what remained of Katie's head and, enraged by what he saw, squatted over her chest and started hammering away with his fists. Dan lunged forward, throwing himself onto Ed and knocking him off Katie's bloody remains. The two men rolled across the Masonite floor, then, in unison, sprang to their feet. They locked eyes and the deadly expression on Ed's face told Dan that if he didn't get out of the house, Ed would kill him, too. So he ran, fled for his life, leaving behind Enos and little Mary.[4] Ed did not pursue him.

Outside the house, Dan sprinted toward the horse shed, mounted the mare, and drove her hard to Jim and Alice DeMatteo's place on the southeast corner of the

Frisbeetown-Sturgis intersection, a snowy, muddy half-mile ride that took less than three minutes. The DeMatteos, a young English couple who had been friendly with Ed and Katie, had a telephone. Ed had used it many times.

Instead of chasing after his younger brother, Ed put on his jacket, opened the kitchen door, and stepped out onto the back porch. He pulled on his knee-high barn boots then reentered the house, where he found Enos and Mary standing frozen in the kitchen next to their mother's corpse. They backpedaled a few feet when their father approached her body. Too shocked to cry, they stood erect with numb expressions on their tiny faces. With the children blankly looking on, Ed, using his foot, pounded their mother's head until the right side of her face caved in and was pulverized. The top of Katie's head split open, her brains squirted onto the floor, and were stomped into pulp. Darkness fell upon the blood-splattered kitchen.

The DeMatteos happened to be home that Thursday afternoon. Dan came to their door in a state of shock and panic. He asked to use their telephone. There was a problem, he said, at the Gingerich house. Although he was vague and a bit incoherent, it was obvious to the DeMatteos that something terrible had happened. Had one of Ed's children been injured? Sensing the emergency, they said, yes, Dan could use the telephone, certainly.

The 911 operator came on the line. What was the emergency? she asked.

"A murder is being occurred at the Gingerich house," Dan said. "My brother is killing his wife! There is violence at the Gingerich house."[5]

The operator, unclear as to whether this was a medical emergency, the report of a killing, or both, said she'd send ambulances and the police. She asked the caller to identify himself.

The caller said he was Daniel D. Gingerich.

Where was the emergency taking place? The operator wanted an address.

Rockdale Township, the home of Edward D. Gingerich, an Amish house next to the sawmill at the crossing of Frisbeetown and Sturgis roads.

Was this Edward D. Gingerich the man who was killing his wife?

Yes.

Had shots been fired?

No. He was beating her with his fists. Dan added that two of Ed's children were in the house.

Have they been injured? the operator asked.

Dan said he didn't know. He had run out of the house to save his own life. Before hanging up, he said he'd meet the police at the Frisbeetown-Sturgis intersection. He'd go straight to the intersection and wait for them.

Dan's 911 call devastated the DeMatteos. Ed killing Katie was impossible. This had to be some kind of mistake, a huge and tragic misinterpretation. Katie must have been injured and Danny, for some reason, was incorrectly blaming Ed. When the dust settled, the truth would come out—a terrible misunderstanding.

Ed wasn't finished with his wife. There in the kitchen, with the children standing a few feet away, he began to undress the body, placing Katie's shoes, stockings, purple dress, apron, and underwear in a neat pile next to the cooking stove. When she was nude and still stretched out on her back, he removed a steak knife from a kitchen drawer and used it to slice a vertical, seven-inch incision in the lower left side of her abdomen. Since her heart was no longer beating, the slit in her body produced very little blood. Through this abdominal incision, Ed thrust his hand, all the way to her lungs, which meant immersing his arm into her body up to his elbow. He then proceeded to pull out, through this cut, her internal organs. He piled these bloody parts—lungs, intestines, kidneys, stomach, liver, spleen, bladder, uterus, and so forth—next to her body. He left her nothing. Having completed his work, he stuck the knife into the top of the slimy mound. Now finished with the body, Ed got up and walked to the sink and rinsed off his face, arms, and hands in the water Katie had just been using to wash the dishes. The water turned red.[6]

In the bedroom, Ed picked up his Bible and carried it into the front room and dropped it into the flames in the wood-burning stove. He returned to the kitchen and instructed the children to find their coats; they were walking to Granddad's house. He put on his summer straw hat and, as the children were slipping into their coats, peeked into the stove to see if his Bible was on fire. He saw that it was, dispelling the myth that Bibles won't burn.[7]

With little Mary up on his shoulders and Enos holding on to his hand, Ed and his children walked down the driveway toward Sturgis Road. "I'm taking you to Granddad's," he said, "then I'm coming back to burn down the house."

"Please don't burn down our house, Dad," Enos replied.[8]

At the foot of the driveway, Ed encountered Ron Alexander, a sawmill customer who had gotten his car stuck in the snow along the side of the road. Ron had come to the mill to see if his order of cucumber wood had been cut. He didn't know about the wedding and had been surprised and disappointed that the place was closed. "Do you know if my lumber is ready yet?" he asked Ed.

"It'll be a while," Ed replied. "It's too cold to cut cucumber wood. Did you get your car stuck?"

"Yes," Alexander replied.

"I'll push you out," Ed said, lifting Mary off his shoulders.[9] He told the children to stay back while he helped this man get his car out of the snow. Ron, behind the wheel rocking the car back and forth as Ed pushed from behind, managed to get the vehicle back onto the road. The Englishman rolled down his window and was thanking Ed when Richard Zimmer came toward them in his pickup truck. Ron drove off as Zimmer, heading west toward the intersection, pulled to a stop alongside Ed. He lowered his window.

"Hello," Ed said as he gathered up the children.

"Where are you going?" Zimmer asked.

"To my dad's house."

"Get in the truck; I'll give you a lift."

"Thanks," Ed replied, "but I think I'll walk. I can use the fresh air."

"See you later," Zimmer said.[10] He stepped on the gas and pulled away. Ed seemed perfectly normal, much better than he'd been that morning coming back from Doc Terrell's. If Terrell had made Ed better, Zimmer wondered, why did his neck still hurt?

Dan Gingerich's 911 call had been received at the Crawford County Emergency Center in Meadville, Pennsylvania, at five-thirty in the afternoon. The 911 dispatcher radioed the Pennsylvania State Police station located in Vernon Township just outside of Meadville, a twenty-minute drive from Ed's house. She also notified the Mill Village Volunteer Fire Department and a paramedic unit headquartered in Union City.

Assistant Mill Village Fire Chief Andrew McLaughlin, driving his black Chevy Blazer topped by a red emergency light, arrived at the intersection first. He had come directly from his home in Mill Village, just three miles away. Crossing Frisbeetown Road, he saw a couple of English people talking to an Amish man who stood next to a horse. McLaughlin came to a stop along the side of Sturgis Road, two hundred feet west of the driveway leading back to the sawmill and Ed's house. The 911 dispatcher had instructed the emergency personnel not to enter the dwelling before the arrival of the state police. They were, after all, responding to a possible domestic situation that involved violence. Andrew McLaughlin had no intention of entering the Gingerich house alone. He had been there before, knew the territory, had seen Ed in action. A year before he had helped tie the crazy Amish man to the body board they had hauled in the Mill Village ambulance to the hospital in Erie. There was no telling what they would find when they walked into that house.

Fire Chief Ron Peters, driving the Mill Village ambulance, parked the orange-and-white Ford off Frisbeetown Road a few yards north of Sturgis. A few minutes later, he was joined by David Dowler, who arrived at the scene in his own car. Peters and Dowler, having helped deliver the mad Amish man to Hamot Hospital the previous March, also respected his potential for violence. The two paramedics left their vehicles and climbed into McLaughlin's Blazer, where they waited for the arrival of the state police.

In the fading minutes of daylight, as the paramedics nervously watched and waited, a tall angular man, wearing a straw hat, a blue denim jacket, dark-hued work trousers, and knee-length boots, rose into view as he ascended the gentle rise in the road before them. Set against the steel-gray sky, he could be seen carrying a little girl and leading a small boy by the hand. The paramedics recognized this figure as Edward Gingerich.[11] He had the children, but where was his wife? The boy and girl did not appear distressed; they were not crying and they seemed unhurt. When Ed reached the Blazer, one of the Mill Village men asked him where he was heading. "I'm going to my dad's house," Ed replied calmly. Upon closer examination, the children, their little faces blank and their eyes glazed over, looked shell-shocked. Ed, on the other hand, seemed normal enough and the emergency men, had they not noticed the specks of blood on his face and beard, his cut right hand, and the wet knees of his trousers, might have wondered if the 911 call had been a mistake, a false alarm. When asked where his wife was, Ed said, "You wouldn't understand."[12]

Ron Peters decided to stay with Ed and the children until

the police arrived. Ed seemed to be in a docile frame of mind, posing no threat. In the meantime, Andrew and Dave would enter the Gingerich house to see about the wife, Katie.

Carrying their medical kits, the emergency volunteers walked into the darkened house through the front door. They switched on their flashlights. In the kitchen, they found Katie Gingerich on the floor, stretched out nude on her back. It was immediately apparent that they would not be needing their medical tools and equipment. A quarter of her face was gone and her skull had been broken open. She was awash in blood and her internal organs lay piled in a wet heap on the brown Masonite floor next to her hollow, blood-smeared body. Also on the floor, stomped into pulp not far from her head, lay what used to be her brain.

The stunned emergency men stood speechless in the spartan Amish kitchen, breathing the damp, metallic air of violent death. There was nothing left to do but leave. Outside, one of the men, speaking into his radio, reported that Katie Gingerich was dead.

30

The Wedding Announcement

At dusk, Ed and the children, accompanied by Mill Village Fire Chief Ron Peters, reached the intersection, where they found Dan, his horse, and a handful of English folks standing along Sturgis Road not far from the foot of Dan's driveway. The state police had not arrived.

Dan, relieved to know that the children were safe, walked up to his brother. Distressed but not surprised by the sight of blood on Ed's face and beard, he asked, "Did you actually do it?"

"Yes," Ed replied. "Dad will understand."

"You killed her?"

"Yes."[1]

Eager to separate Ed from the children, Dan asked one of the bystanders to escort Mary and Enos to their grandfather's house across the way. "You have to stay here for the police," Dan said to Ed as the children were led off. Seemingly calm and unconcerned that he had just killed his wife, Ed didn't object. The children, still in shock, would be reunited at their grandfather's house with their older brother, Danny, who was not aware that his mother had been killed.

Trooper Robert A. Rowles, a young Pennsylvania state patrolman out of the Meadville station, was the first officer to arrive at the scene. In his mid-twenties, Rowles had been on the job three years. He had been notified, while on routine patrol, of a domestic disturbance at an Amish residence next to the sawmill near the crossing of Frisbeetown and Sturgis roads in Rockdale Township just south of the Erie County line. He proceeded directly to the scene.

Trooper Rowles alighted from the cruiser and approached the two Amish fellows standing beside the horse. Dan, pointing to his brother, said, "He had a fight with his wife."

"Yes," said Edward. "I'm the bad man you're looking for."

"Did you really fight with your wife?" asked the trooper.

"Yes," Ed replied. "I may have killed her."[2]

Rowles took Ed by the arm and walked him to the police car. The officer opened the rear door and Ed climbed into the backseat. He sat quietly in the cruiser as Rowles radioed headquarters for assistance. He advised the dispatcher that regarding the Rockdale call, an Amish man might have killed his wife. Rowles said he needed an investigator to take charge of the case. Two detectives were on their way, the dispatcher replied. In the backseat, Ed started to weep. "I believe I really killed her," he sobbed. "And I don't know why I did it."[3]

Rowles climbed out of the car, opened Ed's door, and told him to step out. Wiping his eyes with his fingers, Ed complied. "Is that blood?" the officer asked, pointing to Ed's face.

"I don't know," Ed replied.

"Take off your boots and remove your coat," Rowles said.

As Ed shed his coat, something bloody and moist fell out of a sleeve. The blob hit the ground with a slap and made the snow around it red. "What is that?" Rowles asked, bending over for a closer look.

"Don't know," Ed mumbled.

"It looks like a hunk of flesh or something," the officer said. "Where did it come from?"

"It dropped out of his coat," Dan said. He turned to Ed and asked, "What did you do to Katie?"

"I think I killed her," came the reply.

Rowles glared at Ed. "Get back into the car," he snapped. Ed virtually jumped into the vehicle.[4]

At six twenty-eight, when he arrived at the scene, Patrolman Lon E. Pierce, a young state cop stationed at the regional state-police headquarters in Erie, found Ed seated in the back of Rowles's cruiser and a small crowd hanging around the intersection. Cars, trucks, and a couple of buggies were parked along both roads. People were trying to determine what had happened at the intersection. Had there been an accident? Did a vehicle hit a buggy? Was somebody in the ambulance? Who was the Amish fellow sitting in the police car? Was he the one who got hurt?

Trooper Pierce parked his cruiser and went directly to Officer Rowles, who briefed him on what he knew so far.

The detectives were on their way from the Meadville station, but in the meantime Pierce could question Dan Gingerich, the complaining witness and the subject's brother. Gingerich was the Amish guy standing next to the horse.

Patrolman Pierce scribbled furiously in his notebook as Dan Gingerich told the story of entering his brother's kitchen and finding him sitting on his wife's chest beating her head with his fists. He said he fled the house when Ed made a threatening move toward him and called 911 from a neighbor's telephone. As Dan was describing his brother's demeanor and activities that day prior to the killing, including the emergency run to Doc Terrell's, Atlee walked up to his side and introduced himself to Officer Pierce as Ed's oldest brother. The interview continued with Atlee helping Dan with the details. The two brothers proceeded to enlighten Trooper Pierce with details of Ed's two hospitalizations for mental illness, his recent preoccupation with religion, and the nature of his troubled marriage. According to Dan and Atlee, Ed had been saying that he hadn't been living right and that he and Katie didn't get along. Ed and his wife hadn't been doing things together lately and the children weren't behaving like they should. Ed had been recently confessing to things he had done that violated Amish principles, including arguments with his wife about how to raise the children. Rather than work things out with Katie, Ed would leave the house and not come home for long periods of time. According to the brothers, everyone in the Gingerich family believed that Katie was a bit too "strong-minded" for an Amish woman, implying that her own combativeness had perhaps contributed to her death.[5]

Ed sat quietly in the backseat of Rowles's patrol car seemingly oblivious to the activities around him and the fact that he had caused it. The moment Trooper Pierce had finished with him, Dan walked over to the cruiser to see how Ed was doing. He was about to speak to his brother when Ed looked up at him and said, "You are next."[6] The expression on his face startled Dan so much he took a step backward. Ed stuck his head out of the car window and gazed out at the sky. "That's the North Star," he said. "We must leave here. It's getting close to earth; it'll kill us all."[7]

Once it became clear that the 911 caller from Rockdale Township had actually reported a killing, two investigators from the Pennsylvania State Police station in Vernon Township, six miles west of Meadville, were dispatched to the scene. The detective who would be in charge of the case, Trooper Danny P. Lloyd, happened to be in the barracks working at his desk when the call came in. The brown-haired, medium-sized, forty-six-year-old detective possessed clean-cut good looks and an air of confidence. A graduate of a local, small-town high school, Lloyd had been on the job twenty-two years, handling criminal investigations, mostly theft and burglary cases, for the past nine years. Since he'd been out of uniform, he had been involved in ten homicide investigations, about one a year. Lloyd had joined the army out of high school, became an MP, then three years later got into the state police. Now he was married, had a family, and was a detective—a local kid who made good.[8]

Pulling up to the Frisbeetown-Sturgis intersection at six thirty-five in his unmarked state car, a 1992 gray Chevy Caprice, Detective Lloyd came upon the Mill Village and Union City ambulances, two marked patrol cars, a couple of pickups, a barebacked horse, two Amish men talking to Trooper Lon Pierce, and a small gathering of civilians standing about in clusters. The Amish guy who had supposedly killed his wife was seated in the back of one of the police cruisers. It seemed that everything was under control.

Ron Peters, one of the Mill Village emergency men, informed Detective Lloyd that the Amish man in the patrol car had, in fact, killed his wife. She lay dead on the kitchen floor of their house just down the road next to and behind the sawmill. According to the paramedics at the scene, it looked like the woman had been stomped and gutted. She was also nude.

As Trooper Jerry Bey, the second state police investigator from the Meadville station, pulled into the intersection, Detective Lloyd walked over to Trooper Rowles and instructed the young patrolman to drive the suspect back to the barracks. Following their crime-scene investigation at the death site, Lloyd and Bey would return to the station to interrogate the Dutchman. In the meantime, since the suspect had not been advised of his Miranda rights, he was not to be questioned about the killing or anything else.[9]

Having received his orders, Trooper Rowles slid in behind the wheel and was about to pull away when Ed started violently kicking the back of the driver's seat. Up to this point, in the presence of police authority, he had acted the way one would expect an Amish man, even a crazy one, to act—a bit befuddled but docile. The kicking startled and angered Rowles, who considered it a sign that Ed either didn't appreciate the seriousness of his situation or had no respect for police authority. Whatever the case, Rowles put an end to this silliness by yanking Ed out of the car and spreading him out facedown in the snow. Ed didn't resist as the officer tied his wrists together behind his back with those plastic strips that serve as handcuffs. He also bound Ed at the ankles, then, with the help of others, placed him back into the car. A few minutes later, Trooper Rowles and his prisoner were on their way to the Vernon Township Police Station, a trip of about twenty-five miles.

"I know I killed her," Ed said from the backseat of the cruiser as it headed south toward Meadville. "I can't believe I did it. I really killed her, didn't I?"

"Yes, you did," replied the officer.

"I killed her in front of my children. Maybe God made me do this."

Rowles didn't respond.

"I will tell you a secret," Ed said. "You may tell this to your family. The Lord and Jesus Christ are planning a new way of life. No one will have to work."[10]

Trooper Rowles said nothing as Ed, muttering softly to himself, peered through his window at the passing countryside. Then he wept.

On the morning of Thursday, March 18, 1993, the day Ed ended his marriage by killing his wife, Noah Stutzman, the head man at the Gingerich sawmill, married Lovina Hertzler. The wedding ceremony, attended by one hundred Brownhill relatives, friends, and neighbors, as well as fifty guests from other Amish settlements in Pennsylvania, Ohio, Indiana, Ontario, and New York, commenced at nine o'clock at the Smith Road home of the bride's parents, Amos J. and Rebecca N. Hertzler.

Bishop Shetler, following ninety minutes of song, prayer, and Scripture, delivered an hour-long sermon on the virtues and responsibilities of marriage. At eleven-thirty, as Doc Terrell down in Cambridge Springs cracked his knuckles over Ed's head, the groom, wearing a sparkling white shirt and his three-piece Sunday suit, and the bride, a frail, china-doll-faced, strawberry blonde in a pristine blue dress, stepped forward to take their vows.

Following the marriage ceremony, the second phase of the all-day wedding celebration began. The first involved a one o'clock dinner and the second a six-thirty feast. Both events would be hosted by Dan and Mary Stutzman, Noah's parents.

Jake Hertzler, the bride's twenty-five-year-old brother, and their twenty-four-year-old cousin, Rudy, who had traveled with his wife, his parents, and others from Lucknow, Ontario, to be at the wedding, were among several young men who left the Stutzman party early in the afternoon to attend to chores. They rode out at two-thirty, leaving their wives behind to help prepare the evening dinner, a meal

The Gingerich house on the night Ed Gingerich killed his wife, Katie. (Jim Stefanucci, *Meadville Tribune*)

Brownhill Amish on the night of the Gingerich murder not far from the killing site. (Jim Stefanucci, *Meadville Tribune*)

Pennsylvania State Police obtaining details from the local Amish on the night of the murder. (Jim Stefanucci, *Meadville Tribune*)

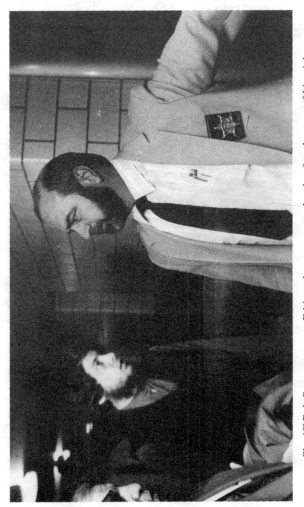

Sheriff Bob Stevens escorts Ed into the courtroom shortly after the start of his trial.
(*Meadville Tribune*)

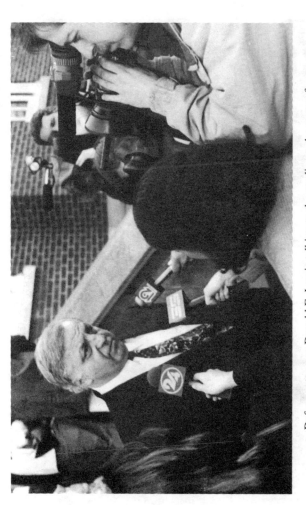

Defense attorney Donald E. Lewis talking to the media on the steps of the Crawford County Court House. (*Meadville Tribune*)

Ed Gingerich escorted by sheriff's deputies into court for his sentencing.
(Chris Horner, *Meadville Tribune*)

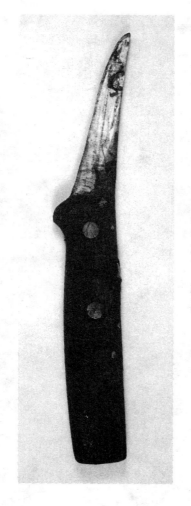

Ed Gingerich's knife.
(Daniel C. Barber)

Sturgis Road looking west from in front of the sawmill and toward the Gingerich family farm. (Jim Fisher)

they wouldn't miss if they worked hard and fast.

Shortly before six o'clock, Jake and Rudy climbed back into the buggy and, from the Hertzler farm on Smith Road, turned south on Frisbeetown on their way back to the wedding reception. As they approached Sturgis, they saw an orange-and-white ambulance parked along the road just north of the intersection. Drawing closer, Jake recognized the Amish man with the horse as Danny Gingerich. Danny was talking to a young English couple. As they pulled up to Danny, an English fellow in a blue pickup drove up, stopped, and got out of the truck.

"What happened?" Jake asked Danny. "Did someone get hurt?"

"Ed hurt Katie," Dan replied. "He might have killed her! Get my mother and Levi Shetler."[11] The man who owned the pickup said he'd follow Jake and Rudy to Dan Stutzman's and ride Mrs. Gingerich and Levi Shetler back in his truck. With the English fellow, a man Jake Hertzler didn't know and had never seen, following close behind, the buggy rolled south as fast as the horse could run. At six-thirty, Jake and Rudy pulled up the driveway and came to a stop in the turnaround in front of Dan Stutzman's barn. Dan Stutzman had just gone into the barn to fetch something and just happened to be coming out when Jake's buggy and a set of headlights behind it shot up the driveway. Jake jumped out of the carriage and ran up to Dan. "Ed Gingerich went haywire," he said. "We need help!"

"What happened?" asked Dan.

"Ed might have killed Katie!"

"He what?"

"Hurt Katie!"

"How do you know?"

"Danny Gingerich."

"When?"

"We don't know. Danny wants his mother and Levi."

"I'll get Levi's team," Dan said. He started for the barn. "No," said the man with the pickup. "I'll drive them back in my truck." The man stepped closer to Dan and whispered, "She's dead. He killed her."

"How do you know?"

"I know she's dead. She's dead."[12] Dan entered the house. The men were taking their places at the dinner tables. Dan found Levi seated at one of the tables in the living room. He walked up behind Levi's chair, whispered in his ear, then accompanied him to a corner where they could speak in private. "Ed has killed Katie," he said.

Levi grabbed his chest with both hands and issued a loud gasp. "I'll get the women," he said.

"There's a man outside with a truck," Dan said. "He'll take you to Danny."[13]

Levi walked into the kitchen, pulled Emma aside, and whispered, "Ed isn't being nice to Katie; we have to go."[14] He approached Mary Gingerich and whispered the same thing to her. The three of them hurried out the door without uttering a word to anyone.

Outside, Mary and Emma climbed into the cab, leaving no room for Levi, who had to be hauled in the back. At six-fifty, the blue pick-up pulled to a stop at the southeast corner of the intersection. Trooper Rowles and his prisoner had just departed. Levi climbed out of the truck bed and accompanied the women as they walked toward a state trooper who had just arrived at the scene. "What happened?" Emma Shetler said to the officer.

"Who are you?" he asked.

"I'm Katie's mother," she replied. "This is Ed's mother, Mary."

"You'll have to speak to the officer in charge," the patrolman said. Pointing toward Detective Lloyd, he said, "He's over there."[15]

Emma introduced herself, Mary, and Levi to Detective Lloyd, then said, "Tell us what happened."

To Mary Gingerich, the detective said, "I'm sorry to inform you that your son has just killed his wife." Emma suddenly felt numb; Levi moaned loudly; and Mary Gingerich fainted, collapsing into the snow at the officer's shoes.[16] Quickly revived and lifted to her feet by Levi and the detective, Mary was helped to her house across the way by the parents of the woman her son had just killed.

Lizzie and Clara Gingerich were with Danny, Enos, and little Mary when Mrs. Gingerich and the Shetlers trudged into the house. Danny's wife, Fannie, who never made it to the wedding, was there as well. Although the children, particularly Enos and Mary, had been talking about what happened to their mother, no one knew Katie was dead until they were told by Mrs. Gingerich.

Emma, in search of details, asked little Mary what she had seen. "Dad grabbed Mom by the hair and pulled her down," the little girl said. "Mom really screamed. He jumped on her face. Her tore her dress and took off her clothes."

"He didn't do that!" Danny yelled. "He wouldn't do that!"

"You weren't there," Mary said.

"No, Dad didn't do that! That's not true!"

Enos spoke up: "Dad took a knife and cut Mom's flesh."[17]

Dan Stutzman stood in front of his barn door and watched the blue pickup, with Levi Shetler bouncing in the back, turn right at the foot of his driveway and head west on Dean Road. Inside the house, men and boys were consuming large quantities of ham, roast turkey, pork chops, and leftovers from the earlier meal. Still in the kitchen were the six wedding cakes and the homemade ice cream. The house was filled with lighthearted talk, sounds of hearty eating, and laughter. Dan Stutzman dreaded what he had to do; he had no choice but to interrupt his son's wedding party and drop the bomb that, in one second, would kill the happiness. From this day forward, Noah and Lovina's wedding anniversary would also be remembered as the day Katie Gingerich died at the hands of her husband.

Dan walked slowly, casually, into the house and took a position in the living room, where he could be seen and heard by everyone. It took him a moment to find the courage, then he spoke: "Could I have your attention? I have an announcement to make." The expression on his face, coupled with the tone in his voice, froze everyone, causing a terrible silence to descend on the house. "Ed Gingerich just killed Katie. He killed his wife."[18]

No one said a word, uttered a sound, or moved a muscle. They all just looked at Dan as though they expected him to say more, perhaps to finish off the announcement with something that in some way would mitigate what he had just said. But there was nothing else to say and nothing anyone could do, so everybody just froze. A minute crawled by, and then another. Finally, a handful of the men carefully and quietly resumed eating. Others followed. Still, no one spoke, and in the kitchen, the women and their daughters stood frozen like Amish figures in a wax museum.[19]

Twenty minutes later, the Stutzman house was empty except for the bride and groom, the groom's family, and a kitchen full of dirty dishes and uneaten food, including the wedding cakes and the homemade ice cream. Upstairs, scattered about three bedrooms, sat the gaily packaged wedding presents, still waiting to be opened.

For the Stutzmans and the tiny, obscure community in which they lived, the party was over.

31

From the Killer's Lips

Detectives Lloyd and Bey had completed their crime-scene investigation at the Gingerich house. They had questioned Ed informally at the state police barracks in Meadville. After being advised of his Miranda rights, he had signed the waiver form "Lord Willing." Following this initial, unrecorded session in the interrogation room, the detectives drove Ed to Cambridge Springs, where he was arraigned. At one in the morning, the three men were back at the police station sitting at the interrogation table. Trooper Lloyd had brought a tape recorder, which he placed in front of Ed. He punched it on and asked, "Ed, do you know what a tape recorder is?"[1]

Ed, sitting opposite his interviewers with his cuffed hands resting on the table, muttered, "Uh-huh."

"This is a tape recorder. We're going to tape what you are saying. Do you understand that?"

"Okay."

"I explained to you and I read you that form that says you have the right to remain silent, and whatnot. You remember that? Do you understand?"

Ed stared at Lloyd with a dreamy expression, then shook his head no.

"You do not?" Lloyd asked. "You understand that stuff you say can be held against you—about what went on today. Do you understand that?"

"How do you mean?"

"Well, things that you say could be held against you in a court of law. You understand that."

"Yeah, and religion," Ed replied, obviously trying to get a handle on the conversation.

"And religion; law and religion. And that you have the right to have an attorney. You understand what an attorney is?"

"Yeah."

"Okay. And you understand you have the right to have an attorney and I explained to you that if you cannot afford to hire one, then the courts would give you one free."

"I know what you mean," Ed said.

"Okay. So you understand that?"

"Yeah, but in our religion we will not have done that."

"In your religion, maybe not, but we have to go by our law."

"Okay, the law, the law."

"We have to go by the law and the law says I have to tell you this. Do you understand?"

"No."

"You have the right to an attorney; you understand that?"

"Yeah. What I'm thinking, my mind is confused, I'm going to tell you that right now, but the reason we don't use the number, the Social Security number . . ." Ed paused as though he had been interrupted by another thought, another voice. The room grew quiet.

"Yeah?" Lloyd prompted.

"Because of the beat, the beats somewhere, the computer."

"Right," Lloyd said.

"In fact, we feel we can track our minds."

"Okay, but let's get back on track and back on track is that you understand what I've explained to you on that piece of paper."

"Yeah."

"I explained that you do not have to talk to me if you don't want to."

"Yeah."

"And you understand that?"

"Yeah."

Apparently unconcerned that Ed's willingness to talk had to do with the fact that he was insane, Trooper Lloyd, satisfied that he had covered all the Miranda bases, pushed on. "Okay, now I know you've told myself and I know you told Trooper Bey enough times, but I want to try to understand this one last time. Exactly what happened, why you killed Katie. Explain that to me again."

"Because, for some reason I felt, I just felt that—what is going to happen after we die?"

"We don't know that," Lloyd replied. "We only presume that we're going to heaven with God and we will be with God the rest of our lives after we are—"

"For eternity," Trooper Bey said.

"For eternity after we have died," Lloyd added.

"Is that what your bishop tells you?" asked Trooper Bey.

"No, I'm so lost. I just don't know what. I'm lost."

"Why don't you just explain to us," Trooper Bey asked, "why Katie had to die tonight."

"For some reason, I think we could still save her," Ed said.

"No, we cannot," Lloyd replied. "I have seen Katie and we cannot save her. Katie is dead and you know Katie is dead."

"Yeah, I know. Why did I kill her? I felt it was a gain."

"A gain for who?" asked Trooper Bey.

"A gain for us, the people," Ed replied.

"All the people?" Lloyd asked.

"Yeah, not just my religion."

"Why?" Trooper Bey asked.

"Because, if I can get back on track, it will come yet."

"Okay," Trooper Lloyd said. "Maybe you can explain why you felt that you had to remove Katie's brain and work your way from the brain down. Explain that to me."

"You know how we, the human being, were made?"

"Yes," Lloyd replied. "From the top down."

"That's right. I had it in my mind that if I worked from the top down . . ." Ed wiped his face with a cuffed hand, then said, "I'm so lost. I don't know what to say."

"But why Katie?" asked Trooper Bey.

"How did you get Katie's brain out?" Lloyd asked.

"I knocked it out, didn't I? . . ."

"But why Katie?" Lloyd asked, still looking for a motive that could be understood, articulated.

"She was my wife."

"Yes, but why did she have to die?"

"I don't know. But I thought she was trying to get me . . ."

"Do you need some sleep?" asked Lloyd.

"No, I have to get my mind back. Now, what else? What other questions do you want to know?"

"Well," Lloyd replied, "I want to know why you felt that Katie had to die? Where did you get the knife?"

"Somewhere in the kitchen there."

"And the children were there when this was going on?"

"The children cried to start with, but then I must have pulled my hair out. I think I'm gaining, but I'm losing. You know what I'm saying?"

"Uh-huh," Lloyd lied.

"That's what I'm doing," Ed said. "I'm actually losing 'cause I think I have to try to find myself."

Trooper Bey, realizing that the interview was going nowhere, asked, "Are you sorry what happened to Katie?"

"Yeah," Ed said, "but I can't cry. I wish I could cry."

"Why can't you cry?" Lloyd asked. "Are you sorry for what you did?"

"Yeah, I'm sorry."

"You have forgiven yourself for what you've done?" Lloyd asked.

"That's my problem. I'm trying; I can't forgive myself.

I haven't come down to that yet. Ah, gee, I never thought I could get messed up this way. I never ever thought I'd get messed like this. We'll have to counsel over this. Sleeping is my problem . . ."

"Did you ever dream that you were going to kill Katie?" Lloyd asked, fishing around for a little premeditation perhaps.

Ed shook his head no.

"Did you ever dream you were going to kill anybody?"

Before Ed could answer, Trooper Bey broke in: "When did you decide that Katie had to die?"

"When my hair started prickling . . ."

"Well, Edward, I think it's time we got you some sleep. Okay?"

"I would like to talk a little longer. You are getting me back on track."

"Okay, sure."

"Have you ever done this before?" Bey interjected.

"Have I ever done this before?" Ed asked.

"Right."

"You mean kill somebody?"

"Yeah."

"Nooo," Ed replied.

"Then how could you do it this time?" Bey asked.

"I do not know. Maybe it is anger."

Now they were making progress. "Were you angry at her?" Lloyd asked.

"Yes. I just told her that all—I told her that she—I just seemed like, ah, everything that—she was just working against me. Do you know what I think? It was me; it was me. I was going backward instead of ahead. That's what it seemed like."

"But now Katie is dead," Lloyd said.

"Yeah—I feel like I did—I don't know—now I'm starting to realize I did a criminal offense."

"Yes, you did," Lloyd replied.

"Do you remember killing her?" asked Trooper Bey.

"I remember, yeah. And I thought I was doing a good deed—I mean I thought I was responsible to do it. You know, I cannot believe I did something like that . . ."

"Edward, I think it's time we took you to the jail so you can get some rest and some food."

"I have to talk to myself some more. Why did you take my fingerprints?"

"Well, that's just part of the law. Anytime—"

"When you were doing that, I was suspicious of you. I thought you were—"

"I could feel that."

"Because my nervous system is out of whack is what it is."

"Our law says that when somebody is arrested for a crime, we have to take their fingerprints and we have to take their photograph. It is just part of the procedure. Edward, we're going to have to go."

"I'll just try to sit it out. I'm going to have to get out. This is not going to slow me. Well—they don't want me at home, do they?"

"Not at this stage, no. But that's not an option open to you at this stage."

"I'll try to sit my time out in prison."

"Okay. It's time for us to go."

"Okay."

Just before two o'clock, Danny Lloyd turned off the tape recorder and brought one of the strangest interrogations he had ever conducted to a close. There was no reason to continue the questioning, even though Ed didn't want them to quit. Apparently baffled by his own crime, Ed didn't seem able to explain why he had butchered his wife. If the only motive he could articulate involved thinking that Katie was the devil or that business about his prickling hair, the officers were wasting their time talking to this man. Since he wasn't sure why he had killed her, there was no way he could explain kicking out her brains then pulling

her organs out of her body through a slit he had made in
her stomach with a kitchen knife. The guy looked crazy,
talked crazy, and had killed his wife in a crazy way. It
was, therefore, not surprising that his confession didn't
make any sense. The poor guy couldn't separate his hallucinations, fantasies, and dreams from reality. Because the
detectives had confirmed for Ed that he had actually killed
his wife, that she was really dead, he had learned more
from the interrogation than they had. At times, it was hard
to tell who was being questioned.

The detectives felt that from an investigative point of
view, Ed's interrogation was not a total loss. He admitted
killing his wife; he said he remembered doing it and the
entire questioning was recorded on tape. The man was obviously dangerous and belonged in an insane asylum. Now
that he had confessed and was on his way to jail, there
wasn't much left for the detectives to do. The case was
now in the hands of judges, prosecutors, defense lawyers,
and shrinks. The criminal investigation, except for a little
mopping up the day after and some paperwork, was over.
Case solved, case closed.

32

Jail

Troopers Lloyd and Bey, accompanied by their confused and babbling prisoner, arrived at the Crawford
County Jail at two in the morning on Friday, March 19,
1993. Under cover of darkness, the trio entered the old,
stone lockup that is attached to the rear of the courthouse
building. They slipped into the basement through a hidden,

alleyway door. On each of the two floors above, inside clusters of white, paint-chipped cells built in 1849 to accommodate thirty, slept one hundred boozers, drug users, women hitters, and petty thieves either doing time for minor offenses or awaiting trial for more serious crimes. Most of these inhabitants were churlish, cigarette-smoking white males with greasy hair, wiry frames, cheesy tattoos, and bad grammar. Ed was under the same roof with a child rapist, a handful of burglars, a man who got caught robbing a convenience store, and a drunk who had squeezed off a harmless shot in a bar, all of whom were in custody because they couldn't make bail. A rough trade. At the moment, Ed was the jail's only homicide suspect; but what really made him unique was the fact that no other Amish person had been inside these walls, a life experience most English people managed to avoid as well. Ed may have thought he had killed the devil, but in reality, he was as close to hell as one could get in Crawford County.

The detectives, whom Ed had slowly come to trust and need, suddenly walked out the door without a good-bye, leaving him in that crumbling, brightly lit, paint-peeling, white-walled place that was sterile but not clean. Here he was again fingerprinted, then stood against the wall and photographed with a camera that made its own pictures. This place was not a hospital; the workers didn't dress in white and were not as friendly as the health-care people in the mental wards he had known. Wearing brown shirts, gold badges, shoulder patches, heavy black belts, and dark trousers with tan piping, the jail guards reminded Ed of the security men he had wrestled at Hamot.

Having been booked, Ed was temporarily housed in one of two basement holding cells, a white, six-by-ten steel box featuring a stainless-steel toilet bowl, a drain in the middle of the gray, cement floor, and, bolted to the wall, a gray steel bench that passed for a bed. There was no mattress or blanket, just a slab of steel drilled with holes and equipped with handles to accommodate restraining straps.

The four-foot fluorescent lamp, bolted to the wall opposite the bunk, lit the place up like an operating room. As the guard backed out of the cell, Ed, standing in the middle of this white box, holding his eyes shut against the light, asked, "Are you going to shoot me?"

"Relax," the guard said, "no one is going to hurt you."[1] He shut the big steel door then peeked at Ed through its tiny, chicken-wired window. Ed hadn't moved; he stood frozen in the middle of the cell with his eyes squeezed closed and his arms held straight and rigid against his sides. He stood there like a man facing a firing squad. The guard had orders to check on him every fifteen minutes, and for the first hour or so, every time he peeked through the little window, he saw the same thing: this gangly Amish man—this overgrown boy—standing at attention with his oversized hands, killer's hands, hanging at his sides like a pair of spent weapons. The guard peeked in at four A.M. and saw that the skinny Amish man was no longer standing in the middle of the cell. He was stretched out on the floor—sleeping under the bed.[2]

At sunrise Friday morning, while Ed slept soundly under the bunk in the basement of the Crawford County Jail and his wife lay cold in a refrigerated hospital vault with her insides bagged up beside her, Noah Stutzman began the first day of his married life by showing up at the sawmill minus two of his employees. Katie's older brother Emanuel and Emanuel Hershberger, her brother-in-law, had quit. They could no longer work for Ed Gingerich, not after what he had done. The two Emanuels were gone for good and that left the entire enterprise in the hands of Noah Stutzman and his younger brother Henry.[3] Within a period of twenty-four hours, Noah had gone from celebrated groom to overworked sawmill operator. For that, he could thank Ed Gingerich.

That morning, on the heels of the previous night's television reports, newspapers in Erie, Meadville, and to a lesser extent Pittsburgh hit the stands with bold, front-page accounts of Katie Gingerich's homicide. Accompanying these stories were photographs: snowy, farm-country scenes depicting horses, buggies, and the shadowy frames of Amish folk, their backs to the camera, talking to state troopers. In one of these eerie, misty pictures, a small dog can be seen relieving himself against the tire of a police car. There were shots of Ed's house, the sawmill, the Frisbeetown-Sturgis intersection with the Gingerich place off in the distance, and a picture of Ed, wearing handcuffs and a straw hat, walking out of the district magistrate's office between State Detectives Lloyd and Bey.

Ed woke up at eight o'clock and had no idea where he was or how he had gotten there. He crawled out from under the bunk and tried to get his eyes used to the light. He had been on his feet a few seconds when the door opened and two guards walked into the cell. "What happened to Katie?" he asked.

"You killed her," replied one of the guards.

"I killed her?"

"Yes, she's dead."

"I can't believe I did it," Ed groaned.

"Are you hungry?"

"No," Ed said, rubbing his eyes. "I killed her."

"We're taking you upstairs to a different place," the guard said. "We're putting you in the isolation cell."[4]

The isolation cell looked a lot like the holding cell where Ed had spent the night, except it was a little bigger, had two bunks with mattresses, and featured a chipped, concrete floor that had been painted red.

Ed didn't stay in the isolation cell very long. At nine-thirty, a couple of guards took him up another flight of stairs to a place they called the nurses' station, which was nothing more than a chair, table, scale, and medicine cabinet squeezed into what used to be a supply closet. Ed sat stiffly on the chair and waited for the visiting nurse whose job it was to measure his heartbeat, blood pressure, temperature, and so forth. Following that, she'd obtain from him a quick medical history to determine if he was allergic to anything, was on medication, or in need of special medical attention. It was all quite routine: a form to be filled out, a signature to be acquired, then filing the paperwork in the proper place. Bureaucracy, the lifeblood of the system. Everybody took it for granted, even the prisoners. Because there wasn't enough space in the nurses' station to accommodate the guards, they left Ed in the chair and waited outside for the nurse.

The nurse, a young woman sporting red hair and a white outfit, had to squeeze past Ed to get to her equipment. He watched her closely as she made preparations for his examination.

Everything seemed to be going smoothly until the nurse looked at Ed and was struck full force by the wildness in his eyes. His double-barreled, predator stare hit her like a shotgun blast. "Can you tell there is something wrong with me?" he asked. "Can . . ."[5]

The nurse *could* tell, but she wasn't telling him. Instead, fearing for her life, she ran out of the former supply closet, flying past Ed so fast he was left in the room speaking to himself.

Ed was still on the chair when the two guards returned. This time they were accompanied by Jack Brickner, the young, college-educated warden—the boss. It was Brickner who told Ed there would be no physical examination; they were taking him back to the isolation cell on the first floor. Ed said he didn't like that place, the light was too bright. So, if they didn't mind, he'd stay right where he was; he wasn't going anywhere.

Jack Brickner and his men did mind, and in about three seconds, they had Ed off his chair and onto the floor. Following a very brief struggle, they bound his ankles with a leather strap and were carrying him down the stairs toward the isolation cell. The Crawford County men looked like zookeepers and Ed looked like a tranquilized alligator. He had just learned a harsh but valuable lesson about life in jail: no one gave a damn what he wanted or didn't want. He was no longer in control. Once again, the English had him and they had him good.[6]

At nine o'clock, about the time Ed was moved upstairs to the cell with the red floor, Katie was being driven by a private ambulance from the hospital in Meadville to the county coroner's office in Erie. At ten, Dr. Takeshi Imajo, a forensic pathologist contracted by the Erie County Coroner's Office, began her autopsy. The doctor noted the extensive damage done to her skull, her partially destroyed face, and the seven-inch abdominal incision on her lower left side. He found no bruises, lacerations, or incisions suggesting a struggle, nor did he find any old evidence of physical abuse. Cause of death: "Blunt force trauma to the head."[7]

A local psychiatrist named Frank J. Yohe, accompanied by a nurse, arrived at eleven o'clock to examine Ed, who had been placed into a regular cell where he could be talked to through the white, paint-chipped bars. Brickner had ordered the removal of his restraints, and although Ed certainly was disheveled, he didn't look particularly crazy. After greeting the doctor and his nurse with indifference, he walked to the cot and lay down on his back. He ignored the doctor's attempts to open him up with small talk and, in response to questions about his history of psychiatric treatment, said he'd been treated for a nervous breakdown in Jamestown, New York. He didn't elaborate other than to say the drugs they had prescribed didn't agree with him and had caused him problems, so he quit the medicine. Ed suddenly sat up and looked at Dr. Yohe. "Did they have the funeral yet?" he asked.

"Your wife's?" asked the doctor.

"Have they held the funeral?"

"No yet—she died yesterday. What happened to her?"

"I don't want to talk about it," Ed replied. "Not with you."

"Who would you talk to?" the doctor asked.

Ed didn't reply.

"Do you hear voices?"

"I hear Danny."

"Who?"

"My brother."

"What does he say?"

"Never mind," Ed said. "What day is it?"

"It's Friday, March nineteenth."

"I thought it was the eighteenth," Ed said.

"Have you been thinking about hurting yourself?" asked the doctor.

"Nooo," Ed replied.

"Have you thought about hurting others?"

"Nooo," Ed said, then suddenly burst into tears. "I don't want to hurt anyone," he cried.[8]

The interview lasted fifteen minutes. Dr. Yohe had seen and heard enough; Ed was probably mentally ill, probably psychotic. The doctor would recommend further evaluation at the forensic unit at the Warren State Hospital in North Warren, Pennsylvania.

33

Cleaning Up

Since its birth in the spring of '83, the Amish enclave called Brownhill had been known mainly to the English of LeBoeuf and Rockdale townships and the residents of the other Amish colonies dotted throughout northwestern Pennsylvania, a population of perhaps ten thousand. Their houses, barns, and outbuildings spread thin and inconspicuous over nine square miles of English farmland in the heart of a lightly traveled, eventless section of Crawford and Erie counties, the Brownhill Amish had escaped notice. They would have had it no other way. When Ed Gingerich killed and eviscerated his wife, people in Erie, Meadville, and the villages and townships in between realized they had Amish neighbors and the real thing, too—men, women, and children who rode in buggies and wore old-fashioned clothes and looked just like what they had seen in eastern Pennsylvania or on postcards in Wal-Mart.

By Friday afternoon, the Sturgis-Frisbeetown crossing was clogged with cars, pickups, off-road vehicles, and minivans carrying adults and children of all ages eager to lay eyes on the now historic house where the Amish man had murdered his wife then performed his own autopsy. Amid the sound and fury of English tourism out on Sturgis Road, Ed's sisters, Clara and Lizzie, went about their business of feeding Ed's animals. Several drivers, having pulled their vehicles off the road, were disgorging gawkers. Some were stomping about the lot in front of the mill, while other, more cheeky sightseers pressed themselves against the house, trying to look inside through the windows. Seeing nothing—no body, no blood, no guts—they fell away, only to be replaced by others. The tourist situation, unseemly and disruptive, had gotten out of hand. Danny and Atlee had no choice but to confront the crime buffs. Didn't they know they were on private property? What were they looking at? What did they expect to see? Would they please leave and not come back? The intruders, proclaiming that they meant no harm and slightly offended and surprised by this Amish unfriendliness, walked to the road and climbed back into their vehicles.

Having driven off the trespassers, Dan and Atlee closed off Ed's driveway by stringing a rope across the two points of access off Sturgis Road. This barrier, although flimsy and easy to defeat, served notice that the mill and house were off-limits to strangers. The brothers also hung cardboard, hand-scrawled KEEP OUT posters on the barbed-wire fence along the foot of the property. The Gingerich sawmill, Brownhill's version of the country store where locals gathered to socialize and do business, was no longer friendly and, at the moment, not open to the public. Ed had transformed his house and, to a lesser extent, the mill, into a pair of roadside attractions. Murder could do that.

Katie's unembalmed, autopsied remains were delivered to Dannie and Mary Gingerich's house in a station wagon provided by a man who owned a funeral home in Union City. Had she been killed in an accident or been taken by illness, her wake would have been held in the house she had shared with her husband and their children. Because she had been murdered by her husband in her own home and her father, Levi, didn't want the funeral at his house because it would have drawn the media and the public to his door ("Keep it there," he had said, referring to the attention focused on Ed's parents' house and the mill), the wake would be held at the Gingerich place.[1]

Emma Shetler and two of Katie's sisters were waiting at the Gingerich house when the man from the funeral home delivered the coroner's body bag containing Katie's remains. Following the autopsy, the forensic pathologist, according to standard procedure, had placed her brains and internal organs, bagged up in plastic, into her chest cavity before sewing her up. Katie returned home with more of herself than she had possessed when the county men had carried her remains out of the blood-splattered kitchen.

The coroner's men laid the black plastic body sack on a table in one of the first-floor bedrooms that could be shut off from the rest of the house by a delicate blue curtain. Emma unzipped the bag and almost fainted at the sight of her daughter's ghastly white skin and the crudely stitched, Y-shaped scar left by the pathologist's scalpel—the coroner's signature—the universal sign of violent death. The right side of Katie's face was gone, leaving a jagged ridge of bone and torn, ragged skin. This was a wound of war, not murder. Although Emma had prepared herself for the worst, the sight of Katie's demolished head struck her dumb with revulsion, shock, and a fear of Ed Gingerich she would never shake. Thank God Levi was spared seeing the obscene aftermath of Ed's murderous rage. This sight of his beloved daughter would have crushed his heart, killed him on the spot.

Emma and the girls removed the death bag, washed Katie head to toe, combed her auburn hair, and then wrapped her body, save her neck and face, in delicate strips of black linen. They cocooned her back into the coroner's bag, zipped it over her face, and, with the help of Mr. Gingerich and Atlee, lowered her into the pine-smelling coffin bridged across the seats of a pair of straight-back chairs sitting nearby. Katie would rest in the unlined, unfinished box with the one-piece lid that slid back for viewing, until it was time, following her wake the next afternoon, to transport he body to the woodsy cemetery above the swamp, where she would join the two young women, the old man, and her niece Mary, the infant.[2] As Emma and the others tended to Katie's body in the Gingerich house, Enos J. Yoder, the former bishop of Conewango Valley, New York, oversaw the digging of her grave, a job performed by hiring an English neighbor who owned a backhoe.

The state detectives had finished their work at the killing site; the Gingerich kitchen was, therefore, no longer the scene of a crime—at least not officially. But the murder room, where stains of Katie's blood, chunks of her flesh, and fragments of her skull bore silent witness to what had happened there, and still reeking of death, had to be washed away before anyone could live in the house again. Cleaning up the murder debris was not a task for a Shetler or a Gingerich, a person of weak heart or stomach, or an

English outsider. It fell upon a party of three—Robert Hershberger, Jake Hertzler, and Rudy Hochstetter—a team of life-hardened adults handpicked by Deacon Ben Stutzman. An hour before the overcast, gray afternoon gave way to nightfall, the deacon's crew entered the house carrying their soap, pails, mops, and scrubbing brushes.[3] Less than twenty-four hours earlier, these men were celebrating the marriage of Noah and Lovina Stutzman. The next day they were cleaning up after Ed Gingerich—one of their own—who had destroyed his wife in front of his children. The men who crawled on their hands and knees on Katie's floor that evening came to know Ed in a way others would not. They sensed his power, touched and smelled his evil, and would live to regret the experience— this intimacy with violent, sudden death.

The mess Ed had left on his kitchen floor could be cleaned up by soap, water, and elbow grease; but the mess he had made of his life and the lives of others could not be scrubbed away. By Amish thinking, he had, by his own actions, ruined himself and his life completely and forever. However, by his murderous act, he had delivered himself into the hands of English "helpists"—entire professions that existed to give hope to the hopeless, forgive the unforgivable, and make whole the most shattered lives. He had fallen into the clutches of lawyers, correction officers, psychiatrists, psychologists, and the omnipresent social worker. He would be studied, tested, talked to and drugged, assured by experts that no one judged him harshly for killing his wife. Yes, he had taken her life with his own hands, but it was not his fault. Ed would learn about "society" and how the cruelties of life drove some people to do the most awful things. He would learn to blame the Amish and, if all went according to plan, the victim—Katie. Poor dead Katie. A backbencher in life, second fiddle in death. It went like this: Forgive Ed, forget Katie.

•   •   •

The documents, the printed forms associated with sending a prisoner to the state mental hospital in North Warren, Pennsylvania, had been filled out. They had been signed and sworn to by all the bureaucrats necessary to make Ed's commitment right, proper, and legal. Under the rules, Ed could be incarcerated in this facility as long as it took to render him mentally competent to stand trial for the killing of his wife. If that day ever came, and thanks to modern pharmacology it almost always did, Ed would be returned to the Crawford County Jail, where he would remain in custody until his trial. As one of the sheriff's deputies shackled him for the seventy-five-mile ride to North Warren, Ed looked at Jack Brickner, the warden of the jail, who was glad to see him go, and said, "I remember what I did—my wife—I just killed my wife!"

Out in the parking lot behind the jail, just before dark, a deputy sheriff clad in khaki and brown, climbed in behind the wheel of the blue county van while his partner, a hefty blond-haired officer in his twenties, slid into the backseat next to Ed. The deputies and their prisoner headed northeast out of Meadville, toward Corry on State Route 77. Ed, sitting on the passenger side of the vehicle next to the window, sat rigid, with his bulging eyes trained on the road ahead. "Oh, boys," he kept saying in his high-pitched voice, "you can't be doing this!"

"What can't we be doing?" the deputy next to him finally asked.

"It's like a puzzle," Ed said. "But the picture is coming clear. You boys can't be doing this!"

"Doing what?"

"You boys are going to shoot me!"

"Where did you get that idea?" asked the young deputy. "No one is going to lay a finger on you. We don't do that kind of thing."

"Then where are you taking me?" Ed asked. "I think you're taking me to the woods."

"We're taking you to a hospital," said the older, more

experienced deputy driving the van. "We don't shoot our prisoners." He laughed. Amish people were something else.

"Will I see a doctor?"

"Oh, yes," said the backseat deputy.

"Okay," Ed replied. "Maybe the doctor can cure my itches." He giggled, relaxed by the realization that he wasn't being executed.

"Be sure to tell him that you itch," the driver said, suddenly serious.

"Okay, I will," Ed muttered.[4]

The county van pulled up to building number twelve, the forensic unit, located on the eastern edge of the state hospital complex. The senior deputy climbed out of the vehicle and ascended the long flight of steps leading to the ornate front entrance. Instead of entering the fifty-year-old building through the front door, he strode down the sidewalk past the snowcapped shrubs toward the corner of the building where a blue sign with yellow letters said FORENSIC. Following the sign's yellow arrow, the deputy rounded the corner and disappeared through a side door.

The young deputy, sitting next to Ed in the van while his partner checked their prisoner into the facility, was getting antsy. He didn't enjoy sitting alone in the dark with a man who had just slaughtered his wife. Not only that, Ed didn't smell very good. Time dragged. How long did it take to check a person into this place? Ed's shackles jangled as he adjusted himself on the seat. He stared out the window. The deputy was about to say something to lighten things up when Ed turned to him and said, "I wish I was in your shoes."

"Why is that?"

"Because I am the devil!" Ed screamed.[5]

The novice deputy damn near jumped out of the van. He wondered if Ed—bug-eyed, wild-haired, and grinning like a drunk who had just bopped someone with a beer bottle—could hear his heart thumping inside his chest. Jesus, this guy was *nuts*! There was no telling what he would do. Regaining enough composure to speak, the deputy said, "It will be all right, Ed. They have doctors here."

"Can they fix my itches?"[6]

34

The Funeral

It is Amish custom, when a death occurs, to put a non-relative in charge of the funeral arrangements. Deacon Ben Stutzman asked his brother-in-law Dan, the man who had announced Katie's death at his son's wedding, to take charge of her funeral. The deacon assigned a crew of young men to handle chores on the Shetler farm while the family mourned. A party of six made up of Katie's aunts and teenage nieces were running the house and looking after the younger children. Ed's offspring were being cared for by his mother and his two adult sisters.

On Saturday morning at ten, forty-one hours after Katie's death, three chartered buses, a dozen sedans, and four vans could be seen parked along Sturgis and Frisbeetown roads. These vehicles had brought Amish mourners from Ohio, New York, Indiana, eastern Pennsylvania, and Ontario. Horses and buggies from the Brownhill and Spartansburg settlements lined Frisbeetown from the intersection north to a hundred yards beyond the schoolhouse and were clustered off the road in front of Dannie Gingerich's imposing red barn.

To accommodate the unusually large number of mourners, funeral services were being held simultaneously at three locations. Katie's closest relatives and Brownhill acquaintances, eighty-five in all, were packed inside the Gingerich house, where Rudy Shetler, the dead woman's uncle and Brownhill bishop, delivered the main sermon. Kim Kerstetter and Alice DeMatteo, Katie's closest English friends and the only non-Amish people attending her funeral, were among this group. Ed's English friends—Jim DeMatteo, Jake Powers, Richard Zimmer, Dave Lindsey, and Lazar LeMajic—although no less stunned and saddened by Katie's death than Alice and Kim, were not on hand to say good-bye. No one felt worse than Jake Powers. Katie's death had knocked him into a state of shock and depression. He had lost more than a friend and a job; he had lost his surrogate family. He would miss Ed, the sawmill, Katie, and the children. He'd really miss the kids. The loss was devastating. None of these men would have been comfortable at Katie's funeral, a ceremony they considered private and Amish. Jake and Richard Zimmer would have been embarrassed by all the singing and the praying. They would have felt like intruders. Dave Lindsey and Lazar LeMajic, had their religious mission been known, would not have been welcomed guests. Not wanting to risk being exposed as predatory evangelists, they stayed away. In fact, neither man had known Katie very well, because their attentions had been so focused on Ed. Spiritually, Katie had been a lost cause. The Amish had co-opted the poor woman's soul, and as a result, she had died without knowing Jesus. There was still hope for Ed and the evangelists had not given up on him.

The mourners who were not congregated at the Gingerich house, about one hundred and twenty distant relatives and family friends from other enclaves, were gathered at a pair of auxiliary sites. One group was assembled across the street in the little gray house where Deacon Ben Stutzman was in charge of the service. Minister Dannie Gingerich officiated up the road in Mahlon Hochstetter's house across from the lane leading back to the Frisbeetown cemetery.[1]

Bishop Shetler's opening message included the biblical admonitions offered in his standard introductory sermon. They were gathered on this special day because God had spoken through the death of a loved one. Yes, Katie was needed by her family and would be terribly missed by her children and her parents, but God needed her more. No one knows when their time will come; therefore, the important thing is to be ready when the Lord calls. Although Bishop Shetler spoke of Katie's life—her good deeds as a mother, daughter, and wife—his message was less an eulogy than an appeal to live a righteous, unworldly Amish life. The Amish do not praise their dead because to do so would make the deceased person special and that would violate the Amish ideals of uniformity and humility. Being the first Amish woman to be murdered by her husband made Katie's death special in the English world. The Amish, however, would not celebrate her passing differently. Hers would be accorded the understated respect that marked all Amish deaths. Nothing more, nothing less.

Bishop Shetler spoke for forty-five minutes, then, as the congregation knelt, read a long prayer, in high German. At the end of the prayer, the audience rose to its feet for the benediction. At the conclusion of the benediction, with the congregation reseated, Rudy Shetler, on behalf of the bereaved family, thanked all of those who had shown special kindness to Katie's loved ones following her sudden and untimely death. The bishop recited a hymn, then brought the service to a close by inviting everyone, following the burial ceremony, back to the Gingerich house for dinner. It was now time to view the body.

Dan Stutzman, in the roles of funeral director and head usher, walked to the coffin and slid back its lid to expose what was left of Katie. Her parents, grandparents, brothers, and sisters, seated in the front rows, remained in their chairs while Dan led the rest of the congregation past the casket, out the front door, and around the house, where they entered the basement through a side entrance. The group would remain there until mourners from the other two houses joined them after filing past the body. Following the mass viewing, the three units, now assembled as one, would be led back upstairs to witness members of Katie's immediate family take one last look at the body before she was put underground.

Kim Kerstetter wasn't sure what she would be seeing when it came her time to look into the coffin. What she saw shook her to the core. She almost fainted. It would be days before she could free herself of that awful image. It was a frightening, haunting sight that revealed the violent, obscene nature of Katie's death. Had Kim known she would be seeing this, she would have stayed home with Richard.[2]

Katie's face was covered by a thin, white handkerchief that fell off sharply along a ragged edge into the void that once had been the rest of her head, revealing in a startling way what Ed had done to her skull. If the handkerchief had been placed there to disguise the gruesomeness of the wound, it didn't do the job. In a way, the piece of cloth, by simplifying and highlighting the damage, made it worse. It was like seeing a hand sticking out of the ground. And that wasn't all. The rest of Katie's body was still in the black plastic bag. On top of the bag lay a white dress covered, in part, by a blue blanket.[3]

When the mourners from the basement regrouped upstairs, they found that the chairs had been put away and the coffin moved to the center of the room. Surrounding the coffin were Katie's closest kin. At this moment, there were no audible signs of grief—no sobbing, weeping, or bawling. Emma Shetler, Katie's mother, suddenly reached into the coffin and unzipped the coroner's bag and started groping for her daughter's body. She had to be pulled away in order that the coffin lid be slid shut. Sobbing loudly, Emma threw herself onto the coffin and had to be pried from it by two of hers sons.[4] She was not ready to say good-bye. She had not accepted her daughter's death.

Using leather straps, four pallbearers carried Katie's coffin to the hearse, a horse-drawn, spring wagon with the seat pushed forward. The pine box, braced by sacks of grain for the half-mile trek up Frisbeetown and across the Hochstetter land to the *Grabhof* (the graveyard), was followed by a procession of mourners and a dozen buggies carrying those who were unable to cover the ground on foot. The black-clad cortege inching its way along the snow-covered path at the edge of the woods, created the image of infantry troops marching into battle behind a rolling cannon. The ghosts of previous battles, the chalky-white headstones tilted among the trees where the original cemetery had been, looked on in silence.

Katie's coffin, strapped to a pair of hickory poles, hung suspended over the freshly dug grave on the knoll above the frozen swamp. Using a pair of long, felt straps, the pallbearers lowered it slowly into the pit, where a younger Amish man, straddling a wooden frame at the bottom, guided the box to its final place. From above, one of the pallbearers handed the young man in the grave several planks, which he laid across the frame. The young Amish man, having boxed in the coffin, was helped out of the hole by one of the men at the edge of the grave. Each pallbearer picked up a shovel and started pitching dirt into the hole. At first the soil could be heard thumping against the roof of the rough box. The shovelers half filled the grave then laid down their tools. Katie's immediate family joined Bishop Shetler at the foot of the grave. The rest of the congregation closed in around them. Sounds of snorting horses and restless buggies came out of the woods as Bishop Shetler opened his book to read a hymn. The men took off their hats.[5] When Bishop Shetler closed his hymn book, hats returned to their heads and the pallbearers picked up their shovels and completed the burial as the mourners dispersed and headed on foot and in buggies back to the Gingerich house and the feast scheduled for three o'clock. About half of the mourners, eager to return to their faraway farms, would soon be departing on buses, cars, and vans, unable to attend the funeral dinner.

That evening, following the big meal, at Danny Gingerich's request, Emma, Levi, their married children and their spouses, as well as Mr. and Mrs. Gingerich and their grown children and spouses, gathered in the living room of Ed's house—the killing site—to hear Danny's account of Katie's death. Danny said he would tell it one time and one time only, then never talk about it again. What he had seen, what he had experienced, was so terrible he had to get it off his chest, then do his best to forget. He had asked God not to let what he had witnessed haunt him the rest of his life. He was afraid that it might.

Danny and his wife were the last ones to enter Ed's house that evening. To those in attendance, he explained how difficult it had been for him to walk through that door; it had taken all the strength and courage he could muster. He didn't mind telling them that he was afraid. He would say his piece then answer questions if there were any.

Danny began his account by relating how he had been summoned to Ed's house by his nephew and namesake. At the house, he was greeted by Enos, who was crying. He burst into the kitchen, where he found Katie lying on the floor being punched in the face by Ed, who sat straddled across her chest. Dan yelled something, then pushed Ed off her body. Katie didn't move. Ed jumped to his feet and that's when Danny saw the other figure. Terrified, he ran out of the house, leaving the children behind. He prayed that God would forgive him for not trying to save the children. But Danny was afraid.

"What did you see?" someone asked.

"He was standing right next to Ed," Danny replied. "In the flesh. I saw him."

"Who?"

"Satan. The devil himself, standing right there next to

Ed. He came out of Ed and stood there. I was scared. I ran for my life."[6]

No one spoke. There were no questions about the devil. Danny finished his story, ending it with the arrival of the police at the intersection. They all knew the rest. Were there any questions?

There were none. They all went home.

35

Loose Talk

Saturday morning, Ed woke up in a strange room tied to a bed. He had no idea where he was and he didn't recognize either of the men looking down at him when he came to. Thanks to the Ativan and Haldol, he didn't particularly care where he was or who these men were. He was confused but not afraid. The scene was vaguely familiar; he'd been through this before: the men wore white, the room was white, and the place smelled disinfectantly clean. Ed was in the hospital again. He was back with the English.

One of the guards asked him if he was ready to be untied. They didn't want any trouble and if Ed acted up, they'd strap him down again. He had killed his wife and he was in their custody. They were there to help him, but he'd have to behave. This was a state hospital; he was not a private patient. If he didn't obey the rules, he'd have to be restrained. Everybody followed the rules. Until Ed proved that he could be trusted, he'd be subject to what they called a one-to-one watch. He'd have a guard who never left his side. If all went well with that, he would be upgraded to "close observation," consisting of periodic, around-the-clock checks. After that, assuming he responded well to treatment, he'd be more or less free to move about his area.[1] Did he understand? Ed nodded that he got the message. They'd have no trouble with him. No sir.

He was untied.

That afternoon, about the time they were lowering Katie into her grave, Dr. Alex Romulo A. Ziga, a Warren State psychiatrist, had his first talk with Ed. It took a while for Ed to warm up to the doctor. His responses to the psychiatrist's preliminary questions were brief and to the point. Ed asked the doctor what he knew about Amish people. Dr. Ziga replied that although Ed was the first Amish man he had ever spoken to, he had read about the Amish and their ways in newspapers and magazines. Loosening up a bit, Ed said that he and his father owned a sawmill that employed three people. His schooling, an eighth-grade education, was typically Amish. The doctor asked him if he liked school. Did he get good grades? Ed replied that his grades averaged somewhere between 60 and 70 percent— good enough to pass. School was okay. What about mental illness—had Ed ever been treated for that before? Yes, he had been mentally ill. His brain was out of balance electrically; it had something to do with his right side being positive and his left charged negative. He had been hospitalized twice, once in Erie and the second time in Jamestown. Dr. Ziga was curious why Ed had been rehospitalized. What had gone wrong? That, Ed explained, had to do with the drugs. He quit taking his medicine and started treating himself with herbs. His doctors told him not to, but he did it anyway. What do you suppose, asked the doctor, made you so ill? Well, Ed replied, just before being hospitalized in Erie, he had been hearing, in his head, his brother Danny's voice. He was also hearing a woman who told him she owned the universe. "My mind was triggered by the greaser," Ed said, referring to the Gunk he'd been working with in his machine shop.[2]

Speaking of Katie and her death at his hands, Ed said, "I helped her close her eyes and I took her brains out and now they are somewhere else."[3] Dr. Ziga wanted to know what was going on in Ed's mind when he killed his wife. Instead of answering the question, Ed explained how one's immune system was controlled by one's eyes. It all started with the eyes then moved downward to the feet, he said. To keep his own system pure, he closed his eyes and passed greenish stools.[4] Dr. Ziga asked him to describe what he was thinking when he killed his wife. He was thinking, Ed said, that he was Judas. Judas Iscariot, the disciple who betrayed Jesus? Yes, that's why he felt he had to burn his Bible. In response to Dr. Ziga's question, he didn't think that anyone in his family was or had been mentally ill, but thought someone may have committed suicide. He was pressed for more details on that, but didn't elaborate. Did Ed ever try to kill himself? Nooo, Ed replied. Never.

Doctor Ziga diagnosed Ed as paranoid schizophrenic. It was not a close call. There were, however, positive aspects to Ed's prognosis. He was an attractive young man who was physically healthy and with a large family who'd give him support. Reasonably intelligent with an outgoing pleasing personality, he was a man who commanded respect, loyal friends, and sympathy—traits that would help him recover and serve him well in court if he regained enough sanity to be tried for killing his wife.

By Monday, the newshounds were chasing other stories, the sawmill was back in action, Ed's children were being cared for by grandparents, and the gawkers were off rubbernecking car wrecks, fire scenes, and other sites of disaster and misery. At least on the surface, Brownhill was back to normal.

Regarding the sawmill, Mr. Gingerich had made an important decision: his oldest son, Atlee, would take charge.

That meant Atlee would move off his rented farm and take up residence in Ed's old house, which was now his. Noah and Henry Stutzman would stay on at the mill, but Atlee would be the boss, a role he didn't relish. In fact, there was nothing about the deal Atlee liked. He was a farmer not a businessman. He hated the mill, but made no complaint.[5] In the Amish world, fathers were obeyed. It was God's will.

Ed's English friends—Dave Lindsey, Lazar LeMajic, Richard Zimmer, Lawrence Kimmy, Sid Workman, and others—didn't believe for one second that Ed was a dangerous person or even mad. They knew him; he was not a killer. They blamed Katie's death, what Richard Zimmer was referring to as the "accident," on the degreasing solvent Ed had been using, improperly, in his machine shop. The Gunk fumes had simply destroyed Ed's mind. What other explanation could there be? Why else would a sane, decent man kill the woman he loved? The notion that Ed's behavior was physiological rather than pathological and, therefore, could be corrected medically by, in essence, degreasing his brain of the degreaser, had obvious appeal to those who liked and supported him. Katie's death was nothing more than a tragic accident.

Outside of Ed's immediate family, no one knew of his sudden obsession with religion and the subsequent spells. Except for Jake Powers, no one knew of Ed's failure as a husband, including the fact that he was hitting Katie. The English, who knew of Ed's friendship with Debbie Williams, paid it little mind and the Amish boys at the mill chalked it up to the bad-boy antics of an Amish rebel. Beyond Brownhill, no one knew of the Gunk. What the outside world knew was this: A perfectly healthy, happy, outgoing Amish man who was respected in his community had, without warning or cause, murdered his loving wife in a most brutal and ritualistic way. Why? Aspects of English culture blamed for all the violence and crime—television, movies, drugs, alcohol, gangster rap, poverty, and child abuse—didn't apply to the Amish. So had what happened to Ed? Well, he must have gone insane. What other reason could there be? The poor man went nuts and killed his wife. But what would cause an Old-Order Amish man to blow his mind? Again, no urban stress, Vietnam syndrome, drug abuse, alcohol, problems at work, unemployment, loneliness, or love gone sour.

It had to be genetic. All that Amish inbreeding caused some people like Ed to be missing a gene, chromosome X, or something like that. The problem was growing into an epidemic. Amish people all over the country were gong nuts. Pretty soon, Amish murder would be commonplace. Ed's family tree, as rumor had it, was full of insanity. He had an aunt somewhere up in Michigan living in an apple cellar, a couple of batty uncles over in New York State, and there were disturbing tales about Ed's youth in Norwich.

There were English folks and a few of the Amish over in Spartansburg, people who knew Ed casually and some who had never met him, who believed he had known exactly what he was doing when he killed his wife. He had ripped out her guts to fool the police into thinking he was insane. Clever guy that he was, Ed was setting himself up for an insanity defense. The fact that he was an Amish man made it all the more believable. Ed was crazy like a fox. So why did he kill her? What was his motive?

Ed always had a pocketful of cash. He had money and lots of it. He wasn't getting rich from the sawmill, which was just a front. Ed was into drugs. He was a broker, a middleman between Amish farmers and local marijuana growers who cultivated their crops between rows of Amish corn. The farmers picked up a few bucks and Ed took a percentage. The cops didn't have a clue and everything was running smoothly until one of Katie's relatives found out and came to her with the information. Katie made Ed promise to get out of the business. If he didn't, she'd go to the bishop. Ed planned the killing all winter, and with spring just around the corner, he took her out.

Another theory, no less cold-blooded but widely held, featured Ed being in love with an English woman he wanted to marry. Katie refused to play ball, so he killed her, taking great pains to make himself look crazy. Following Katie's death, Bishop Shetler, Deacon Stutzman, Levi Shetler, and others within the Brownhill and Spartansburg enclaves heard stories about him that fit in nicely with the theory that Katie had been the victim of a love triangle. According to these rumors, Ed's drivers, principally Jake Powers and Lawrence Kimmy, regularly dropped him off at night in Union City, Waterford, and Erie so he could rendezvous with his mystery lover. He'd climb out of the truck on a street corner or at a traffic light and simply walk off. Jake Powers or Lawrence Kimmy would drive away and return for him later when he called. No one ever saw the woman or exactly where Ed walked to after he got out of the truck.[6] Jake Powers and Lawrence Kimmy repeatedly denied doing anything of the kind which did not squelch the rumor.[7] One would expect friends, sworn to secrecy, to lie. Ed had a certain power over his English friends that made them fiercely loyal.

If there was such a thing as a prevailing theory, a rumor completely untrue, it was this: Katie and Ed's brother Danny had been having an affair for years. Ed caught on when he found out he was sterile and that the children were not really his. He blew his top and killed her. He took out her insides to see if Danny had made her pregnant again. Some of the comments Ed had made to his English friends about having drawn straws with Danny to see who got stuck with Katie, although made in cruel jest, lent credibility to the rumor.

Emma Shetler, still in a state of shock over her daughter's sudden death, wasn't sure what to think of Ed or why he had done such a horrible thing. He may have found another woman; Katie herself had considered this a real possibility. Their marriage had been in trouble for years. A few months before her death, in a letter to relatives, Katie had written: "It's one in the morning and Ed is still not home. I don't know where he is."[8] But why did Ed kill her? He didn't have to kill his wife to start a new life with another woman. It didn't explain the murder.

Although Emma hadn't sorted it all out in her mind, Katie's death was in some way connected to Ed's turning into a religious fanatic. Shortly before the murder, he had announced to a roomful of people that he was thinking about leaving the church for a new religion. Perhaps it was a satanic cult. Katie may have been some kind of sacrifice to Satan. Ed may have been possessed by the devil. According to Danny Gingerich, the devil was there, standing next to Ed in the bloody kitchen. Danny saw him and Danny wouldn't lie.

Ed's family had already made plans to visit him at the state hospital in North Warren. Others in the community were talking about going up there as well. Mr. Gingerich had spoken to one of Ed's doctors by phone and the news was good: Ed was coming around. No one was worrying about Katie. There would be no "coming around" for her.

36

Shunned

In the forensic unit, patients and their visitors met in a spacious room containing tables and chairs. The place resembled a hospital cafeteria without the food counter. There were, however, candy, soft-drink, cigarette, and coffee machines. The Gingerichs took seats at a table in the center of the room and waited. Mrs. Gingerich took comfort in the security men posted at desks near the two doors on opposite ends of the room. A third guard circulated among the tables as the patients huddled in muted conversation with wives, girlfriends, and relatives. Mrs. Gingerich tried not to imagine who these people were or what they had done to end up in such a place. Several of the visitors were wearing suits and ties—probably lawyers. Ed, accompanied by his own security guard, approached the table. The two men pulled up chairs and sat down. Ed was pale, looked slightly addled, and was concentration-camp thin. His shoulder bones were outlined through his denim shirt that, although buttoned to the top, hung loosely around his neck. The only thing about him that looked normal was his hair and beard. He was thin, he was pale, he looked a little goofy; but he was still an Amish man. They made an odd-looking group, the Gingerichs, but nobody seemed to notice. It was, after all, a mental institution.

Ed greeted his parents warmly if not enthusiastically. He clearly recognized who they were but seemed a little confused. Mary Gingerich, sitting stiffly in her chair, tried to hide her fear and apprehension. She wasn't doing a very good job but Ed didn't seem to notice; he was focused on his father. It was a little awkward at first, but following a short prayer offered by Mr. Gingerich, things loosened up a bit, even for Mrs. Gingerich. So, are they treating you well at this place? Oh, yes, they're all very nice. How did you get up here? George Brown. How is George doing? Fine. Was it a good ride up? Yes. Are you taking your medicine? Yes, they see to that. And so it went until Mr. Gingerich decided the time was right for the big question— what in God's name had possessed him to kill Katie? Why? In front of the children, yet. And why did he take a knife to her body and remove her parts? What was going on in his mind?

Ed replied that he had been asking himself those exact questions. He recalled being angry with Katie because she wouldn't let him go to the wedding. "I just couldn't find myself," he said. "I guess they don't want me back."

Mr. Gingerich told Ed that no one was holding him responsible for Katie's death. "We should have gotten you help," he said. "I shouldn't have gone to Indiana that morning. We didn't realize you were so sick. No one thought you'd hurt anyone. It wasn't your fault."

"Do I have a lawyer?" Ed asked.

"You'll have to speak to the English about that."

"I'll have to sit in prison for a while," Ed replied. "I'll have to do my time."

When told that his children were being cared for by his sisters, Lizzie and Clara, and living under the Gingerich roof, Ed said, "Don't let Levi have them."[1]

Ed asked how things were going at the sawmill and was told that the two Emanuels—Katie's brother and her brother-in-law—had quit. After what Ed had done, they couldn't work there anymore. Atlee was running the mill; he and his family had also moved into Ed and Katie's old house. Ed might as well know that now because he'd soon hear about it from others. Everybody, including Emma and Levi Shetler, were planning to come and see him. If it bothered Ed that Atlee had taken over his job and his house, he didn't show it. He had other things to worry about. For good or bad, life as he had known it was over. He didn't need a shrink to tell him that.

It was time for the Gingerichs to leave. Mr. Gingerich said another prayer. Ed seemed unwilling to end the visit as the guard helped him to his feet and took him away. The only words Mrs. Gingerich had spoken were hello and good-bye.

Emma and Levi Shetler, accompanied by the bishop and Deacon Ben Stutzman, rode up to North Warren on April 2. Katie had been dead fifteen days. Ed's contact with the outside world had been limited to his parents' earlier visit and a letter he had received from a relative in New York. Ed knew they were all coming because the deacon had called the hospital to arrange the visit. He wanted visitors, but he was not looking forward to seeing Bishop Rudy Shetler. He was also nervous about Levi and Emma, particularly Emma. What could he say to them; what would they say to him?

Emma and Levi had discussed, at length, the pros and cons of visiting Ed. Levi wasn't sure it was a good idea; Emma thought it was the only Christian thing to do. When Levi assured Emma his ailing heart was strong enough to call on the man who had killed his daughter, the decision was made. They'd visit Ed, but not alone. They would take the bishop and the deacon along for support. Under the influence of a Xanax pill, but still drawn tight, Emma walked stiffly into the visiting area carrying a rhubarb pie.[2] It was for Ed; she had made it herself.

Ed ended the preliminary phase of the visit—a nervous exchange of pleasantries and Amish small talk—with a point-blank question to Levi Shetler that shocked everyone. "Have you forgiven me for what I have done?" he asked.

Unprepared for such a direct question, Levi could only manage: "We can only forgive you as much as we can. For what you did, only God can forgive you."

"I've asked Him to forgive me," Ed replied.

"And has He?" asked the bishop.

"I don't know. I don't feel that He has," Ed said. "I wasn't home many evenings when I should have been, and me and Katie had fights."

"I'm not the one who can forgive you," Levi reiterated. "Only God can do that."[3]

Since they were getting down to the nitty-gritty, Deacon Stutzman fired off a question that had been burning inside him since the killing: "Did you plan this?" Now it was Ed's turn to be surprised. He hadn't expected that question.

"No," Ed replied. Then, in what seemed to his visitors as an attempt to shift the blame from himself to Katie, Ed said, "She wouldn't let me go to a *real* doctor."[4]

Although it was true that Katie was the driving force behind pushing Ed to Merritt Terrell and Jacob Troyer, Emma was angered by what she considered Ed's despicable attempt to blame Katie for her own death, to establish her as the villain. What kind of man criticized the woman he had just killed to her parents? "But they did take you to real doctors," Emma replied. "You stopped taking your medicine."

"That's because Katie wanted me to," Ed said. "She believed in herbs."

"Katie did everything she could to help you," Emma said. "You shouldn't talk about her that way."

"She was spoiled," Ed replied. "You didn't raise her right. She always had to have her own way."

"That's not true," Levi said.

"I hope the children are all right," Ed said. "I don't want this to trouble them later."

"The children *are* troubled," Emma said. "What did you expect?"[5]

There was a pause in the conversation. No one knew what to say. This was not what Emma and Levi had expected. Ed broke the silence. Apparently no longer interested in talking about Katie, he launched into a long monologue describing his first two weeks in the forensic unit. He talked about his doctors, the nurses, the other patients, and the food. He described, in great detail, what the meals were like. It was a far cry from good old Amish cooking. But it was all right. He wasn't going to starve. At least his appetite had returned. But the best news was this: His doctors had determined that he only required one-tenth as much medicine as typically needed by others with his kind of chemical imbalance. The doctors at Hamot and Jamestown had overdosed him and with the wrong drugs!

Finally, he was getting the care he needed, the proper treatment.[6] It was on this narcissistic note—some good would come out of this tragedy—that the visit ended. Ed, energized by the visit, was escorted out of the room while his stunned and embittered visitors remained seated at the table with the half-eaten pie. They got to their feet and, without a word between them, started for the exit.

That night in the Shetler living room, with children and in-laws present, Emma and Levi talked about Ed, his illness, his marriage to Katie, her murder, and the visit that day to the state hospital. Levi was still upset over what he considered Ed's outrageous request for forgiveness. The nerve of him to ask them for forgiveness so soon and to make that bold request in the presence of others. Levi didn't think Ed cared if they forgave him or not. It was clear he felt no remorse for what he had done. He had even tried to shift the blame from himself to Katie and, now that she was dead, could think only of himself. That's the way Ed was, always putting himself ahead of others. He can only think of himself. He had killed his wife and was in English custody. He was in trouble and figured to get out of this mess, it would help if the dead woman's parents forgave him. Levi decided not to be used by Ed. They would not lift one finger to do him harm, nor would they do anything to help him. They would let God and the English legal system determine Ed's fate. They would put their trust in God and, to a lesser extent, the English. There would be no more visits to North Warren, and if Ed wrote them letters, they would not write him back. The bishop, the deacon, Ed's family, and others in the Amish community could maintain a relationship with Ed if they so pleased. Levi would not hold that against them. But as far as he and his family were concerned, Ed was no longer a part of their lives. Ed didn't know it, but he had been shunned.

Hiring the Head Doctors

On April 13, 1993, Donald E. Lewis, one of the most experienced and successful criminal defense attorneys in the region, was appointed by the court to represent Ed. Ed didn't realize it, but he had gotten lucky.

With his schizophrenia in remission, Ed left the Warren State Hospital on July 9 after being there sixteen weeks. His prognosis: "guarded." Because he depended on drugs for his sanity, Ed was not cured. Since there was no more they could do for him at the hospital, he was going back to jail. It was like moving from the New York Hilton to the Bates Motel.

Don Lewis had not taken the Gingerich case for the money; no one got rich on court-appointed cases. This was especially true in murder defenses, where the standard fee rarely came close to covering the time that had to be put into these cases. Lewis could easily spend $20,000 to $30,000 worth of his own time and another $10,000 for expert witnesses and a private investigator. He'd ask for more, but probably squeeze a mere $10,000 out of the judge. So why did he take Ed's case?

Ed Gingerich was a young, attractive, God-fearing white male with a pleasant demeanor, no history of crime, a supportive family, sterling reputation, and a severe mental illness that responded well to pills. He was a defense attorney's dream. If there were such a thing as the perfect murder defendant, Ed Gingerich was it. Lewis, a veteran trial attorney who'd worked both sides of the street, had never prosecuted or defended an Amish man. Eventually, experience leads to boredom because there are fewer and fewer surprises. This case was different, refreshingly so. It also offered the chance to defeat the opposition, to strike a blow for justice, and to humiliate lazy, heavy-handed cops. Winning was one experience that never got boring. This case could be won, and Ed, a defendant worthy of victory, could be returned to his people. The criminal defense lawyer as hero was an opportunity that didn't come down the pike very often, a chance Don Lewis didn't want to miss. Don Lewis and his sympathetic wife-killer—a winning team.

Don Lewis's father, a former all-American football player at the University of Pittsburgh, became a dentist and raised his family in a well-groomed, suburban neighborhood on the north side of Pittsburgh called Manchester. Don dropped out of college, became a Green Beret, and fought in Vietnam. He returned to college, graduated from law school, and became an assistant prosecutor in the Crawford County District Attorney's Office.

Following one term as the Crawford County district attorney, Lewis, in 1985, joined the United States Attorney's Office in Tampa, Florida, as an assistant federal prosecutor. After three years of prosecuting drug cases, he returned to Meadville to enter private practice. He grossed more than $100,000 his first year, fees from criminal defendants who walked in the door. Although he hadn't planned it this way, Lewis soon became Meadville's busiest and most successful criminal defense attorney.[1]

A partner in the firm Peters, Lindsay, Lewis and Gagliotti, with offices in a converted house just off Courthouse Square, Don Lewis in the fall of 1993 was at the peak of his career. His belly had outgrown his hips, his thinning hair was turning gray, and he needed glasses to read, but beneath the middle-age girth lived the frame of an athlete who could still move with grace and speed. Don Lewis's wide-set eyes, hawkish nose, and puffy face gave him a look of a man who was unpretentious, friendly, quick-witted, and fierce. He was also tough, emotionally volatile and shrewd. Don Lewis was not a man to take lightly, mentally or physically, particularly if you were opposing him in court.

Don Lewis knew his law—procedural and substantive—good as or better than most. But his real talent showed up in court, where he could charm a jury into seeing things his way. He won them over by playing the underdog, at times acting a little confused, overwhelmed, befuddled by the mindless power of the state. He was just a humble attorney trying his best to protect his clients from neo-Nazi cops and prosecutors who would send their grandmothers to jail if it furthered their illegitimate careers.

For a small-town lawyer, Lewis lived well. He owned a nice house, drove a Cadillac Fleetwood, regularly took his wife to Hawaii, maintained a boat on Conneaut Lake, and supported three kids in college. He didn't drink alcohol, listened to classical music, and played computer football. He had recently cracked a vertebra in a skydiving accident when the main chute failed to open. The backup chute saved his life.[2]

Don Lewis's philosophy of law was summed up on a sign that hung in his office. It read: FRIENDS DON'T LET FRIENDS PLEAD GUILTY. In Ed Gingerich, Lewis had a client for whom he could, in good conscience, plead not guilty—not guilty by reason of insanity. Under the law, taking a life was not a crime unless it was done with intent, criminal intent. In Ed's case, the question wasn't did he kill his wife but rather what was he thinking when he did it? The law was not concerned with Katie Gingerich's state of mind or the fact that she was just as dead, and probably a lot more innocent, than the victim of a Mafia hit. This was not God's law, as Ed Gingerich understood it; this was Pennsylvania's law, and in time, thanks to Don Lewis, Ed Gingerich would know it well.

Insanity, as a total defense, was a tough sell. No one

knew that better than a veteran courtroom lawyer like Don Lewis. Nationally, it was raised in less than 1 percent of homicide trials and in 75 percent of those cases, it failed. It was particularly unpopular in rural, conservative regions like Crawford County, where people believe that all killers, at least to some degree, are crazy. Therefore, being nuts is no excuse. In places like Meadville, people were getting tired of criminal excuses. Had Erik and Lyle Mennendez been tried in Crawford County, they'd still be telling their sob stories to sympathetic TV interviewers, but they'd be doing it on death row. Pennsylvania's version of the insanity defense—its statutory definition of *legal* insanity—reflects the principles set down in the famous 1843 M'Naghten case in England. According to the so-called M'Naghten Rule, a criminal defendant is not insane under the law unless: "At the time of the commission of the act, the defendant was laboring under such a defect of reason, from disease of the mind, as not to know the nature and quality of the act he was doing, or if he did know it, that he did not know what he was doing was wrong." Popularly referred to as the right/wrong test, this meant that Don Lewis would have to prove, by a preponderance of the evidence, that Ed either didn't know he was killing Katie when he stomped her brains out, or if he did, that he didn't realize it was the wrong thing to do. In other words, just being medically insane was not enough. The defendant had to be very crazy in a specific kind of way, a kind of insanity that prosecutors and a few psychiatrists don't believe exists. The serial killer Ted Bundy, for example, was as crazy as one can get, but because he knew exactly what he was doing, he wasn't legally insane. They eventually got around to executing him, an event that disturbed very few in Crawford County or, for that matter, New York City.

Lewis was already laying the groundwork for Ed's insanity defense, working on his pitch to the jury. In a memorandum to himself he wrote:

Within a time period of approximately 40 hours prior to the murder, Ed was crying out, begging for someone to help him. He talked with at least 6 different people. Two of which are supposed to be doctors. He went to his father on two different occasions, his brother Daniel, Sid Workman (an Amish driver), Dr. Troyer, and Dr. Terrell. No one helped. If anything they fueled the fire in his mind, by coming right out and telling him that his thoughts were right; that he was in fact sick, and had a diseased mind. The doctors never told his family to take him to a hospital. The family never discussed taking him back to the hospital. Ed fell victim to his own crazed mind. THERE WAS NO INTENT TO HURT KATIE OR ANYONE. He never tells anyone that he had any desire to kill anybody. The man was calling out for help. He knew something was wrong, but couldn't do anything about it. Ed was just as much a victim of this horrible circumstance as was his wife, Katie.[3]

In the same document, Lewis made a list of factors he could highlight to establish Ed's lack of malice and murderous intent:

1. Violence is not a way of life in the Amish community.

2. Autopsy report states there were no marks or scars that would show prior abuse to the spouse.

3. Had people with him minutes before the murder took place. He never suggests he is going to kill anyone.

4. He is an avid hunter, but he doesn't use a gun.

5. Leaves the knife; doesn't try to hide it.

6. Statement to the police proves how deranged he really was. He didn't understand his rights.

7. In-laws stayed in contact with him after the murder. Came to see him and wrote him letters.

8. He had nothing to gain by killing his wife (no insurance, they do not believe in insurance).[4]

About half of these points, however, could be factually challenged by the prosecution. If they were, it would be up to the jury to sort out the truth. For example, the autopsy report did not actually state "there were no marks or scars that would show prior abuse to the spouse." In fact, the forensic pathologist who performed the autopsy, Dr. Takeshi Imajo, found bruises, lesions, and abrasions on Katie's right hip, right elbow, lower back, and behind her right armpit that certainly did not cause her death and may have been inflicted sometime before it. Dr. Imajo did not specifically identify these marks as evidence of spousal abuse, but as a prosecution witness he could possibly be pressed into such a conclusion. Of particular interest was a bruise on Katie's hip described as "bluish."[5] Could this have been made at the time of her death?

Lewis's chances of success depended in large measure upon how prepared the prosecution was and how hard they intended to attack. In the end, it would boil down to who had the facts or at least what looked like the facts. Since trials are designed to produce justice, the truth doesn't always prevail. There is evidence and there are facts; the two aren't always the same. Indeed, they are rarely the same.

Lewis was looking for plausible explanations—causes—for Ed's mental illness. It would help, in establishing that he was in fact insane, to offer the reason why. The lawyer had his sights on two possibilities: Ed had either inherited his psychosis from Amish inbreeding or had destroyed his brain inhaling toxic fumes from Gunk, the undiluted degreasing solvent. The next step in the process involved finding credible experts willing to develop these hypotheses into full-blown theories that would sound good in court.

The trial, scheduled for September, was pushed back to November to accommodate Lewis, who needed more time to prepare Ed's defense. Lewis had asked for but hadn't received Ed's psychiatric records from Hamot, Jamestown, and Warren and still had to find a battery of shrinks to portray the killing as sheer madness. The prosecutors, nowhere near being prepared themselves, welcomed the delay.

On October 2, at a routine pretrial discovery hearing, Don Lewis, according to standard legal procedure, informed the court that he planned to plead his client not guilty by reason of insanity. The prosecutor was already considering the possibility of digging up a head doctor who would testify that although Ed may have been medically insane when he killed his wife, he knew exactly what he was doing and that it was wrong and unlawful. The prosecutors would then point out that the inability to control one's rage, regardless of the reason, was not a defense to murder. Don Lewis's disclosure of his intended plea surprised no one.

At Lewis's request, the trial was postponed again, this time to the January 1994 term of court. In the meantime, Ed was becoming increasingly restless, impatient with the uncertainty of his future. He couldn't plan his life because he didn't know how much of it would be spent in prison or in a mental facility

Levi and Emma Shetler were living under a cloud of uncertainty as well. The Shetlers had no idea what they would do if the lawyer found some way to get Ed out of jail. The mere thought of him coming home pushed Emma to the brink of panic. Having no one to inform them of the progress of the case or explain how the system worked, the Shetlers waited and worried in the dark. On the legal insanity front, Lewis pushed forward by hiring, in January, Dr. Lawson F. Bernstein, Jr., a thirty-six-year-old assistant professor of psychiatry with the University of Pittsburgh School of Medicine. Dr. Bernstein had been teaching since 1991, the year he completed his three-year residency in psychiatry at the New York Hospital in New York City. Associated with the Western Psychiatric Institute and Clinic in Pittsburgh as director of general psychiatry training, a position he had held less than two years, Dr. Bernstein had not been board-certified as a forensic psychiatrist.[6] Following his review of the coroner's file, the transcript of Ed's confession to the state police, as well as other documents Don Lewis had sent to him, Dr. Bernstein drove to the Crawford County Jail where he and Ed talked for five and a half hours. On January 31, Dr. Bernstein wrote an eight-page report in which he concluded, based upon what he knew of Ed and the killing itself, that Ed, at the time of Katie's death, ". . . lacked the mental capacity to appreciate the nature of this act [the killing] . . . and therefore could not discern right from wrong."[7] Bernstein had found the language—the magic words—to thread Don Lewis's legal needle. Don Lewis, courtroom warrior that he was, knew that in the worlds of tort law and legal insanity, doctors and lawyers sounded the same.

Dr. Bernstein's enthusiasm for Ed Gingerich's legal insanity was boundless. He concluded that Katie "was essentially a random victim with the bad fortune to be in closest proximity when Mr. Gingerich's psychotic state exploded."[8] Fair enough, but what about the children, Enos and little Mary? When Ed's psychotic bomb went off, they were both standing well within the blast area. Dr. Bernstein had an answer for that: Ed didn't kill his children because he falsely believed that Katie, not the kids, by refusing to let him attend the wedding, was denying him the chance to wrest his soul from the devil. The doctor wrote: "I can detect no evidence, either during my exam or from review of the records provided me, that Mr. Gingerich acted out of anger at his wife per se. Rather, I believe that at the moment he would have killed anyone he perceived as attempting to thwart his psychotic plan for 'redemption.' Since his children did not thwart his acts, they were spared."[9] But the *way* Ed killed his spouse, the desecration of her body, didn't that reflect a white-hot rage, an uncontrollable hatred? Was this the behavior of a man, an insane man, who loved his wife? Why didn't Ed kill *himself*? Assuming that Ed loved his wife, or at least didn't hate her ("Mr. Gingerich recounts no history and the records do not reflect any significant marital discord between him and his wife"), Dr. Bernstein accounted for Ed's postmortem rampage as follows: "Mr. Gingerich killed his wife in a ritualistic fashion, 'from head down' to reflect biblical doctrine regarding creation. In addition, he removed her brain and viscera with a knife to reflect the stigmata Christ received while on the cross (details revealed in my clinical interview with Mr. Gingerich)."[10]

In his eagerness to cleanse Ed of even a trace of responsibility in his wife's death, Dr. Bernstein stepped out of psychiatry into the field of sociology, where, as an apparent expert in the ways of the Amish, he boldly professed the following:

Unfortunately, Mr. Gingerich's case illustrates the strong cultural biases against medication treatment for the mentally ill, especially among religious sects such as the Amish. This reticence to seek medical care is evidenced by the severe preincident traumatic injuries Mr. Gingerich suffered, which were never medically evaluated or treated! Such practices are apparently common amongst the Amish, as evidenced by the fact that Mr. Gingerich was brought to psychiatric attention only under the most dire of circumstances. In addition, when Mr. Gingerich went off his medications, it appears to have been with the tacit approval of his religious community. Indeed, when subsequent care is sought, it is at the hands of a chiropractor who engages in what can only be charitably termed "uninformed" care. These many factors conspired to leave Mr. Gingerich's psychiatric illness unmedicated; a tragedy in retrospect given the fatal outcome, and his current robust response to antipsychotic medication. If Mr. Gingerich had received more timely and ongoing psychiatric care, it is quite possible that Mrs. Gingerich would be alive today.[11]

Dr. Bernstein signed onto Don Lewis's two-pronged causation hypothesis, noting that Ed had showed no signs of psychosis until he had "sustained a significant toxic exposure to a petrochemical solvent 'Gunk.'" Regarding Ed's state of mind at the time of Dr. Bernstein's examination, the psychiatrist noted:

Mr. Gingerich denied current suicidal/homicidal ideation, auditory/visual hallucinations, and there was no evidence of formal thought disorder or grossly psychotic ideation. Mr. Gingerich did evidence overvalued ideation in the thought that his illness was "part of a divine plan" for him to discover the essence and cure for it . . .[12]

Levi and Emma Shetler were much more familiar with Ed's "overvalued ideations" than Dr. Bernstein. They were convinced that Ed's "divine plan" was to get out of jail. In their eyes, he had been overvaluing himself for years. Katie got in his way and he killed her. Now it was God's plan.

On January 19, Don Lewis arranged to have Ed examined at the Western Psychiatric Institute in Pittsburgh by a Ph.D. in neuropsychology named Lisa A. Morrow. Dr. Morrow had been recommended to Lewis by Dr. Bernstein. The purpose of the examination: to determine if Ed's exposure to the Gunk fumes significantly contributed to his psychosis and the resultant death of his wife.

Dr. Morrow, an assistant professor of psychology at the University of Pittsburgh Medical Center, in concluding that the Gunk fumes triggered Ed's psychotic behavior, relied on Ed's account of his all-day exposure, in March of '92, to the degreasing solvent. According to her report:

> *He states that he used this chemical initially from early in the day till around four P.M., at which time he left the shop because he felt ill and "not like himself." Symptoms on that day were headache, dizziness, and tingling and stiffness in his hands. He states that he returned the next morning to continue cleaning motor parts and finished cleaning around three P.M. At that time, he stated that he continued to feel unwell and that the smell of the chemical was "getting to him." He stayed in the shop until eleven A.M. and* reports having a discussion for several hours about religion with another man. *That night he states that he had a nightmare and awoke around five A.M. feeling "very scared."*[13]

Ed awoke that morning obsessed with Jesus and the idea of leaving the Amish for a new religion that offered salvation. He landed in the mental ward a few days later, one year before he killed Katie. Dr. Morrow, enamored with the Gunk fume theory of causation, didn't ask Ed more about the religious discussion he had in the machine shop that day, ignoring a possible variable in the explanation of Ed's subsequent behavior. In Dr. Morrow's report, Dave Lindsey never became more than "another man." He was not even identified as an English friend. The fact that Ed was talking religion in his machine shop, particularly with an outsider, would have grabbed the attention of a person more knowledgeable about the Amish. That alone would have been a clue that something unusual was afoot, something that might help explain what happened later.

Perhaps the key to Ed's murderous behavior involved more than the Gunk, more than heredity, even more than insanity. Ed said it was God's plan, the Shetlers thought it was the devil's, and Don Lewis, as long as the cause of the killing constituted legal insanity and a verdict of not guilty, didn't care what it was. Trials are about winning or losing, not about truth, religion, or the secrets of life.

38

Beating the Bush for Witnesses

Prosecutors Douglas Ferguson and J. Wesley Rowden didn't object when Don Lewis asked for another postponement. Rescheduled for March of '94, the trial would be held one year after Katie's death. Ferguson needed the extra time to line up a shrink who would take the stand and say that although the defendant may have been insane according to the general definition of the term, he knew he was killing his wife and that what he was doing was wrong. Ed's insanity merely released his pent-up hatred for his wife, allowing him to act out his murderous rage. The defendant, therefore, had no defense under the law. At the moment, however, Don Lewis was ahead in the game with two experts who believed Ed was so crazy he *didn't* know what he was doing when he killed his wife. If the prosecutors couldn't counter Lewis's doctors with at least one of their own, the defense attorney would have the preponderance of evidence he needed to prove Ed *legally* insane. Jurors, when confronted with expert testimony that conflicts, generally reject all of it which tends to hurt the side that needs it the most—in this case the defense. Finding a prosecution expert, if not essential, was, therefore, extremely important.

Assistant DA Rowden, in February, sent the Bernstein/Morrow reports, the transcript of Ed's state police confession, and his forensic-unit file to Dr. Phillip J. Resnick, a professor of psychiatry at Case Western Reserve University in Cleveland. Dr. Resnick, in a letter dated March 8, gave Rowden the bad news: "It is my opinion that the authors of the reports [Bernstein and Morrow] had a reasonable basis for concluding that Mr. Gingerich was severely ill and did not know the wrongfulness of killing his wife at the time of the homicide."[1]

Perhaps it was time to negotiate. Maybe a deal could be struck that would satisfy both sides—a legal compromise—a bargained plea. The prosecutors risked letting a homicide conviction slip through their fingers while the defense, given the brutality of the killing, was vulnerable to a long prison sentence. Trials were unpredictable, why did it have to be all or nothing? The prosecution offered this: They would accept a plea of mentally ill but guilty of murder in the third degree. Maximum sentence: ten years. While serving his time in prison—with parole in five or six years, Ed would be treated for his illness. Not bad for killing your wife. A real bargain.

No dice. How about this: mentally ill but guilty of voluntary manslaughter? Ed had already spent a year in custody. He'd do one more, be paroled, and they'd call it even. The prosecution had no chance of proving murder—where was the malice? Where was the criminal intent? If a jury got hold of this case, Ed could walk. He wasn't bad, he was sick, and now he was well—healthy enough to take his place in society. If they went to trial, Ed would win, the prosecution would lose and look bad doing it. Lewis's offer: voluntary manslaughter, take it or leave it.

No dice, no deal. They were going to trial.

• • •

The Gingerich trial would not be a case of reasonable doubt, the prosecution didn't have to prove that Ed killed his wife, that was a given. Since the law presumes that defendants are not insane, the burden of proving Ed not guilty by reason of insanity fell upon Don Lewis. In other words, this was not the usual case where the defense attorney can simply sit back and poke holes in the prosecution's evidence. Don Lewis would have to develop a strategy, put on a case. To win for Ed, Lewis would have to convince the jury that it was pure insanity that killed Katie Gingerich, not his client. To do that, he would have to show that Ed had no malice toward his wife, no motive, therefore, no *intent* to kill her. Lewis wanted to paint Ed as a loving, devoted husband and to do that, he needed character witnesses from the Brownhill settlement. Who knew Ed better than his Amish friends and neighbors? Lewis planned to fill the courtroom with Amish folks who would testify that Ed had been a kind and gentle husband, father, and friend.[2] Since the Amish are known to be truthful, they would make credible, cross-examination-proof witnesses. What choice would the jury have but to conclude that the Gunk fumes or heredity had turned Ed into a mindless monster of death, the Amish version of Dr. Jekyll and Mr. Hyde.

With the trial date approaching, Don Lewis sent his friend Randy Fyock, a public-school teacher and part-time investigator, into the Amish community in search of character witnesses. Fyock spent several days driving around Brownhill talking to Ed's parents, his brothers, Levi and Emma Shetler, Deacon Ben Stutzman, and Bishop Rudy Shetler. Expecting to be warmly received by grateful friends and relatives, Fyock was met with indifference bordering on hostility.[3] He didn't understand this attitude. Where was the loyalty to one of their own? No one agreed to voluntarily participate in Ed's defense. Ed's trial had nothing to do with them. They were leaving Ed's fate up to God. If subpoenaed, they would testify, otherwise they would not. And don't expect any of them to be on hand as courtroom spectators either. The Amish found Fyock's solicitations puzzling. Ed Gingerich had murdered his wife. Dangerously insane, he was obviously a threat to himself and society. What exactly was there to resolve in this case? What could an Amish person say that would alter the only decision that made sense: long-term medical incarceration. Why would anyone, including Ed's lawyer, want to put a dangerous man back into society? If medical science had worked on Ed, Katie would not have been killed. Surely Randy Fyock did not expect anyone from the Amish community to do anything that might help the court justify Ed's premature release. They were not out to punish Ed, that was up to God; the Amish were simply taking a neutral stance, hoping that the medical experts and the judge, with guidance from above, would make the correct decision.

Don Lewis had taken it for granted that the Amish would come forward on Ed's behalf. He was building his defense around Ed's insanity and his good character. What would it look like if no one from the Amish community took the stand for Ed? What inferences would jurors draw from this glaring omission? Ed was being tried for murder, his life was on the line, and this was war. There was no such thing as neutral; the Amish were either on Ed's side or they weren't. Infuriated over this development, Lewis went to Ed for an explanation. Had he seen this coming? No, Ed said, he hadn't. He was as shocked and disappointed as Lewis. What about his parents, Lewis asked, his own family—how could they be neutral when their son, their brother, was being prosecuted for murder? Who was behind this policy? Who was enforcing it? That would be the bishop, Ed said. Bishop Rudy Shetler, Katie's uncle. His word was law.[4]

As a murder defendant in need of character witnesses, Ed's principal weakness as an Amish man, his being "too

English," was now his strength. No one in the Brownhill community was more popular with the English than Ed. When Don Lewis asked for a list of potential witnesses, people who would say nice things about Ed and his marriage, Ed gave him Richard Zimmer, Kim Kerstetter, Jim DeMatteo, and Jim's wife, Alice.

Lewis also needed a witness who could establish a connection between Ed's use of the degreasing solvent and his first mental breakdown, someone to back up the machine-shop account he gave Dr. Morrow. Lewis asked for the name of the man who had been in the shed that day with Ed. Dave Lindsey, Ed replied, the Gunk fumes had gotten to him as well. Who was Dave Lindsey? Lewis asked. Dave Lindsey was a sawmill customer and a friend who had come to the shop that day to buy a saw blade. In characterizing his relationship with Lindsey, Ed failed to mention Dave's role as his spiritual mentor, nor did he identify Lindsey as a soul-saving evangelist or describe the nature of their conversation in the fume-filled shed. Had he done so, Lewis may have seen the connection between Lindsey's religious assault and Ed's subsequent obsession with Christ and the devil that preceded, and maybe even caused, his mental crack-up. Had Lewis been aware of Ed's quest for redemption outside his faith, his perception that Katie stood between him and salvation, and Dave Lindsey's attempt that day in the machine shop to break Ed free, the attorney may have had second thoughts about Gunk fumes being the cause of Ed's madness. Lewis would have also stayed away from Dave Lindsey, a potentially dangerous witness. Don Lewis wasn't aware of any of this because Ed hadn't enlightened him. If Lewis and his client were lucky, the prosecution didn't know these things either and wouldn't find out. If Lewis got Lindsey on the stand as a Gunk causation witness and it somehow slipped out that he and Lazar LeMajic had been trying to convert Ed, Lindsey would blow Dr. Morrow's Gunk testimony sky-high and hand the prosecution the motive, malice, and intent they were so desperately looking for. If that happened, Ed's chances for legal insanity would be slim to none and he could be nailed for murder instead of manslaughter. Dave Lindsey was a high-order bomb, a booby trap that, if carelessly handled, could go off in Lewis's face. What the defense attorney didn't know, what his client hadn't told him, could sink them both.

Don Lewis wanted the jury to like and feel sorry for Ed. Ed was a victim. It wasn't his fault he went mad. Yes, he had quit his medicine, but he did it to please his wife. He cried out for help, real psychiatric help, but instead was given herbs in Punxsutawney and a toe-pulling in Cambridge Springs.[5] Had the Brownhill Amish, under the thumb of an unenlightened bishop, been more open-minded about mental health, Katie Gingerich, Ed's beloved wife, would not have died. The killer in this case was ignorance.

The best witnesses—that is, people who possess important information about a defendant—don't always surface to tell their story under oath. Defendants know who can hurt them. If a defendant doesn't want a particular person to testify and this individual doesn't come forward, testimony that might help a jury render an informed verdict is lost unless the other side puts this person on the stand. Jake Powers was such a witness. Jake loved Ed like a brother; he meant him no harm, but he had seen Ed hit his wife, and in general behave like a man who wanted nothing to do with domestic life. Jake Powers had secretly delivered bourbon to his best friend's wife, a woman who was distraught because she thought her husband had found another woman. This was a far cry from the picture Ed was letting Lewis paint, through witnesses like Richard Zimmer and Kim Kerstetter, of his marriage. Unless the prosecutor flushed him out, Jake Powers would remain in the bushes holding his breath until the trial was over. He wasn't going anywhere near the courthouse, not even as a spectator.

Jake Powers wasn't the only potential witness who could damage Ed's image. Regarding the hitting and the physical abuse, Emma Shetler had seen Ed's violent side as well as the bruises on Katie's arms. And no one knew what Mr. Gingerich might say if asked about such things. Dr. Takeshi Imajo's autopsy report, notwithstanding Lewis's belief that it contained no evidence of a battered wife, may have suggested otherwise. If it did, the forensic pathologist would be given the chance to elaborate when called to the stand by the prosecution. In addition to the autopsy report, the prosecution possessed another document that cast doubt on Lewis's idyllic portrait of Ed's marriage. Trooper Lon E. Pierce of the Pennsylvania State Police, shortly after the killing, questioned Ed's brothers and wrote the following:

> *His brothers [Atlee and Danny Gingerich] stated that the subject didn't feel that he and the victim did enough things together, that they didn't get along the best. Danny said that the suspect had said about a week or so ago that his children wouldn't behave like they should. They state that when the subject was too depressed to get himself up, he would talk about everything, like make a confession, and that he would also talk about disagreements he had with the victim. They stated that some of the disagreement would be about the children's upbringing; that the suspect didn't help with the children and that his interests were not with the family. They stated that during disagreements, the suspect would just leave, that he would not try to work things out. The family felt that maybe the victim was too strong-minded . . .* [6]

The outcome of a criminal trial depends more on the facts than it does the law. To a large extent, Ed's fate depended upon what the prosecutors knew, what they had learned about Ed's marriage, what they knew about him. Did they know about the evangelists? Had they found Jake Powers? Lewis's case and Ed's future were in the hand of the Pennsylvania State Police. If they had conducted a thorough follow-up investigation into Ed's background and into his life, Ed Gingerich could be in trouble.

It had been a slow, hard-fought winter for Emma Shetler. January and February brought icy winds that howled outside her windows and ripped through the barns. Unrelenting, blinding snow piled up and drifted into every corner of her life, bogging her down, sapping her strength, and suffocating her spirit. The animals, at the mercy of nature, were her responsibility. The winter had also worn Levi down. His sickness had returned, settled into his chest. He coughed, fought for breath, and grew weak. Some days he didn't bother to get out of bed. Emma stood between him and death.

The Shetlers had survived many hard winters; it was a matter of holding out for spring. But this year, the coming of spring was not a rising ball of fire but a menacing black cloud advancing low on the horizon. In a matter of weeks, Ed Gingerich would go on trial for killing their daughter. As the trial approached, rumors started dropping out of the sky like funnel clouds. Every day there was something new about Ed. He had escaped; he had tried to kill himself; his lawyer was making him a deal that would get him off; he had attacked a guard; he had flipped out again and was back in the hospital at Warren; he was coming to take his children away, and so on. It had been a winter of fear and, as spring came, uncertainty.

Early in March, a car pulled up the driveway and came to a stop in the turnaround area bordered by the house and the two Shetler barns. A man wrapped in an overcoat climbed out of the car and walked through the slush to the Shetler side door. Emma watched his advance through the kitchen window. She and her daughters were preparing lunch. Emma knew instantly that this slightly tall, slightly overweight, slightly bald, mid-fortyish man wearing business shoes, a tie, and an expressionless face was some kind of cop, lawyer, or government official and, in one form or another, represented the trial. This officious-looking man, this harbinger, had come to tell them something or perhaps to ask them questions about Ed. Katie had been dead a year and this was the first official to come to their door. Emma pulled herself together, answered his knock, and invited the man into her house. He was Douglas Ferguson; he said he was in charge of prosecuting Ed for Katie's death. He needed Emma's help and Mr. Shetler's, too. They would have to testify at Ed's trial, on the prosecution's side of the case. The thought of speaking against Ed, with him in the same room looking on and listening, scared Emma to death. She would do what she had to do, but Levi couldn't. His heart was too weak; the ordeal would kill him. Emma would have to testify for them both. What did they have to know?

Mr. Ferguson said he was interested in two things, mainly. How did Ed and Katie get along, and the last time Emma saw Ed before the killing, was he acting crazy? Regarding the first thing—the how-they-got-along-part—how could she even begin to answer a question like that? Where could she find the vocabulary to describe, to an English person, a stranger, Ed Gingerich's relationship to her daughter? Emma didn't have the words to describe her own marriage to Levi. Amish people rarely speak of relationships, and when they do, they express themselves in ways an English person wouldn't comprehend. Katie hadn't burdened her parents with her marital problems. She protected Ed, suffered in silence. Emma and Levi had witnessed her suffering and knew its source. They knew what kind of man Ed was. Their opinion of Ed and his suitability as a husband and father had been formed, over many years, by hundreds of events, clues, hints, and stray comments, each one a tiny dot like the dots that come together to form a picture in a newspaper. How did Ed and Katie get along? That was an English question that called for an English answer. The question about when they had last seen Ed, Emma could answer. Yes, when she and Levi were last with Ed before the killing, they saw no sign that he was crazy.

Ferguson, apparently misinterpreting Emma's tentativeness as a desire not to cooperate with the prosecution, tried to scare her into taking sides against the defendant. "If Ed gets out," he said, "he might hurt his son Danny. He might kill him because he ran for help."[7]

Emma had already heard rumors that if and when Ed got out, he'd take revenge on his oldest child. Hearing it from an official of the court filled her with dread. Even worse was the realization that this man was so desperate for her cooperation, he felt he had to scare it out of her. The fact that Ed's fate, in the English court, depended so heavily on her testimony was the scariest thing of all.

Mr. Ferguson solemnly informed Emma that she would be receiving a document—a subpoena—that would summon her to the courthouse in Meadville on the day she'd take the stand. He thanked her for her cooperation and was gone. She watched his car roll down the driveway, pull onto Townline Road, and then disappear over the rise just west of the house. She left the window to check on Levi.

Emma Shetler couldn't characterize her daughter's marriage to Ed Gingerich any more than the prosecutor could explain to her why he needed to know how Ed and Katie had gotten along. When a man murders his wife, what difference does that make?

39

Brainstorming

Sunday afternoon, March 6, two weeks before Don Lewis and the prosecutors would begin their tricky, iffy, but crucially important game of selecting a jury to their mutually exclusive likings, Lewis was huddled in his office with his defense team. Lewis's schoolteacher friend and amateur private investigator, Randy Fyock, was present in the cramped and cluttered room with Lewis's free help, Chris Hauber and Kathy Easly, a pair of interns. Chris, a senior political science major at nearby Edinboro University, a smallish, muscular kid with clean-cut looks and eyeglasses that made him look studious, had been supporting himself through college by working as a farmhand. He was smart and mature beyond his years. Kathy, a thirty-year-old business school paralegal student with brassy blond hair, a slender, workout parlor body, and the slightly cocky demeanor of a young woman who thought she was moving up in the world, would be helping Lewis on *voir dire* by collecting background profiles of the prospective jurors. The Gingerich dream team, a public-school teacher and a pair of interns, although not very professional, was hardworking, devoted to the client, and led by one of the best trial lawyers in the state. Compared with most Crawford County criminal defendants, Ed Gingerich would be well served by Don Lewis and his crew. Lewis had assembled his team on one of those wet, cold, gray afternoons so common to northwestern Pennsylvania, for the purpose of discussing his strategy for Ed's defense.

The core of Lewis's defense was this: The only reason Ed killed his wife was because, through no fault of his own, he went completely nuts. Dr. Lawson Bernstein, the Pittsburgh shrink who'd examined Ed in January, in the jargony lingo of his profession, had concluded that Ed was crazy at the time of his wife's death. Bernstein had, therefore, emerged as the central, most important witness for the defense, which meant he would become the prosecution's main target. Like an aircraft carrier in enemy seas, Bernstein had to be protected. In courtroom wars, key witnesses are protected by carefully preparing and tailoring their testimony and leading them with questions on direct examination that fortify their positions without exposing their flanks. In his report, Dr. Bernstein identified the Gunk fumes as a possible cause of Ed's insanity. Could this be a problem? The prosecution could attack this point in one of two ways: to weaken the causation link between the Gunk and the killing, they could point out that Ed had inhaled the fumes a full year before the murder. The prosecution, on the other hand, might accept the Gunk connection and try to use it against Ed, suggesting that he had become an addicted solvent sniffer who, in effect, had killed his wife after voluntarily intoxicating himself. Ed Gingerich as a homicidal dope addict was not a possibility Lewis wanted the jury to consider. The Gunk element was tricky and Lewis knew it.

Later in the meeting, Lewis raised the subject of Dr. Bernstein's fact base. They were vulnerable to attack on this point and it obviously worried him. "If I were prosecuting this case," Lewis said, "I would ask the doctor what he did to check his information out . . . where he got this information and what he did to check it out for truthfulness. Information is only valid if it is accurate."[1]

Kathy Easly said, "I definitely think we are going to need a family history. I am not sure where he [Bernstein] got that information about the father, the brothers, and his [father's] sisters." Kathy was referring to Dr. Bernstein's findings that these relatives had suffered from schizophrenia.

"He probably got it from Gingerich," Lewis replied.[2]

It wasn't enough for Dr. Bernstein simply to declare that Ed was crazy; he'd have to articulate his conclusions just the right way in order to satisfy the legal nuances of the insanity defense. Another Lewis concern: "He has to make his decisions on the basis of legal conclusions, not medical conclusions . . . Heat of passion, for example, we are not defending on heat of passion. Psychiatrists have difficulty when they are confronted with heat-of-passion defenses. Irresistible impulses, another interesting defense that psychiatrists usually have a difficult time with. We are not discussing irresistible impulse. They may try to turn this into an irresistible impulse case—he [Ed] had this impulse that was irresistible. No, irresistible impulse is not what this is; this is a psychotic misadventure."[3]

Referring to Ed's Gunk fume exposure as the cause of his mental condition, Kathy Easly raised an interesting point: "I have a problem with him [Ed] saying that he was completely well until then [the Gunk exposure] because the report from Dr. Terrell shows clear back in 1988, Ed was complaining of poor appetite, dizziness, itchy skin, and things like that . . . Does the Commonwealth [prosecution] have this report?"

"No," Lewis replied. "They didn't get it from me. I have no duty to give it to them as discovery material because Bernstein is not basing his conclusions on this and I have no intention of calling this guy. I don't want these guys [Terrell and Troyer]; this guy is a chiropractor practicing psychology . . . Let's say they get his report. Now they approach Dr. Bernstein on cross-examination and they say: 'Dr. Bernstein, do you know who Dr. Terrell is? Do you know that Dr. Terrell was treating the defendant?' Then Bernstein will kill them—'I was told that man was a chiropractor; what was he treating the defendant for?' I hope they say that Terrell was treating Ed for his mental condition. Bernstein is too much of a pro; he'll take them apart on this. I hope they bring it up. I am half tempted to ship this [Terrell's medical record of Ed] over to them and let them try to get Bernstein. Bernstein will kill them."[4]

Amish cooperation on Ed's behalf, or lack of it, was still a problem. Fyock had been out and around Brownhill, and as far as he could tell, attitudes hadn't changed. Referring to Ed's father, Fyock said, "Daniel, Sr., indicated that he would not be at the trial. He is not coming down, nor does anybody in his community plan on coming down, unless they are forced to be here. And while I'm thinking about it, they do not plan on raising their hands on the Bible and swearing to the truth, the whole and nothing but the truth, and swear to God. Instead, they can affirm that when they say yes, they mean yes, and when they say no, they mean no. They will not swear on the Bible."

"Well," Lewis replied, "they are not required to." Later in the meeting, alluding to the lack of Amish cooperation, Lewis said: "We got a bunch of people who want to play zombie with us. They don't even want to answer questions. They are getting downright nasty now."[5]

The discussion turned to Ed's delusions and hallucinations and how important they were to his insanity defense. Randy Fyock said: "Daniel, Sr., told me that Edward felt that if he didn't go to that wedding, that meant that he would go to hell. If he would go to the wedding, his soul would be saved and he would go to heaven."

"Well, then," Lewis said, "we will have to subpoena that guy, and whether he wants to drive his little buggy here to town or not, he is going to have to put his little ass in it and do it. He is going to have to say it. I understand about him and the courts, but I don't sympathize when it's his son's life we are talking about here. I don't care what religion you belong to, your son's life ought to mean more to you than that . . ."

"If the wedding was so important," Randy asked, "and the only way he can get to the wedding is if he kills his wife, can they turn that around and show that this is intent?"

"That is the concern, sure," Lewis replied.

"He has planned for a day to kill his wife, to get to this wedding."

"The thing that scares me," Lewis said, "and I have already raised this with Dr. Bernstein, that if there was an intent to kill anybody, I am in trouble. He tells me it didn't matter that his wife was trying to keep him from going to the wedding. Anybody standing in his way was in danger of being killed. Ed didn't understand the nature and quality of his act. He didn't understand that it was wrong; what he was doing was wrong. He thought it was right. In other words, if a prudent man believes, let's forget about mental condition, that his life is in danger, they can find him not guilty. Now, let's talk about a guy with a psychological condition and let's talk about a situation where he thinks he is strangling a turnip. Well, it is not unlawful to strangle a turnip, however painful it may be for the turnip. In that situation, the ordinary-man test doesn't apply because of the mental condition. We have a guy who was delusional . . . this guy thought he had to do this to be saved and didn't appreciate that what he was doing was wrong, that he was actually killing his wife . . . that's all I need to show.

"Now, practically speaking, you're right; the jury is going to hear an argument from the Commonwealth that even the psychiatrist testified that his [Ed's] wife was in the way of getting this done and that's why he killed his wife or anybody who stood in his way . . . and that involves intent . . . that he killed for a purpose; he killed for a reason . . . His wife stood in the way; that was the mistake she made, therefore, she is dead. If they [the prosecution] are smart, they will say that what she did didn't justify being killed. I don't know if they will use that or not, but if I were them, it's what I would say. He felt that he was going to die and he had to do something."

Chris Hauber said, "Now, all of his activity reflects the Amish belief. Like you said earlier, it is almost a religious defense."

"Yeah, but don't say this is a religious defense because there is no such thing as a religious defense. You can't kill somebody because your religion tells you to kill them. The Supreme Court has decided that if your religion says you have to smoke pot, then you can do it. This isn't the same thing; ritual killing is still murder. So we have to avoid any suggestion that this is a religious defense."

Two weeks later, on the eve of the trial, Don Lewis and his helpers were killing another Sunday afternoon in the lawyer's document-cluttered office discussing Ed's defense. The focus of this meeting concerned the immediate problem of picking the right jury. Kathy had studied the list of seventy-three potential jurors—twenty-eight men and forty-five women—pooled for the current term of court. Kathy wanted to know to what lengths they should go to exclude women from the jury. Lewis wasn't sure that was a good idea in this case: "The old traditional idea of keeping married women off the jury when the victim was a married woman doesn't hold up in this case because there is no evidence of a conflict—I mean there is no marital discord. This thing didn't come about as a result of his (Ed) being the husband and her being the wife or any action having to do with that . . ."[6]

Kathy asked Lewis what relevance the Amish factor had in their selection of a jury. Specifically, did this mean they should try to stack the deck with religious types? "Our client's defense," Lewis said, "is as much about a religious defense as it is an insanity defense. I mean from the layman's point of view. Now, do we want the Unitarian type, do we want the born-again Christian, or do we want to stay away from the super-religious?"

"The only advantage of having really religious people,"

Kathy said, "is that they are like the Amish; they are very forgiving."

"Okay," Lewis said, "let me give you my reason for not wanting the super-religious. My problem with super-religious is the verdict guilty but mentally ill. These people are the first ones to find you guilty . . . They tend to be very prosecution-oriented, very law-enforcement-oriented and at the same time are also very forgiving. What better person for a prosecutor to want on his jury than one who was going to say he's guilty but mentally ill."

"On the other hand," Kathy said, "most of these people—these Holy Rollers—have been on the other side of the law at one time. So generally, they're going to be more forgiving."

"That's not the way I see then," Lewis replied. "I don't see them as forgiving people; I see them as very self-righteous people . . . I don't trust them because I think they are wackos . . . We have decided that we don't want super-religious."[7]

Don Lewis would have been surprised to know that his opinion of the super-religious harmonized with Amish attitudes about such people. Had Lewis known that his client, a shrink-certified "wacko," had been converted into a super-religious person by Dave Lindsay and Lazar La-Majic, he might have changed his mind about keeping "super-religious" folks off Ed's jury.

Addressing the question of how intelligent Ed's jurors should be, Randy suggested they avoid brainy types. "Not somebody too smart," he said. "Not a college professor, not a high administrative worker because they will be trying to analyze everything too much."

"What's too much?" Lewis asked.

"I think they lack common sense. I think that the person who is really smart lacks a lot of common sense."

"Is insanity really a commonsense defense?" Lewis asked. "I don't think so . . . It's those people that are way up there that acquit on insanity defenses because they are not down there where murder is. It's an abstract thing to them; they don't see it; they don't feel it; they don't understand it; and they don't know people who are likely to commit it. It is just something that happens in another world to them. So they are more likely to disassociate themselves from any emotional reaction to the crimes and are more inclined to acquit on the basis of insanity. Plus, they are people who are not bound to the norm; they are not going to say, 'Gee, he killed; we really have to find him guilty.' They don't feel that way about it. That's the kind of people I want. I don't want the street law-enforcement-type guy, even though law enforcement credibility isn't an issue here."

Randy, with the jury list before him, said, "We have a lot of secretaries, laborers, truck drivers, mechanics, registered nurses, retired people, a janitor, a principal, a couple of bankers, a welder, and a manager of a restaurant . . . We don't have anybody with that high of an intellect by the sounds of it . . . What particular occupations do you want to keep off?"

"Let's start with the clergy and the medical people," Lewis replied.

"What about registered nurses?" asked Randy.

"Well, I don't like registered nurses to start with. Registered nurses are a little too registered to me. Registered nurses think that the next thing beneath them are physicians and that they know all there is to know about medical stuff. I don't want some medical giant getting into the jury box trying to change the emphasis of this case. I want to downplay the general nature of this incident and play up the psychological nature of it. I want to do exactly what the defense attorneys did in . . . what's the name of that guy that assaulted President Reagan?"

"John Hinckley, Jr.," someone said.

"Hinckley . . . here is a guy that attempted to commit a crime in front of the whole world on television and yet during the trial you never read about the facts of the case of what he did. The whole trial was about his mental condition . . . they played up the psychological aspects. That was a case about Hinckley's mental condition, not about whether he shot the president. Nobody cared by the time the case was over; nobody cared if he shot the president of the United States . . ."[8]

The strategy session ended at nightfall. It was snowing again, but the large, wet flakes were only sticking to the shade-placed snow that hadn't melted. The new layer would hide the filth, at least for a while. With a tough, stressful week ahead of them, Lewis and his people went home to rest. They felt they were ready.

40

Commonwealth v. Gingerich

Meadville, a town of eighteen thousand in the hilly, snowbelt region of northwest Pennsylvania, had once been the center of a thriving tool-and-die industry that had brought thousands of highly skilled, well-paid blue-collar workers and a managerial class to the area. Although the town had seen better days, Meadville, the county seat, was still a vital place, with its light industry, private liberal-arts college, commercially active downtown district, hospital complex, and daily newspaper. Ed Gingerich, one year and three days after killing his wife, would be tried in the Crawford County Courthouse, a steepled, four-columned, three-story Greek Revival building overlooking a village green dotted with flower beds, park benches, a fountain, and, in its center, a gazebo. Courthouse Square, consisting of the courthouse, the jail, and several office buildings that housed private companies and government institutions, sat adjacent to the downtown area. The park itself was enclosed by a fence line of parking meters standing guard over their diagonal parking slots.

On Monday morning, just before nine, a pair of brown-clad Crawford County deputies walked Ed from his cell to courtroom number two on the third floor. Unshackled and dressed like an Amish man, Ed joined Don Lewis and his interns at the defense table. A couple dozen spectators, including a handful of newspaper and television reporters (TV cameras are not allowed in the courthouse), sat scattered about the pews on the gallery side of the balustrade. Prosecutors Douglas Ferguson and J. Wesley Rowden made their entrance. Don Lewis, looking spiffy in a slate-gray suit, white shirt, and yellow-patterned tie, walked over to the prosecution table at the jury-box side of the room and shook hands with the enemy. The court crier materialized through a door in the paneling behind the bench, signifying the arrival of the judge. "All rise," he bellowed. The black-robed judge walked into the room through the same door and ascended to his exalted, flag-framed seat on the bench. "Here ye, here ye, the Court of Common Pleas for Crawford County is now in session, the Honorable Gordon R. Miller presiding," cried the crier. "All those having business before this court draw near and ye shall be heard. God save the Commonwealth and the Honorable Court. Please be seated."[1]

"Good morning, gentlemen," said the judge, a tall, thin fifty-three-year-old with short brown hair, a straight, prominent nose, and long, artistic hands. Judge Miller had been on the bench four years and this was his third homicide trial.[2]

"Good morning, Your Honor," the lawyers chimed like three brownnosing college students.

"Are we ready for *voir dire*?" the judge asked.

"We are," came the reply.

Of the twenty-two prospective jurors questioned on Ed's

first day in court, sixteen were excused either for cause (for example, a drug conviction) or because one side didn't want them on the jury. One woman said she didn't think much of psychiatrists and another had managed a doctor's office. They were both scratched by Lewis. By the end of the day, three men and three women had been seated on the jury.

Thursday morning, Judge Miller greeted everyone with, "Good morning. It's a nice sunny day in paradise."[3] The fact that they were under a blue sky in March, in Meadville, was indeed rare and worthy of judicial notice. Judge Miller's quip left everyone but Ed smiling.

Prospective jurors, one by one, were led into the room and questioned, first by Ferguson and then by Lewis. Four came in and four went out, and at ten o'clock, Judge Miller called a ten-minute recess. During the break, Ed's guards told him he could get up and walk around, stretch his legs. He could do this now because there were only a few people in the courtroom. Ed, with a deputy at his side, walked over to the wall of windows on the jury-box side of the room. He looked out onto the street and said, "It sure looks nice out there." Chris Hauber, one of Lewis's interns, joined him at the window. Ed turned to Chris and said, "We need more men on the jury."[4]

By noon, four more prospective jurors had been excused. Lewis and Ferguson were already getting on each other's nerves. Tempers flared and hot words started bouncing around the arena like ricocheting bullets. Judge Miller broke for lunch.

The prospective jurors kept coming and more were rejected, but that afternoon the twelfth member was accepted. Two alternates were selected before Judge Miller adjourned for the day. Ed's six-man, six-woman panel—white, small-town, middle-class, high-school-educated nonprofessionals, ranging in age thirty to seventy—was the typical Crawford County jury, devoid of doctors, lawyers, clergymen, college professors, entrepreneurs, and Amish.

Wednesday morning, the third day, the jurors, sporting ridiculously large campaign-style buttons that read JUROR entered the packed courtroom. Stern-faced, they all looked straight ahead (perhaps looking around would somehow contaminate their judgment) as they snaked into the jury box. If looks meant anything, they were aware they were making history as the first American jury to pass judgment on an Amish man charged with homicide.

Ed's parents and his brothers Atlee and Joe were sitting in the first-row pew behind the defense table. Danny and Emma Shetler, scheduled to testify that morning for the prosecution, were waiting in the district attorney's office. On the other side of the room, behind the prosecution table, sat Levi Shetler and Ed's three children. Ed made no attempt to acknowledge the presence of his family or his in-laws, the only Brownhill Amish there. Kathy Easly, wearing a pair of large, golden earrings, leaned toward Ed and said something. She was really speaking to the jury. "See," she was saying, "I'm not afraid of this man. He's nice."

There was a buzz of excitement in the room that sounded a lot like the murmur of a boxing crowd before a big fight. The gallery on this first day of testimony consisted of an unusual mix of Mennonites, New-Order Amish, evangelists, Old-Order Amish from Spartansburg and other enclaves, Mill Village English, people down from Erie who'd been following the case in the papers, folks from the print and TV media, regular courthouse hangers-on, and seventy-five field-tripping high-school seniors from Cambridge Springs and Meadville.[5] The high-school teachers had brought the kids to see the mad, wife-killing Dutchman on the day the forensic pathologist would describe the gory details of Katie's death and evisceration.

Douglas Ferguson, facing the jury from a lectern,

opened for the prosecution with a short address consisting of a chronological account of the killing that began twenty-four hours before Katie's death and ended with Ed's arrest at the Sturgis-Frisbeetown intersection. The prosecutor characterized Ed, just before he killed his wife, as a "highly functional person who, after the deed, behaved quite rationally by washing his hands, dressing his children for the cold, then leading them out of the house. At the foot of his driveway, Ed had a conversation with two acquaintances and to the state police had said, 'I'm the bad guy you're looking for.'" Ferguson pointed out that perfectly sane people can do horrible things, and even if Ed was mentally ill at the time of the killing, he was not *legally* insane. Being completely mad and out of one's mind is one thing, being mentally ill and unable to control one's anger is another story, something the law does not excuse.[6]

Replacing Ferguson at the lectern, Don Lewis took his shot at the jury. "We are about to hear testimony that will remain with us forever. I am honored to be able to represent Edward Gingerich, to protect his rights during this traumatic time in his life. Together we will search for the truth because that is what a trial is all about, a search for the truth." The truth, as Lewis presented it, was that Ed became sick from the Gunk, was hospitalized, stopped taking his medication at the urging of his people, relapsed into madness, and killed his wife, simply because she was there. "You will sit there in frustration," he said, "and wonder why someone didn't answer the call and take Ed back to the hospital, where he needed to go." Lewis closed by assuring the jurors that because Ed was so mentally ill, he did not intend to kill his wife. He simply didn't know what he was doing and, therefore, should not be held criminally responsible for her death. The defendant was sick, not bad.[7]

Following his brief but passionate speech, Lewis thanked the jurors for their attention and returned to his chair at the defense table. Several of the jurors were now staring at Ed and from their expressions, which appeared sympathetic, Lewis had gotten off to a good start.

The jurors returned from a ten-minute recess to find the Commonwealth's first exhibit resting on an easel a few feet from the jury box. It was a drawing, a primitive outline on a large sketchpad, of Katie's corpse. The courtroom sketch depicted a void where Katie's head and brains had been stomped away, a simple line represented the abdominal incision Ed had made to get his hand inside her, and the place on the floor where he had piled her organs was shown as a crudely drawn enclosure. This childlike, almost whimsical exhibit, in lieu of the crime-scene photographs, patronized the jury and insulted the victim. This drawing of what looked like a gingerbread cookie with a bite taken out of its head, was a huge benefit for the defense because it trivialized the killing by sanitizing the effects of the homicidal fury. It also dehumanized the victim. The idea of the drawing, surprisingly enough, came from the prosecution, who didn't want the jury to see the brutality of the killing for fear it would help prove the defendant's insanity.[8]

The drawing on the easel heralded the prosecution's first witness, Dr. Karl E. Williams, a board-certified forensic pathologist from Elwood City, Pennsylvania. Although he had not performed the autopsy, Dr. Williams had studied Dr. Takeshi Imajo's autopsy report as well as the crime-scene photographs and pictures taken at the morgue after the blood had been hosed off Katie's body. The fact that Dr. Imajo wasn't on the stand (he had left Erie County to work in another state) suggested that the prosecution placed little importance on this evidence other than to prove that Katie had been killed by the defendant. Dr. Williams had been called, *pro forma,* to establish the main element, the *corpus delecti,* of the homicide charge, and nothing more.

Testifying that all of the victim's internal organs had been removed through a seven-inch incision in her lower left abdomen, and that Katie's brain had been "pulpified," Dr. Williams agreed with Dr. Imajo that the cause of death was "extensive blunt force trauma to the head." Ferguson showed Dr. Williams the kitchen knife found stuck in the organ pile next to Katie's corpse and asked if this could have been the instrument used to make the cut in her lower belly. Yes, said the doctor; that could have been the weapon. Ferguson handed the witness a photograph showing Katie facedown on the autopsy table and asked him what he saw. Dr. Williams said the photograph revealed marks, in the form of abrasions and bruises, behind her right armpit, on her right elbow, on her lower left back, and on her right flank near the hip—external injuries also noted by Dr. Imajo in his autopsy report. Dr. Imajo had also found a bruise on the front side of Katie's right hip and described the wound on the left side of her lower back as follows: "Red banklike abrasion one by seven centimeters . . . composed of numerous minute lines mostly oriented vertically." Dr. Williams, in examining the morgue photograph, had found another wound, on the other side of Katie's back, which he described as a "patterned abrasion, a narrow band of crosshatches running horizontally above her flank." Doctor Williams surmised that this mark might have been left by a rope or a cord, noting that a length of twine had been found on the kitchen floor under Katie's right hip.[9]

Dr. Imajo's autopsy report said nothing about this patterned abrasion and the cord or rope under Katie's body. This was new, unexpected evidence. Don Lewis, frantically taking notes at the defense table, didn't like being surprised. He wasn't sure where this was leading. What relevance did these external bruises and abrasions have to the case? Dr. Williams, when asked what he made of the cord found under Katie's body, said that he didn't know what it meant. In his notebook, Lewis wrote:

Other abrasions-band-narrow/cross hatches on it.
Rope, string-*horizontal/flanking.*

> *relatively minor;*
> Rope—*looked to be a cord;*
> *Under right flank.*
> *Used for "Doesn't know."*
> <u>ROPE</u>? ? ?

Dr. Williams, in studying the morgue photograph, had noticed other superficial injuries not mentioned in Dr. Imajo's report. He had discovered "minor abrasions and contusions on the victim's wrists," as well as "bruises about her shoulders."[10] The presence of bruises and abrasions on Katie's back, sides, shoulders, and wrists raised provocative questions regarding when and how they got there, and why. How old were these wounds? Did Katie have them before Ed punched her in the face then stomped her to death? What accounted for the contusions on her wrists? Had Dr. Williams found evidence of prior abuse? What had made the patterned abrasion noted by Dr. Imajo and the ones seen by Dr. Williams? Were these wounds contemporaneous with the homicide? Could they have been impressions made by the bottom of a shoe or boot? Had the bottoms of Ed's tennis shoes and his barn boots been compared with these wounds? Had an expert ruled out the crime-scene rope or cord? Did this evidence in any way cast doubt on Ed's account of the killing? Would Katie have to have been nude when these wounds were made, or could they have been inflicted through her clothing?

Dr. Williams had opened up an interesting can of worms. If Ferguson could prompt the doctor to say that at least some of these injuries could have been inflicted a day or so before the killing, that the dead woman had wounds not unlike those found on battered wives and girlfriends, the prosecution would have laid the groundwork for establishing the malice and intent they needed to convict Ed of murder. Ferguson, instead of inquiring about the possible cause and origin of Katie's bruises and abrasions, asked Dr. Williams if the body bore any injuries that could be termed defense wounds. Don Lewis could not have been more pleased. The witness replied he found no evidence that the victim had tried to defend herself against the fatal assault. Ferguson had no further questions and neither did Lewis. The witness was excused.[11]

Doc Terrell, wearing a blue suit, white shirt, narrow tie, and cowboy-style dress boots, told the jury that on the day of the killing, Ed, accompanied by his wife and an English couple, came to his office complaining of anger, insomnia, and the sweats. Prosecutor Ferguson approached the witness and asked, "And did you treat him on that occasion?"

"Yes. I adjusted the patient's head."

"How do you do that?"

"I manipulated the scalp."

"Did Ed Gingerich appear different that day?" Ferguson asked.

"No."

"He was acting normal?"

"Yes."

"You saw no signs of mental illness?"

"No."

"I have no further questions."

It was Don Lewis's turn. "How long have you been treating the defendant?"

"Several years."

"Regularly?"

"About once a month."

"Have you been treating him the last year?"

"Yes."

"What for?"

"Poor appetite, itchy skin, poor balance, headaches, weakness, forgetfulness."

"Depression?"

"Yes."

"You were treating him for emotional problems?"

"Yes."

"And what was your diagnosis?"

"He had a virus in his brain."

"Are you a psychiatrist?"

"No."

"Are you an MD?"

"No."

"Are you a psychologist?"

"No."

"Then why were you treating Ed for depression?"

"Because he complained about it."

"Because he complained about it?"

"Yes."

"What if he said he needed brain surgery?"

Ferguson rose from the prosecution table. "Objection!" he bellowed.

"Sustained," said the judge.

"Sorry, Your Honor," Lewis said with a thin smile for the jury. Addressing the witness, he asked, "Did you tell Ed's brother Danny that Ed had a virus on the brain?"

"No."

"Did you prescribe blackstrap molasses that day?"

"No."

"You were treating Ed for emotional problems?"

"Yes."

"I have no further questions, Your Honor."[12]

The Pennsylvania Doctor stepped off the stand, strode out of the courtroom, pulled his black, five-gallon Stetson off the hat rack in the hall, and, with briefcase in hand, made for the exit. Doc Terrell didn't have office hours on Wednesday, but he had better things to do than hang around the murder trial of a former patient.

Although Doc Terrell had been a prosecution witness, he helped the defense by showing that Ed was having mental problems just before the killing. Moreover, taking a psychotic man to have his head massaged by a chiropractor who thought he had a brain virus was so pathetically misguided, it made Ed look more like a victim than a killer.

It helped shift the blame for Katie's death from Ed onto his people.

If Dr. Karl Williams had been a missed opportunity and Doc Terrell was a mistake, the prosecution had gotten off to a slow start. But with his next witness, Emma Shetler, Ferguson could turn things around in a hurry. The jury, upon hearing this frail, honest Amish woman tell the story of her daughter's agonizing marriage to a cruel, disturbed man who had never loved her, might start to realize there was more to this case than met the eye. If handled properly, Emma Shetler had the potential of affecting Ed's destiny in a profound way. This was also her chance to have a say in her own future.

Emma Shetler had the answers, but did Douglas Ferguson have the questions?

41

Lord Willing

Emma Shetler, just ten years older than Douglas Ferguson, looked old enough to be his mother as she sat stiffly in the witness chair, her hands folded tightly on her lap, waiting for her ordeal to begin. Levi Shetler sat alongside Ed's three children in the front pew across the balustrade from the witness box. Next to their grandfather, the children looked like dolls. Emma didn't glance Levi's way. In this, she was alone; there was nothing he could do for her. Several of the jurors were looking fondly at the children, wondering perhaps what they were doing in the courtroom. Would they be testifying?[1]

As Ferguson approached his witness, the room fell silent. With the Xanax coursing through her veins, Emma adjusted her granny glasses and raised her eyes to the prosecutor. Responding to Ferguson's questions in her taut, brittle voice, she provided the court with her full name, address, and relationship to the defendant, then named the three grandchildren—Danny, age seven; Enos, age five; and Mary, age four—sitting in the pew next to her husband, Levi Shetler. Her daughter, Katie, had given birth to these children. As Emma spoke, people became aware of another sound. All eyes shifted to the other side of the room, where Ed, his forehead resting on the defense table, sobbed in a most sorrowful way. Don Lewis had laid a consoling hand on Ed's heaving back. For a minute or so, until he regained his composure, the trial came to a halt.

Until that very moment, Ed had shown no emotion. He had sat stone-faced at the defense table as Ferguson and Dr. Williams recounted and described, in gory detail, Katie's death and mutilation. Hearing how he had "overkilled" his wife in front of their children had not made him cry. Now the tears. Why? Who was Ed crying for? His wife? His children? Himself? The jury? Emma Shetler's grip on the jurors had been broken, their sympathy was flowing back to Ed. The moment was lost, the defendant had upstaged his victim. Don Lewis couldn't have been more pleased. One of the jurors had tears in her eyes.

Ferguson, eager to shift the focus back to his witness, asked, "How did the defendant and his wife, the victim, get along?"

"I don't know how to answer that," Emma replied.

"When was the last time you saw the defendant before Katie's death?"

"He was putting up ice," Emma said.

"At your house?"

"Yes."

"Did you notice anything unusual about him?"

"No."

"Was the defendant invited to the wedding on the day of the victim's death?"

"Yes, the groom worked for Ed at the sawmill. Ed and Katie had both been invited."

Ferguson asked a few more questions then turned Emma over to Lewis, who wisely decided not to cross-examine. Emma stepped down.[2] Levi gathered up the children and followed her out the door. She had been worrying about this day for months and suddenly it was over. She had known the defendant ten years, had witnessed the disintegration of her daughter's marriage, had experienced the madness and the violence, and had seen the psychological and physical toll it had taken on her daughter. Since the killing, Emma had been with Enos and little Mary, who had said things about their father, things the prosecution might want to know. They had been present when their father killed their mother, eyewitnesses to the last act of a tragic marriage. Emma Shetler, the witness who knew things that might have altered the course of Ed's trial, profoundly affecting its outcome, had been on the stand eight minutes, just long enough to be upstaged by the defendant.

Danny Gingerich, the prosecution's fourth witness, after being led through twenty minutes of hesitant, reluctant testimony, sat and watched as Ferguson and Lewis argued over Ferguson's attempt to introduce a statement Danny had given Lewis's investigator, Randy Fyock. Judge Miller ruled in favor of Ferguson then broke for lunch. Danny was back on the stand at one o'clock telling the jury what the defendant remembered about the killing two weeks after Katie's death. The occasion was Danny's first visit to the forensic unit at Warren State Hospital. "He talked about it," Danny said. "He remembered some things like she was out washing dishes. He was in the living room. 'I guess I just punched her,' he said."

Ferguson approached the witness. "Can you read?" he asked, handing Danny three pages from the fourteen-page transcript of his interview with Randy Fyock.

"Absolutely," Danny replied.

"Please read, out loud, what you told Mr. Fyock on June eleventh, 1993, about the conversation you had with the defendant at the Warren State Hospital after Katie's death."

Pronouncing each word carefully, like a schoolboy performing for his teacher, Danny read his own words to the jury:

And then the wedding, I think he talked about the wedding that evening again, he was quite upset that he couldn't go to the wedding that evening again. He told us that. The first time when we was up there [the forensic unit] he was feeling mentally ill and not that I can remember, Ed didn't, later, three, four days when we went up again, he said that it's hard for him to talk about it, but he talked about it, you know, he gets relief from it. We asked him how it started and he said that Katie had got up after lunch, went to bed, Katie had got up and said she's going to the wedding in the evening and so she got up, straightening up the house, washing dishes. Ed said she was out there singing, humming to herself and I just can't remember exactly how he said it, I think after a little bit he got up, she was in the kitchen, and I think he came out to her and said that he also wants to go to the wedding. He asked her what she's doing and she said she's cleaning up so she can go to the wedding and then he asked can I go and she said no, you are not well enough and I think he kind of got upset about that. I think there was some more said, I think Ed said more or she said more, I can't remember, but then Ed said he walked over to her and slapped her in the face and she fell on the floor and at that time he said he thinks, he thought that's when Katie told the oldest son, Danny, to come over and get me. Ed, he just stood there; he didn't know what, and then he went out to the porch. Ed went to the porch; she was lying in the kitchen. And he said that she had all kinds of chances to get up and go, that's what he said, and then he went out to the porch and got on his boots and came back in, and by the way he said, think he was on the porch a little bit and then came back in. Before he went out to the porch, I think he said that Katie said, "Why do you do this?" I don't know what he said then, but when he came back in from the porch he said, "Katie, is this the way you want it to be?" And she, I don't think she knew what he was talking about, and then the next thing he said he don't know why he did it. He said he just don't know why; he just did it. He said he stomped on her face and head. I asked him if he remembered seeing me, and he said he remembers seeing me and I asked him if he remembered me pushing him off and he can't remember anything like that.[3]

Ferguson, by Danny's statement, was establishing malice. Ed was mad at his wife, and with the quote—"Katie, is this the way you want it to be?"—his intent was to kill her. Ed didn't think he was stomping the devil's face or squashing a turnip, he had said, "*Katie,* is this the way you want it to be?" He had slapped her to the floor, then walked outside to put on his boots—his stomping boots. She was still on the ground when he came back into the kitchen, so he killed her. Malice and the intent to kill, add them up and you get, mental illness or not, murder. The prosecutor, satisfied that he had made his point through his witness, turned him over to the defense for cross-examination.[4]

To get the jurors' minds off the killing and back onto Ed's insanity, Lewis asked Danny to describe the torturous, last-minute dash to Jacob Troyer's house near Punxsutawney. The story of this paranoid schizophrenic being driven a hundred miles through a nocturnal blizzard to an Amish eye reader and herb dispenser dramatically illustrated the severity of Ed's insanity as well as the lack of good sense in taking someone that sick to a self-described quack. Having characterized his brother as "a man gone wild," Danny Gingerich was excused.[5]

The next witness, Ron Alexander, the sawmill customer Ed encountered at the bottom of his driveway just after he had killed Katie, in referring to Ed's bloody clothing, said, "I knew the Amish did their own butchering." The two men conversed, Ed helped push Alexander's stuck car out of the snow, and as far as the witness could tell, Ed looked, acted, and sounded perfectly normal.[6]

Trooper Robert A. Rowles, wearing civilian clothes, followed Alexander to the stand. Questioned by J. Wesley Rowden, the young officer (on the job four years) said he spoke to the defendant's brother shortly after arriving on the scene. From Danny Gingerich he learned that Ed had killed Katie. When asked if this was true, the defendant had said, "Yes, I may have killed my wife. I'm the bad guy you're looking for." Later, after they had placed Ed in Rowles's patrol car, Ed said, "I really killed my wife. I don't know why I did it." On the way to the Meadville station, the defendant said that his wife had told him he couldn't go to the wedding. He didn't know why she didn't allow him to attend the wedding and said that his hair was tingling, like it was on fire. The defendant knew he had killed his wife, and why, and apparently had the ability to carry on a fairly intelligent conversation.

When turned over to Lewis for cross-examination, Trooper Rowles stiffened like he was about to be stabbed by a fork. Lewis, on the other hand, was menacingly nice. Following a series of rather innocuous, harmless questions that brought guarded, even hostile responses, Lewis asked, "Did you advise the defendant of his Miranda rights?"

"No, but he initiated the conversation."

"Didn't you draw him into it?"

"No."

"Wasn't some of the things Ed said to you off-the-wall?"

"I don't know."

"What about his hair tingling?"

"Maybe."

"What about his warning that the North Star was falling to earth?"

"Yes, that was."

Having pulled this concession out of the surly trooper, Lewis said he was finished with the witness.[7] Young Rowles jumped off the hot seat and, looking a bit sullen, headed for the door.

Prosecutor Rowden called the Commonwealth's seventh witness, Trooper Danny Lloyd, to the stand. Following the customary preliminary questioning, Rowden took his witness back to the night of the killing when Lloyd and state investigator Jerry Bey questioned the bloodstained Amish man at the Meadville station. Rowden asked Lloyd if the defendant had understood that he had the right, under the Constitution, to remain silent, that he did not have to discuss his wife's death with the detectives. "I felt," Lloyd said, "that Mr. Gingerich understood what I was telling him about his rights and he voluntarily waived them and agreed to talk."[8]

Rowden, having laid the groundwork, asked the Court if he could play the audiotape of Ed's statement. If a defense attorney had procedural objections to the introduction of a confession, this was the time to raise them. Lewis was silent. Although Ed's confession was arguably inadmissible under the Miranda doctrine on the grounds he had been in no condition to *knowingly* waive his rights, Lewis wanted the jury to hear it. The defense attorney believed that the confession proved Ed was insane that night. That's why Lewis didn't care if the troopers, in acquiring the confession, had violated the defendant's Fifth and Sixth Amendment rights.

Rowden distributed copies of the fifteen-page confession transcript to the jury, then played the thirty-minute tape. The transcript was necessary because the sound quality of the tape was so poor it was hard to make out what was said. From the gallery, it was impossible, from the recording, to pick up the gist of the interrogation. Nevertheless, from the sound of Ed's high-pitched, supercharged voice, it was obvious even to the casual listener that he was off beam. After the tape had been played, Rowden asked Trooper Lloyd a series of follow-up questions then announced he was finished with the witness.[9]

It was approaching five o'clock, too late to start anything new, so Judge Miller closed shop for the day. Several hours earlier, television crews had caught Levi and Emma as they rushed Ed's children down the courthouse steps following her testimony. The boys, their faces hidden from the cameras by flimsy, blue scarves draped over their heads beneath their hats, looked like miniature beekeepers. Visions of the Shetlers escaping the courtroom with their grandchildren flashed across TV screens that night in northwestern Pennsylvania, northeastern Ohio, and southern Ontario.

The field-tripping high-school students didn't return for the fourth day of the trial. Neither did the Shetlers. Mr. Gingerich and his son Danny, accompanied by Mrs. Gingerich, Atlee, and Joe, were seated in a back pew on the windowed side of the courtroom. They were present because Mr. Gingerich and Danny had been subpoenaed by the defense. The Gingerichs had placed themselves about as far from the defense table as one could get without leaving the room. It had been one year to the day since Mr. and Mrs. Gingerich had traveled to North Warren to visit their son for the first time. It had been the worst year of their lives.

Trooper Danny Lloyd climbed into the witness chair and braced himself for Lewis's cross-examination. "What is the purpose of Miranda?"

Lloyd, an experienced courtroom testifier, replied, "To tell the subject his rights."

"Did the defendant understand his rights when he signed the waiver form 'Lord willing'?"

"I felt that Mr. Gingerich understood what I was telling him about his rights. He voluntarily waived them and agreed to talk."

"But the first words out of his mouth were that he *didn't* understand. You asked him, 'Do you understand that, Ed?' He shook his head no. It's right here in the transcript. Later, you asked, 'And you understand this?' He says, 'No.' Did he understand his rights?"

"Yes, I believe he did," Lloyd replied, confident and unshaken.

"A voluntary, intelligent waiver?"

"Yes."

"And rational?"

"Yes."

"When he signed the waiver form 'Lord willing,' didn't that tip you off that something was wrong?"

"No."

"When Ed said he had to remove Katie's brain and work his way down because that's how humans are made—was that an appropriate response?"

"Yes."

"He said, 'But you see what my problem is my hair prickled and they still prickle.' Was that appropriate?"

"Yes."

" 'I felt I had to kill her to get my conscience clear for everybody else.' What about that?"

"Yes."

"Rational?"

"Yes."

"What about the *tone* of Ed's voice? Did he *sound* normal to you?"

"Yes."

Lewis continued this line of questioning—quoting the

most bizarre statements Ed had made that night. Trooper
Lloyd, unwilling to concede the obvious, refused to acknowledge Ed's insanity. Although he was able to maintain his composure, the witness, by refusing to admit that
many of Ed's responses that night were not rational, was
losing his credibility. Finally, when asked to respond to
yet another bizarre quote, Lloyd accused Lewis of selecting, as examples, Ed's most outrageous statements, ex-
cluding comments Ed had made that were quite rational.
Taken as a whole, Lloyd said, Ed's confession revealed
that he had just killed his wife and was willing to take
responsibility for his act, an act he knew was wrong. Lewis
finished his cross-examination of Danny Lloyd at ten-
forty.[10] Under fire for ninety minutes, Lloyd left the witness box still cool and collected. Judge Miller ordered a
ten-minute recess that stretched to twenty.

When court resumed, Douglas Ferguson rose to his feet
and announced that the Commonwealth had rested its case.
That was it. The jury hadn't heard from Jake Powers, Debbie Williams, Trooper Lon E. Pierce, the children who'd
witnessed the killing, or any of the Mill Village paramedics. No one had explained the contusions and abrasions on
Katie's back or the crime-scene rope. The prosecution had
failed to produce a forensic psychiatrist to say that although Ed was mentally ill, he knew he was killing his
wife and that doing it was wrong. Why hadn't the jurors
heard a prosecution toxicologist debunk the notion that the
killing was somehow related to the Gunk fumes? How
come no one knew about the evangelists and their influence on Ed and his behavior? The jurors had been left with
no idea of who the victim had been. They didn't learn of
her suffering. They knew nothing of the marriage. They
had not been asked to consider the fact that Katie may
have died because she was too strong-minded. Seven witnesses, less than a day and a half of testimony. That's all
the jurors got, an anemic, inchoate prosecution, at best.

Don Lewis must have been straining to hold back his

tears of joy. The defendant, had he not been so drug-addled, might have been dancing on the defense table. People in the gallery were stunned. That was it?

It wasn't over. Don Lewis didn't have all the facts either. There were unexploded mines everywhere, and if Lewis didn't watch his step, the case could blow up in his face. The fat lady hadn't sung.

42

The Gunk Defense

Don Lewis launched his defense with Richard H. Zimmer, Ed's English friend and Brownhill neighbor. The burly farmer, decked out like a barn dancer, was asked, "Are you familiar with degreasers?"

"Yes. I am."

"Do you know whether or not at approximately one year before the death of his wife, Ed Gingerich was fixing machinery or working with machinery?"

"Yes."

"Do you know if he had a special shed for that?"

"Yes. I do."

"Have you ever been to that shed?"

"Several times."

"Do you remember a time when Edward had to go to Hamot Hospital about a year prior to his wife's death?"

"Yes."

"Were you ever in the shed with Edward at a time when he was using a degreaser to clean his engines?"

"Yes."

"Do you know what kind of degreaser that was?"

"It was a Gunk degreaser solvent that you dilute."

"Did you advise him to use Gunk?"

"I did show him. I had him over to my place and I showed him the stuff I was using, and yes. He asked me where I got it and he went and got some, too, for his own use."

"Now, back in those days and for the year prior to Mrs. Gingerich's death, did you see Edward on a fairly regular basis?"

"Yes, I would say so."

"Okay. Did you notice any change in him or difference in him after he came back from Hamot Hospital?"

"Yes. I did."

"Tell us what you knew of him or his demeanor before going to Hamot Hospital that changed after he came back."

"Before he was happy-go-lucky, jolly, and after he came back he was withdrawn, always complaining of his headaches, eyes bothering him, burning, and I told him that when he felt that way, just go out and get some fresh air, that he was using that stuff too much."

"Did you see my client at any time on the day of the death of Mrs. Gingerich or on the day before that?"

"Yes. I did."

"Do you have any feeling about whether or not his behavior was staying the same, getting better, getting worse, over that year?"

"The day of the accident, I knew his problem was worsening. I knew he didn't seem to be in the right state of mind at the time . . ."

Zimmer described the trip he, Kim Kerstetter, Katie, and Ed took to Doc Terrell's that day. He completed his direct testimony at eleven-fifteen. Douglas Ferguson, on cross-examination, asked, "If I understand correctly, approximately a year before the death of Mrs. Gingerich, you told Mr. Gingerich about a degreaser called Gunk."

"Yes."

"And, can we agree that even after that, Mr. Gingerich continued to work at the sawmill?"

"Yes."

"Did he continue to go places with Katie?"

"Yes."

"Did you have occasion to talk to him in the last year after he got back from Hamot?"

"Yes."

"Did you just talk to him about normal things that you are doing at your place and what he is doing at his place?"

"Yes."

"And I believe that you would tell people that Mr. Gingerich was very good with machinery. Is that correct?"

"Yes."

"I think you told somebody one time if he couldn't fix it, he could make the part for it. Is that right?"

"I told *you* that," Zimmer replied.

"Yeah. Okay, and he continued to do that even after he got back from Hamot. Correct?"

"Not as much as he did prior."

"I understand that, sir. But he continued to do it. Is that correct?"

"As far as I know; I didn't see."

"If I remember correctly, Mr. Gingerich's group [the sawmill] made the legs that go on bar stools. Is that correct?"

"Yes."

"And they were doing a lot of work up to the time of the death of Mrs. Gingerich. In fact, the truck had to come, I think, once a week and load up all those little logs and take them away. Is that correct?"

"I don't know what you are talking about, little logs."

"Well, the barstool legs. Didn't it come about once a week and pick them up?"

"I don't know how often it came."

Zimmer, in describing the trip to Doc Terrell's, kept referring to the killing as the "accident." Ferguson asked,

"Is there some reason why you refer to the death of Mrs. Gingerich as an accident?"

"That's the way I look at it."

"Okay. Now, you are good friends with Mr. Gingerich. Correct?"

"And I was also good friends with his wife."

"I understand that. Now, when you were with him on the eighteenth, wasn't there a discussion about going to a wedding?"

"Yes," Zimmer replied, warily.

"And wasn't there a discussion in front of Mrs. Gingerich where it was said to him that he might not be able to go to the wedding?"

"No."

"But there was a discussion about the wedding. Is that correct?"

"Amongst the women."

"And Mrs. Gingerich was present?"

"And so was I. The two ladies, the two ladies that was in the truck, was the ones that was going to the wedding."

Ferguson turned to the matter of Ed's demeanor when he encountered Zimmer at the foot of the driveway after the killing: "And you talked with Mr. Gingerich at that time, didn't you?"

"Yes."

"What did you say to him?"

"I said, 'Ed, where are you going?' He said, 'I am going down to Dad's.' And I says, 'Well, get in the truck, I will take you down.' He walked over toward the truck and he turned around and he said, 'I'm going to take your advice, Richard,' he says. 'I need fresh air. I am gong to walk down, because I need the fresh air.' "

"Now, can we agree, Mr. Zimmer, that when you talked to him on that occasion, he recognized you?"

"Yes, I assumed that he did."

"And, well, he called you by name. Didn't he say, 'Dick,' or 'Richard, I am going to take your advice'?"

"Yes."

"And he responded to your question 'Do you want a ride?' with, 'No, I think I will walk, I need the fresh air.' You understood that, didn't you?"

"It was puzzling to me, but I understood it."

"Well, it was a cold night. You thought maybe he would take a ride?"

"He had to carry one of the little kids."

"He had the kids with him, right?"

"Yes."

"Thank you."

Richard Zimmer stepped from the stand and joined Kim Kerstetter in the gallery.[1] He looked pleased with himself, or perhaps he was just relieved to be out of the grill box.

Dave Lindsey was next. Unaware that Lindsey's relationship with Ed had more to do with religious indoctrination than logging, Lewis asked the witness to describe what it had been like in the machine shed the day before Ed started having the spells that led to his hospitalization at Hamot. Lindsey said the Gunk fumes hurt his eyes and left him with a throbbing headache that plagued him all night.

Following a cursory cross-examination, Lindsey was excused.[2] Douglas Ferguson apparently wasn't interested in why, if the Gunk fumes were so bad, Dave Lindsey had stayed so long in the shed. Lindsey wasn't a diesel mechanic, what were they doing? If they were just talking, what were they talking about? Were they talking sports, discussing the weather, ruminating about their favorite TV shows, what? In discussing his Gunk exposure with Dr. Morrow, the psychologist, Ed reported having a long discussion in the shed that night with a man. He said they had talked about religion. That man was David Lindsey. Apparently Ferguson had not read Dr. Morrow's report, or if he had, had not made the connection to Dave Lindsey. The next morning, Ed awoke as a religious fanatic, then came the spells, and a year later he killed his wife. He had found Jesus, but not in a can of Gunk.

Don Lewis next produced his first expert, Dr. John J. Spikes, a sixty-five-year-old toxicologist working for a private firm near Philadelphia. A bulky, bespectacled man without much hair, a florid complexion, and a pronounced limp, Dr. Spikes, in the authoritative voice of a veteran professor, explained that if not used properly, degreasing solvents could make one ill. That's because these products contain toxic ingredients such as benzene, gasoline, naphtha, kerosene, and mineral-seed oil. Improper exposure could damage the epidermis, liver, and brain, causing skin irritation, headaches, dizziness, fatigue, loss of appetite, irritability, paranoia, and hallucinations. In Dr. Spike's professional opinion, the defendant's exposure to high concentrations of Gunk had caused what he called "organic brain syndrome," a condition that existed at the time of Katie's death.

The afternoon session began with the toxicologist's cross-examination. Had the witness, Ferguson wanted to know, ever spoken to the defendant? No, he had not. "Did you question anybody who saw the defendant on the day of the killing?"

"No."

"Then everything you know about the defendant has come from Attorney Lewis?"

"Yes."

"Do you know if the defendant used other products besides Gunk to clean engines?"

"No."

"Do some furniture-polishing products contain petroleum distillates?"

"Yes. All things are toxic, some more than others."

"Are skin rashes always a symptom?"

"No, but frequently. The organs remain affected after the petroleum distillates have passed through the system."

The witness was dismissed.[3]

Lewis called Ed's brother Danny to the stand. According to Danny, Ed's mental illness started the day after his exposure to the Gunk in the machine shed. "He talked like a kid," Danny said. "He didn't work as much, you could hardly have conversations with him. You could ask him questions but he didn't answer."

"Did Ed ever believe he was abandoned by God?" Lewis asked.

"I believe so."

"Did he think his sickness came from the Lord?"

"As a punishment, I think, yes."

"Did Ed tell you of conversations you never had?"

"Yes."[4]

Danny Gingerich was followed to the stand by his father, who said that as a child, Ed fell off a horse and was knocked unconscious. On cross-examination, Ferguson asked, "Did you ever tell your son he spent too much time with the English?"

"I might have. I don't remember when."

"Did you ever tell your son to spend more time with the Amish?"

"I probably did."

"How old was your son when he fell off the horse?"

"Ten or eleven, maybe twelve."

"Is your son an honest person?"

"Yes."

"When you visited your son in the hospital at Warren, did he explain to you what happened to his wife?"

"I don't recall."

Mr. Gingerich was excused.[5]

Judge Miller, noticing that some of the jurors were suffering from mid-afternoon drowsiness, called a fifteen-minute recess. Mr. Gingerich gathered up his family and made straight for the exit, passing Ed's table without a look or a word. If Prosecutor Ferguson had asked Mr. Gingerich if he'd ever told his son to spend more time with *Katie,* he'd still be on the stand.

Dr. Frank Yohe, the local psychiatrist who'd certified Ed for the forensic unit at Warren, described Ed's appearance and demeanor on the morning after the killing.[6] Sergeant David Bickel of the Crawford County Jail took the stand and said he was on hand the night the state police delivered Ed to the lockup. Ed kept saying, "Where am I? Why am I here?" and "Are you guys going to kill me?"[7] Next came Sidney J. Workman, the man who'd driven Ed and the others across the state that night to Punxsutawney to see Jacob Troyer, the Amish eye-reading herb healer. Kim Kerstetter, put on the stand as a character witness, informed the jury that Ed and Katie had gotten along well as a couple. Kim also described Ed's last visit to Doc Terrell's, describing the defendant as depressed, slow, confused, and complaining of severe burning inside his head.[8]

Ed, slumped in his chair with his head down, seemed oblivious to his surroundings as Debbie Williams, Lewis's tenth witness, took her place in the witness box. Based on her ten-year acquaintance with the defendant, Debbie Williams described him as a nonviolent person with an impeccable reputation with the English. When asked, on cross-examination, when she last saw the defendant before the killing, the witness replied that she'd seen Ed about three weeks before Katie's death. Having been in the witness box less than ten minutes, Debbie Williams was excused.[9] It was too late in the day to start another witness, so Judge Miller brought the session to an end.

Friday, the fifth day of the trial, began with Don Lewis putting Ed's English neighbors Jim and Alice DeMatteo on the stand as witnesses to his character. They had known the defendant eight years and had nothing but good to say about him as a husband and as a father. Both witnesses left the stand without being cross-examined.[10] Neither witness looked at Ed as they exited the sparsely populated courtroom. Outside, it started to snow.

Dr. Lisa A. Morrow, the young, stylish neuropsychologist who had examined Ed two months earlier at the University of Pittsburgh, oozed confidence as she described some of the twenty or so psychological, motor-skill, memory, and intelligence tests she had given the defendant to determine, among other things, if Ed's exposure to the Gunk fumes had damaged his brain. The results of Dr. Morrow's tests showed that Ed had a relatively low IQ, a below-average memory, and poor motor skills. The psychologist concluded her direct testimony by opining that Ed's anxiety, depression, delusions, hallucinations, and paranoia had been triggered, at least in part, by his exposure to the Gunk.

On cross-examination, J. Wesley Rowden asked, "Dr. Morrow, do you know of anyone other than the defendant who has killed from the affects of Gunk fumes?"

Before the witness could answer, Don Lewis objected to the question. Rowden withdrew it and asked, "If a person sees things that aren't there, does that mean that person is schizophrenic?"

"No," Dr. Morrow replied. "But if a person sees angels in the sky, hears a voice chanting 'Kill your wife,' and 'I am the whole white world,' it's a sign they are psychotic."

"Did Ed tell you he ever drank alcohol?"

"Yes, for medicinal purposes."

"Did he ever tell you he was mad about something?"

"Yes, he was angry because his wife refused to let him attend the wedding."

Later in the cross-examination, Rowden asked, "Did you ask for the reports of the other experts who had examined Ed?"

"No," Dr. Morrow answered.

"When you spoke to the defendant in your office, did he act normal?"

"Yes, he was on medication."

"Did you ask him if he knew who Louis Armstrong is?"

"Yes."

"Why would you ask him that?"

"It's a standard test, uniform for all."

"Did he know who Amelia Earhart was?"

"Yes."

"You asked him why dark clothes are warmer than white clothes. Did he know the answer?"

"Yes."

"You asked him if he ever read *Hamlet*. Had he?"

"No."

"Did he know who Martin Luther King is?"

"Yes."

"The capital of Italy?"

"No."

"Did he know why yeast causes bread to rise?"

"Yes."

"How many senators are in the U.S. Senate?"

"No."

"What temperature causes water to boil?"

"He got that wrong."

Prosecutor Rowden next had Dr. Morrow explain and describe her word association, immediate recall, math, and memory tests, then asked, "Is it possible for a schizophrenic person to know the nature and quality of his act?"

"Anything is possible," Dr. Morrow replied.

Rowden, boring the jury to death, kept Dr. Morrow on the stand another hour describing in great detail, all of the other exercises she had made the defendant perform that day.[11] Perhaps this was the prosecutor's way of trivializing Dr. Morrow's work, ridiculing her low-tech, pen-and-pencil, peg-in-hole-type tests. If this had been Rowden's purpose, he may have been better served asking the doctor why she hadn't administered EEG (electroencephalogram) and MRI (magnetic resonance imaging) procedures to determine if Ed's brain had, in fact, been damaged. Why infer this from word tests when the brain itself can be examined for lesions, scarring, and other evidence of physical trauma?

In the wake of Dr. Morrow's testimony, the jury, if not bored, looked unimpressed. Maybe they were just hungry. Judge Miller recessed for lunch.

43

"Whacked-Out"

.

Dr. Lawson F. Bernstein, Jr., Don Lewis's fourteenth witness and the centerpiece of his defense, took the oath looking like a heartthrob doctor in a TV soap. The thirty-six-year-old psychiatrist from the University of Pittsburgh appeared relaxed and confident. Of medium height with impeccably styled, wavy black hair, a meaty chin, and a physique that suggested regular workouts, Dr. Bernstein, like Dr. Morrow before him, had the look of the big city. In Bernstein's case, it was New York City, where he had been born, raised, and educated. He came from a land where there were no cornfields, Agway buildings, John Deere hats, or Amish enclaves. The minute Dr. Bernstein opened his mouth, the jurors knew he was an alien from another galaxy. He was not one of them.

Following his obligatory and essentially meaningless recitation of his professional qualifications (the fact that he wore a suit and tie identified him as an expert), Dr. Bernstein pointed out that the defendant's sister suffered from depression and his uncle was psychotic. This genetic proclivity, coupled with his exposure to the Gunk petrochemicals, had led to mental-ward commitments in Erie and Jamestown after the defendant failed to respond to his "nonmedical chiropractic treatments." Ed was in relatively good health after his second hospitalization, then became ill two months before the killing when he was exposed to the fumes of an oil-based paint. This exposure to petrochemicals triggered a series of delusions and hallucinations: suddenly the devil was after his soul, people were trying to poison him, his internal organs were disappearing, he looked out the window and saw a giant rabbit, and a female voice inside his head told him to kill his wife. Dr. Bernstein's testimony, considerably more graphic and perhaps more relevant than Dr. Morrow's, kept the jurors alert even though it was getting late in the afternoon. At three, Judge Miller called a break until three twenty-five when Dr. Bernstein, back on the stand, started discussing the transcript of Ed's statement to the police, a document the witness called "immensely important" to the diagnosis of Ed's mental state on the day of the killing. Dr. Bernstein cited comments like, "I think we can still save her . . . Are my kids still alive? . . . I thought I was being responsible . . ." and "I felt it was a gain for us, the people," to illustrate Ed's flight from reality. The psychiatrist noted that interspersed among the gibberish, twisted logic, and statements reflecting Ed's inability to follow through on a thought (Bernstein called this "thought blocking") were little pockets of dialogue that made sense. During these passing moments of lucidity, Ed was saying: "Hey, fellas, I'm trying to talk here but there is something wrong with my brain." Testifying with a degree of self-assurance bordering on cocky, Dr. Bernstein said, "If I read this transcript to a ten-year-old child, the child would know that Ed Gingerich was crazy, psychotic. He was whacked out . . . The defendant, due to the severity of his mental illness, lacked the ability to appreciate the nature and quality of the act that led to the death of his wife."

Douglas Ferguson's chance to question the expert came at five o'clock. Normally, Judge Miller would have adjourned for the day, but because he was hoping to hand the case over to the jury within twenty-four hours, he allowed Ferguson to proceed with his cross-examination. "Doctor," the prosecutor said, "did you test the defendant for neurological damage?"

"No."

"Did you interview the police?"

"No."

"Have you spoken to any members of the defendant's family?"

"No."

"When the doctors at the hospital in Jamestown examined the defendant, did they find that Gunk had damaged his lungs?"

"They just gave him a standard X ray," Dr. Bernstein replied, a trace of impatience creeping into his voice.

"How long did you interview the defendant?"

"Five and one-half hours—in this building," the doctor said.

Making little effort to hide his contempt for courthouse shrinks, Ferguson noted that the defendant, after punching his wife to the floor, walked onto the porch to pull on his boots before beating her brains out. "Didn't that show," Ferguson asked, "that the defendant knew what he was doing when he stomped her to death?"

"No. He did *not* know what he was doing."

"But he remembered this. He remembered that his kids were in the room. Wasn't he aware of what he was doing?"

"No, he was not."

Ferguson, trying to keep his anger under control, said, "But he knew his kids were there. Didn't he know that?"

"It's not clear to me that he knew that."

"Okay. If I show you *evidence* that he knew his children were in the kitchen—would you *then* say he was aware of what he was doing and where he was?"

"No. Besides, he may have put this fact together from the police telling him this six or seven times."

"After he killed her," Ferguson said, "he left the house with his children. He helped a man get his car out of the snow. Wasn't he acting perfectly normal?"

"That shows how crazed and removed he was from the event. People can perform normal activities in a psychotic state. He had no idea of what he was doing."[1]

Ferguson was banging his head against a wall. Dr. Bernstein had dug in his heels and wouldn't budge. This wasn't science, it was war. The jury looked tired and bored and it was a quarter to six, extremely late for courthouse people to be working, so Judge Miller closed up shop for the day. Ferguson would get his chance to discredit the doctor in the morning.

Thirty minutes after the court had adjourned, Dr. Bernstein spoke to a TV reporter on the sidewalk in front of the courthouse. Referring to Ed Gingerich, he said, "He was really very ill." That evening, Dr. Bernstein had dinner with Don Lewis before returning to his room at the Days Inn out near the interstate.[2]

Saturday morning, with only a handful of people looking on from the gallery, Ferguson, referring to the fact that Ed had washed his hands after gutting his wife, asked, "Doesn't this show, Dr. Bernstein, that the defendant knew he had killed his wife?"

"No," replied the psychiatrist. "A person can perform automatic motor acts. It doesn't mean that the defendant was functioning in a rational way."

"The defendant spoke to his brother Danny that evening at the intersection. 'I killed my wife,' he said. What does that show?"

"It shows he was aware it happened, but he doesn't know he had done anything wrong."

" 'I'm the *bad* guy you're looking for,' he said. Doesn't that show he knew it was wrong?"

"Not necessarily, no."

"Katie thwarted the defendant's desire to attend the wedding. Wasn't that the reason, the intent behind the killing?"

"He was saving his soul, not killing his wife."

"He didn't kill his children to save his soul, did he?"

"No."

"He didn't harm the children. He wanted to hurt his wife. Isn't that correct?"

"That's an incorrect assessment."

"He didn't want to harm his wife?"

"No. He didn't know he was hurting her. He was out of control. He would have harmed *anyone* standing there. I can't even say he knew she was a human being."

"How do you know that?"

"We have a window into the defendant's brain, a wonderful window, the officers' interview gives us that window, line by line. It showed he was grossly psychotic."

"But the evidence shows us he was aware of what he was doing. Common sense tells us that. Maybe to a psychiatrist he was insane, but a lay person can see he appreciated what he was doing. It is common sense. Isn't that correct?"

"Before I became a doctor, I was a real person," Dr. Bernstein replied with a smirk. "The defendant was so crazy he couldn't hit the ground with his hat."

As an expert witness, Dr. Bernstein was everything a defense attorney could hope for. He was handsome, well dressed, confident, unequivocal, and knew exactly what was expected of him. And he delivered the goods. He could not be shaken because he simply refused to acknowledge there were cracks in his analysis. Ferguson, reluctant to let this smug courtroom shrink survive the cross-examination unscratched, pushed on: "Would you describe to the jury what schizophrenia is?"

"It's a chronic mental disease involving periods of remission and periods of exacerbation, when the patient loses touch with reality."

"Are there schizophrenics who are aware of what they are doing?"

"The issue is capacity," Dr. Bernstein replied. "Schizophrenics lack the capacity to comprehend some activities and have it to understand others."

"Couldn't we conclude, from the evidence in this case, that the defendant was, indeed, mentally ill, but responsible for the act of killing his wife?"

"No. The defendant was out of his mind. Some of the defendant's apparent rational behavior was automatic, like helping the man at the end of the driveway. This acute juxtaposition speaks to the inherent craziness of his mind." Dr. Bernstein, having warmed to his subject and apparently confident that he could make the jury see things his way, pointed out that it was unproductive and misleading to use isolated lines from Ed's police statement to prove awareness, malice, and criminal intent. These isolated comments, taken out of context, meant nothing. Ed's mental condition had to be analyzed in the context of his psychiatric history during the year leading up to his wife's death. A man who looks out his window and sees a giant rabbit is crazy.

Ferguson, losing ground and his temper, asked, "How much have you been paid for your work on this case?"

"I object, Your Honor!" Lewis bellowed from the defense table.

"Sustained," said the judge.

"Did you talk to Mr. Lewis last night about your testimony today?"

"We had dinner, shot the bull, discussed the case generally, but did not talk about my testimony," said the doctor.[3] He smiled to emphasize how unfazed he was, how cool, composed. When you're right, you're right; when you're wrong, you look and sound like the prosecutor. You lose. The poor guy had no style. Ferguson was finished.

Following a short recess at nine forty-five and a brief redirect by Don Lewis, Dr. Bernstein was excused. Except for the possibility that the jury had found his cockiness off-putting, the psychiatrist had been a strong witness. Lewis rose to his feet and said, "The defense rests its case, Your Honor."

Don Lewis had run fourteen witnesses past the jury, twice as many as the prosecution. He had put on a forensic toxicologist, a neuropsychologist, two psychiatrists, four non-Amish character witnesses, Dave Lindsey, the jail sergeant, Sid Workman, Ed's father, and the defendant's brother Danny. The most important person in the case, however, did not testify. Lewis had decided to keep Ed off the stand. If Ed had climbed into the witness box, it could have undermined his insanity defense. According to Dr. Bernstein, Ed's mind was somewhere else when his body killed Katie. Why risk having the defendant contradict his own expert witness? Since there was nothing to gain and everything to lose by calling Ed to the stand, the jury didn't hear from the person whose testimony may have informed them the most.

Judge Miller called a recess and announced that when the court reconvened, Don Lewis would make his closing argument. Douglas Ferguson would get the last word.

Facing the jury from behind a lectern, Lewis, in a loud but conversational voice, said, "One who has been responsible all his life doesn't do something like this. The prosecutors say that Ed Gingerich knew what he was doing when he killed his wife, Katie. They ask you to believe that this Amish man had killed his wife because she told him he couldn't go to a wedding. There is one issue in this case: What was the defendant's mental condition at the time of Katie Gingerich's death? What was in his mind? What was his intent?"

Lewis asked the jurors to think of Ed's statement to the state police as a window into his brain. In the midst of an "intense psychotic storm," Ed has signed the Miranda waiver form "Lord willing." The prosecution had offered no professional testimony to counter the testimony of the two defense psychiatrists who told them Ed was so crazy he didn't know what he was doing. "The Gunk fumes may have been a factor in the onset of Eddie's mental problem," Lewis said. "He was exposed to it. But no matter what the cause, it was the schizophrenia not the Gunk that caused the event. Mental illness makes you a different person . . ."

The jurors' faces did not reveal if they were sympathetic to Lewis's argument. They were, however, paying close attention to what he was saying. He went on: "I have been

twenty-five years at this job. This is a major case and attorneys can get nervous. I hope I didn't miss anything.
The prosecution has an advantage; they get the last word
in closing. Why do they get this advantage? Because of
the heavy burden they have in proving their case—beyond
a reasonable doubt. Another advantage they have is when
I'm finished with my closing argument, I can sit down. I
can't interrupt the prosecution; I can't say they are wrong.
They have listened to me; they will try to tear down my
arguments. I can't do that to them. I have no rebuttal opportunity . . .

"We're not talking about a master criminal. We're talking about a young Amish man who has worked hard all
of his life, a man faithful to his religion and his family.
His reputation was that of a peaceful, nonviolent person.
One of his friends calls the death an accident . . . After using Gunk in his machine shop, he changed. He was given
medication but stopped taking it because it made him sick
and he couldn't work. He was frustrated by not being able
to work. Had he not been reluctant to take the medicine
and had he not been encouraged not to take it, Katie would
be here today . . . The prosecutors say the defendant is a
man who intentionally and with premeditation and malice
brutally murdered his wife. Has this trial shown this? If
so, I've failed miserably . . .

"Eddie Gingerich is as much a victim as Katie—she lost
her life—she's at peace. Eddie did not lose his life—and
may never be at peace. Thank you."[4] Lewis walked back
to the defense table and sat down heavily. He patted Ed
on the shoulder. If the defendant had been moved by his
attorney's speech, he didn't show it. From all appearances,
he hadn't been listening.

It was noon, so Judge Miller recessed for lunch.

Douglas Ferguson stepped up to the lectern and said, "If
I said something you didn't like, please hold it against me,
not the witnesses." The prosecutor asked the jury to apply
common sense to what they knew about the killing. The

defendant's malice toward his wife and his intent to kill her could be reasonably inferred from the evidence, he said. Yes, the defendant was mentally ill, but under the law, an insane person could still be held responsible for his criminal act. The viciousness of the defendant's assault revealed his hatred of the victim. If he had been purely mad, he would have also killed the children. But he didn't hate his kids; he hated his wife, the one he *intended* to kill. When the police came, Ed had said, "I'm the bad guy you're looking for." He knew he had done something wrong. He knew he had murdered his wife. Taking aim at Dr. Bernstein, the heart of Ed's defense, Ferguson said, "Is it—everybody has to believe me because I'm Dr. Bernstein? You can say, 'Dr. Bernstein, you said the magic words but you didn't do your job. I'm not fooled because I'm too smart!' " A few minutes later, Ferguson concluded his summation with, "Our common sense tell us that the defendant was mentally ill, but guilty of first-degree murder. Katie Gingerich's death was no accident; it was *murder*."[5]

Judge Miller, following another short recess, instructed the jury on the law before sending them off to determine Ed's fate. On one end of the verdict spectrum, they could find Ed not guilty by reason of insanity, on the other, guilty of first-degree murder. In between, there were the verdicts of guilty of third-degree murder, voluntary manslaughter, and involuntary manslaughter. If the jury found that Ed, in fact, was insane but still capable of appreciating the wrongfulness of his act, he could be found guilty of murder one, murder three, voluntary manslaughter, or involuntary manslaughter—but mentally ill. A guilty-but-mentally-ill verdict simply meant that while serving his sentence, Ed would be treated for his mental afflictions. He would not be released when cured, but when his sentence ran out. Judge Miller then explained the difference between the degrees of murder and the two kinds of manslaughter: "First-degree murder," he said, "is a murder in which the killer has the specific intent to kill. You may find the defendant guilty of first-degree murder if you are satisfied that the following three elements have been proven beyond a reasonable doubt: first, that Katie Gingerich is dead; second, that the defendant killed her; and third, that the defendant did so with the specific intent to kill and with malice. A person has the specific intent to kill if he has a fully formed intent to kill and is conscious of his own intentions. The specific intent to kill does not require planning or previous thought or any particularly length of time. It can occur quickly. Second-degree murder is often called felony murder because it involves a killing incidental to a felony. This offense does not apply to this case. Third-degree murder is any killing with malice that is not first- or second-degree murder. The word *malice* as I am using it, has a special legal meaning. It does not mean simply hatred, spite, or ill will. Malice is a shorthand way of referring to three different mental states that the law regards as being bad enough to make a killing murder. Thus, a killing is with malice if the killer acts with: first, an intent to kill, or second, an intent to inflict serious body harm, or third, a reckless disregard for the possibility of death. *Voluntary* manslaughter occurs when a defendant kills in the heat of passion following serious provocation or kills under an unreasonable mistaken belief in justifying circumstances. You may find the defendant guilty of *involuntary* manslaughter if you are satisfied that the defendant's conduct was reckless or grossly negligent. A defendant's conduct is reckless when he consciously disregards a substantial and justifiable risk that death will result from his conduct. Compared with recklessness and gross negligence, the malice required for third-degree murder is a more blameworthy state of mind."

Judge Miller, following a lecture on the difference between legal insanity (not guilty by reason of) and insanity, merely justifying a guilty-but-mentally-ill verdict, concluded his instructions by saying, "Do not concern yourself with the consequences of your verdict. For example, do not reject the not-guilty-by-reason-of-insanity verdict because you are afraid the defendant will be confined too long in a mental hospital or released too early. Assume that the authorities will do the right thing."[6]

It was now time for the jury to do the right thing. With the discretion to find Ed not guilty of anything but insanity all the way to first-degree murder, the jury filed out of the courtroom to deliberate on its verdict. A pair of Crawford County deputies escorted Ed back to his cell while Don Lewis and his helpers returned to his offices to wait.

Ed's fate depended upon what aspect of Katie Gingerich's killing mattered most to the jury. Was it Ed's state of mind? Was it fear that a man who had killed once could do it again? Was it gauging Ed's blameworthiness and punishing him accordingly? Or was it something none of the lawyers had anticipated? What if the jurors asked themselves what the victim would have wanted?

What then?

44

The Verdict

The jury foreman, two hours into the deliberation, sent word to Judge Miller that several members of the panel were confused about the difference between not guilty by reason of insanity and the verdict of guilty but mentally ill. Judge Miller, back in the courtroom with the jury and opposing attorneys, distinguished ordinary mental illness from *legal* insanity, the kind of madness that, although the judge didn't use these words, turned defendants into mindless zombies. If they determined that the defendant was legally insane at the time of the act, the jury would have to find him not guilty. He would then be psychiatrically evaluated and, depending on the results of this examination, be treated or released. If found guilty but mentally ill, the defendant would be sentenced according to the seriousness of the jury's homicide verdict and treated while serving his time. Was he sick, was he bad, or was he sick *and* bad?

Having been fully instructed on the application of insanity law to Katie's homicide and Ed's paranoid schizophrenia, the jurors, at three-thirty, filed out of the courtroom to figure it all out. Some of them, if facial expressions meant anything, were still confused.

Don Lewis picked up the telephone at a quarter to six. He rushed out of his office; the verdict was in.

"All rise!"

Judge Miller came through the door behind the bench.

"Be seated," said the court crier.

"Have you reached a verdict?" Judge Miller asked. All eyes turned to the jury box.

"We have, Your Honor," the jury foreman replied as he handed the verdict slip to the clerk, who carried it to the bench. After reading it over, Judge Miller handed the slip to the clerk, who walked it back to the jury foreman.

"Will the defendant please rise and face the jury?" Judge Miller said.

Ed got to his feet and, with his oversized hands hanging at his side, looked glassy-eyed toward the jurors.

"In the case of the *Commonwealth of Pennsylvania* versus *Edward D. Gingerich* on the charge of criminal homicide, how do you find?"

"We find the defendant, Edward D. Gingerich, guilty of involuntary manslaughter but mentally ill," declared the foreman.

Don Lewis sprang to his feet. "Your Honor, I move that the court issue a decree allowing the defendant to be immediately returned to the Warren State Hospital for his presentence evaluation."

Judge Miller looked at Douglas Ferguson. "Any objection?"

"No, Your Honor," the prosecution replied.

"Granted," said the judge. "The defendant will be sentenced on Monday, May second, 1994."[1]

The trial was over.

The jury, by this verdict, had rejected Don Lewis's insanity defense. In so doing, they had also rejected Dr. Bernstein and his expert testimony. They had found that Ed had been mentally ill, but not crazy enough to completely absolve him of responsibility for his wife's death. That made perfect sense. But what didn't make sense was the type of homicide they had found Ed guilty of—*involuntary* manslaughter. Katie's death had *not* been an accident, the result of a negligent or reckless act. The jury could have logically concluded that Ed's mental illness had erased premeditation and malice, the elements required for murder, but finding the killing unintentional didn't square with the facts. *Voluntary* manslaughter, a more serious offense involving intent but not malice, would have been legally more appropriate. The jury had looked beyond the law to the sentence; they wanted Ed punished but not too harshly. In this regard, they had fashioned a compromise verdict. Although by law the maximum sentence Judge Miller could impose for involuntary manslaughter was five years, the typical sentence imposed for this offense was one year, time rarely spent in prison. According to the state's sentencing guidelines, recommendations judges didn't have to follow, the standard manslaughter conviction should bring, *at the most*, eighteen months in prison. Cases involving aggravating circumstances justified a full five-year sentence, while the least serious offenders, cases comprising mitigating circumstances, called for short periods of probation—no jail time at all. In thirty-six days, at Ed's sentence hearing, Don Lewis would make the argument that in Ed's case, due to his mental illness and the fact that he was a nondangerous Amish man, there should be no prison time, merely a short period of probation. Sending Ed to the slammer, for any length of time, would amount to cruel and unusual punishment. The prosecution, on the other hand, would ask Judge Miller for the maximum sentence—five years behind bars—not bad for killing your wife.

The jury's compromise verdict had pleased the defense *and* the prosecution.[2] Lewis was happy because in his mind it meant that Ed would be free to go home after the sentence hearing. Had he been found not guilty by reason of insanity, Ed would have been returned to Warren State Hospital for an undetermined length of time. The prosecutors were happy because, without putting their own shrink on the stand, they had defeated Dr. Bernstein and the insanity defense. They had obtained a criminal conviction and were quite proud of themselves. To a newspaper reporter, J. Wesley Rowden, speaking for the prosecution said: "We're glad he is in the system and he's getting help. He'll either be in a mental hospital or a prison for up to the next five years. The important thing is to get treatment and he'll be in a secure environment while getting treatment."[3]

Don Lewis, when asked by a reporter how he felt about the verdict, replied: "Except for my ego, this is the best possible verdict . . . It hit me like no other verdict I've ever had."[4] When asked how his client felt about the verdict, Lewis said, "Ed doesn't understand our justice system. He is relieved the trial is over. It was stressful for him."[5]

Only three jurors would comment publicly about the verdict. One juror called the deliberations "traumatic" and another said he had a hard time arriving at a decision. The third juror said it was hard for the panel to decipher the law behind the ten possible verdicts in the case.[6]

The decision, rendered on Saturday, was, by Sunday, the main topic of conversation among the Brownhill

Amish. The Gingerichs were not sure what to make of the verdict or how to react, but everyone else in the community was alarmed and shocked by the court's leniency. By killing his wife, Ed had proven himself unpredictable and dangerous. How could such a man not be incarcerated for life? It wasn't a matter of forgiveness or even punishment; those matters were up to God. It was about public safety, acting responsibly to protect Ed's children, his parents, brothers, sisters, the bishop, and others who would cross his path. What kind of courts did the English have? No wonder crime was such a problem in America.

Emma and Levi had assumed that Ed, by doing what he had done, had proven himself unsafe for society and would, in one form or another, be institutionalized for a long period of time, perhaps for life. Having taken this for granted, they were stunned, then angered, by the decision. Emma, afraid that Levi's weakened heart couldn't take the strain, kept him home from church that Sunday following the verdict. She was still terrified of Ed and afraid for his children. In five years, when Ed got out of prison, his oldest boy would be eleven. Enos would be nine and Mary, the baby, would be eight. Bishop Shetler, in responding to the verdict, declared that he did not want Ed back in Brownhill, ever. Seven families in the enclave had already promised to move away if Ed came back and tried to live among them. Apparently the people running the court hadn't considered the well-being of the Amish community when they made their decision. What would happen if the Gingerichs refused to give Ed his children when he came for them? What would he do? The children were afraid of their father. What would they do? How could they live with the man who killed their mother before their very eyes?

That Sunday, Emma expressed her concerns and fears to Bishop Shetler, who told her that he and Deacon Ben Stutzman had decided to take action against the verdict.[7] They had made a terrible mistake in not getting involved with the court in the first place. They should not have assumed that the English authorities would make the right decisions. Bishop Shetler said he would draw up a petition for everyone in the community to sign that would ask Judge Miller to reconsider the verdict and to send Ed back to the Warren State Hospital for the rest of his life. The bishop would present this petition, in person, to the judge at Ed's sentence hearing.

On Friday, March 31, six days following the verdict, Crawford County deputies drove Ed back to North Warren for twelve days of presentence psychological and psychiatric testing. When asked on admission if he knew why he had been brought to the institution, Ed replied, "I feel very well, doctor, and the court sent me here for evaluation before I get sentenced."

One of the psychologists, after giving Ed a Rorshcach Inkblot Test, wrote:

Mr. Gingerich continues to no longer be actively psychotic . . . Mr. Gingerich now appears to have adequate inner resources to cope with current stressors in an adaptive manner. While his self-image may be somewhat negative and his relationships not as rewarding as previously, he appears to have a less pessimistic outlook on life. However, he still may occasionally make unconventional translations of a stimuli[sic] . . . which could contribute to less successful adjustment in the future. Thus, he is considered to continue to be vulnerable to aggression under significant stress and continued regular use of psychotropic medication is highly recommended.[8]

In other words, if Ed quit taking his medicine, he could turn dangerous. Ed had proven this twice before the killing, and according to the psychologist, nothing had changed. At the conclusion of Ed's evaluation at Warren,

Dr. Alex Romulo A. Ziga, the psychiatrist who had treated Ed for sixteen weeks following Katie's death, had this to say:

> *He is no longer depressed. His depression was reactive due to the loss of his wife when, because of his psychosis, he killed her. He was cooperative, coherent, and relevant while on this hospital stay. He did what was expected of him and also he attended and participated in the therapeutic activities that were offered to him even when he was here only for a short period of time. It was observed by the staff that he interacted fairly well with the others on the unit, including other patients, and all throughout, he maintained appropriate behavior and utilized his leisure with no depressive signs and symptoms, and expressed some hope for the future. He is expecting that he will not have to spend too much time in jail.*[9]

While Ed was being reevaluated at Warren, Dr. Bernstein, at Don Lewis's request, submitted his own suggestions regarding Ed's sentencing. Having failed to bring the jury around to his way of thinking, the psychiatrist would try to influence Judge Miller. Dr. Bernstein had four recommendations:

1. Ed be given the minimum sentence, noting that "under medication, Mr. Gingerich should pose no threat to his community. Indeed, I believe he is safe for discharge to the community at the present time . . ."

2. If Ed be incarcerated, he do his time in a place like Warren State Hospital rather than a state correctional facility.

3. If in a regular prison, Ed be placed in a "Special Needs Unit" for inmates with mental disorders and not in the general prison population.

4. When discharged from custody, Ed continue being treated by "mental health professionals familiar with the Amish community."[10]

Bishop Rudy Shetler had a mission. As leader of the Brownhill Amish, it was his duty to protect his people from Ed Gingerich. In furtherance of that responsibility, he drafted a petition that read:

> *About Ed Gingerich*
> We like Ed Gingerich, but absolutely don't trust him and are seriosly [sic] afraid of him because of what he did. We want him to stay in Warren County mental ward.

The bishop was the first to sign his name to this statement. He took the paper to Ed's dad and asked him to endorse it. Mr. Gingerich, torn between his love for his son and his duty to the congregation and the bishop, signed the petition. Atlee, Joe, and Danny, out of loyalty to Ed and perhaps fear of retribution, refused to add their names to the document. Mrs. Gingerich, although in sympathy with the bishop's quest to keep Ed institutionalized, didn't sign the petition. She was afraid to go on record against her son. In the end, sixty persons over the age of seventeen signed the bishop's petition.

Judge Miller, on May 2, 1994, opened Ed's hearing by inviting the prosecution to go on record with its sentence recommendation. J. Wesley Rowden, speaking for the Commonwealth, called Judge Miller's attention to Ed's presentence psychiatric report. According to the psychiatrist at Warren State Hospital, Ed could still be dangerous without his medication. The prosecutor read a letter he had received from the victim's parents, Mr. and Mrs. Levi Shetler. "We will never trust Ed," they wrote. "We are fearful of him."[11] Rowden asked Bishop Rudy Shetler to come forward with his Brownhill petition. "We like Ed," Rudy Shetler said, "but we're afraid of him. We want him to stay in the Warren Hospital. We're just afraid. We don't trust him. We encouraged Ed to get good care, but he didn't do it."[12]

Don Lewis had been taken by surprise. This hearing was supposed to be a cakewalk. Lewis was expecting, anticipating, a probated sentence and didn't like the way things were shaping up.[13]

"Your Honor," Rowden said, "the Commonwealth recommends that the defendant be given the maximum sentence under the law. We have nothing more."

Lewis urged Judge Miller to consider what it would be like in jail for an Amish man. Prison life was violent and dangerous, no place for a man whose religion forbade the use of force. Ed wouldn't last a minute in a place like that. Lewis, therefore, suggested that Ed be placed on probation on the condition that he remain under the care of a psychiatrist. Lewis assured the court that Ed posed no danger to himself or society. The poor man had already spent a year in jail; there was no need for additional punishment. His client had to live with the fact that he'd killed his wife; wasn't that punishment enough? Lewis reminded the court that his recommendations were supported by Dr. Lawson F. Bernstein, the prominent Pittsburgh psychiatrist who had studied Ed and had testified on his behalf. The defense attorney concluded his remarks by expressing confidence that the court would make the right decision with respect to his client, Ed Gingerich.

Judge Miller turned to Ed. "Does the defendant have anything to say?" he asked.

Ed, dressed in his jailhouse blues, rose to his feet. "All I can say is, I'm sorry to all the community that this has happened." He sat down.

"The defendant," Judge Miller said, "committed a brutal killing of his wife by his hands and his feet, then removed portions of her body. He is a danger to society and he must be incapacitated. A lesser sentence would depreciate from the criminal act and would be most inappropriate. The defendant did not adequately deal with his mental illness or problems he knew he was having prior to the event. Accordingly, the defendant is sentenced to pay the costs of prosecution and to undergo imprisonment at the State Correctional Institution in Pittsburgh for a minimum term of two and one-half years and a maximum of five years with credit for presentence incarceration since May 19, 1993. The court recommends that Mr. Gingerich be housed in the Mental Health Unit because of the significant religious and mental overtones he presents."[14]

Don Lewis jumped to his feet. This was an outrageously harsh sentence and would force him to file a motion to modify. The defense attorney, of course, was just blowing off steam. By the time he appealed the denial of this motion and the case was heard, Ed would have served his time. It was over. Ed Gingerich was going to prison. He wouldn't be eligible for parole until December 1995. That meant, at the very least, he had nineteen months of prison time ahead of him, probably in a minimum-security facility. Lewis could afford to be outraged; it wasn't his life that was on the line. Ed was relieved; it could have been a lot worse.

On May 9, a week after Ed's sentence, Levi Shetler got up from the dinner table and said, "I miss Katie; I wish I could see her."[15] Exhausted from his illness, he went to bed. Sometime late that night, he died. A few days later, they buried Levi in the woods next to his daughter. It was spring; Katie's favorite time of year.

End Notes

Abbreviations

ATN	author's trial notes
CC	Crawford County
DA	district attorney
DM	district magistrate
EDT	*Erie Daily Times*
ETN	*Erie Times News*
HMC	Hamot Medical Center
PPG	*Pittsburgh Post-Gazette*
PSP	Pennsylvania State Police
TMT	*The Meadville Tribune*
TYV	*The Youngstown Vindicator*
WSH	Warren State Hospital
WCA	Jamestown Memorial Health Center
ADM	Alice DeMatteo
AG	Atlee D. Gingerich
AMcL	Andrew McLaughlin

ARAZ Dr. Alex Romulo A. Ziga

BS Deacon Ben Stutzman

CB Charlotte Brown

CDC Dr. Craig D. Caldwell

CG Clara Gingerich

CH Chris Hauber

CM Carrie Mowery

CN Carlyle Nobbs

CO Cindy Ormsbee

DF ADA Douglas Ferguson

DEG Dannie E. Gingerich

DDG Danny D. Gingerich

DEL Attorney Donald E. Lewis

DL David Lyle

DLL David L. Lindsey

DP Douglas Peters

DPL PSP Trooper Danny P. Lloyd

DS Dan Stutzman

DW Delberta "Debbie" Williams

EAS Emma A. Shetler

EDG Edward D. Gingerich

EEG Enos E. Gingerich

EG Elizabeth D. Gingerich

EH Emanuel Hershberger

ES	Emanuel Shetler
FY	Dr. Frank J. Yohe
GB	PSP Trooper Gerald Bey
GRM	CC Judge Gordon R. Miller
HP	Social Worker Harry Punia
HW	Hank Williams, Jr.
JB	Jim Brown
JCM	John C. Miller
JDM	Jim DeMatteo
JE	Jan Elliott
JG	Joe E. Gingerich
JH	Jake Hertzler
JO	PSP Officer John Och
JP	Jake Powers
JS	Dr. John J. Spikes
JT	Jacob Troyer
JWR	CC ADA J. Wesley Rowden
KE	Kathy Easly
KG	Katie L. Gingerich
KK	Kim Kerstetter
KW	Dr. Karl E. Williams
LAM	Dr. Lisa A. Morrow
LFB	Dr. Lawson F. Bernstein, Jr.
LJ	Lynn Jobe

LK   Lawrence Kimmy

LL   Lazar LeMajic

LP   PSP Trooper Lon E. Pierce

LS   Levi Shetler

MEG   Mary E. Gingerich

MG   Mary Gingerich

MWT   Dr. Merritt W. Terrell

NS   Noah Stutzman

PJR   Dr. Phillip J. Resnick

RBS   CC Sheriff Robert Stevens

RF   Randy Fyock

RH   Robert Hershberger

RNS   Bishop Rudy N. Shetler

RR   Trooper Robert A. Rowles

RS   Raymond Shetler

RZ   Richard Zimmer

SW   Sid Workman

TI   Dr. Takeshi Imajo

TM   Tim Moriarty

WJB   CC Jail Warden Jack Brickner

Chapter One
The Brownhill Amish
1. The Gingerich family background is based upon interviews of: EG 7/12/94; EAS 7/25/94; EAS 7/25/94; CN 9/19/94, 9/30/94

2. Ed's early schooling: EG 7/12/94; DS 7/28/94;
   9/13/94. For Old-Order Amish schooling generally: Hostetler, John A., *Amish Society,* 4th
   edition, Baltimore, MD: The Johns Hopkins
   University Press, 1993

3. Ed's hatred of farm work and being a slacker:
   EG 7/12/94; EAS 8/1/94; EH 7/25/94; BS 7/26/94;
   DS 7/28/94; RNS 4/11/95

4. BS 8/5/95

5. EG 7/12/94

6. Background and history of the Gingerich sawmill: EG 7/12/94; DS 8/9/94; DL 9/13/94; EH
   7/25/94; BS 8/5/94; JP 8/23/94

7. RZ 12/1/94

8. *Ibid.*

9. *Ibid.*

10. DW 12/5/94

11. DW 12/5/94; JP 8/23/94; JE 8/15/94, 8/22/94;
    DL 10/4/95

Chapter Two
Ed Meets Katie

1. EAS 8/22/94; EG 7/12/94

2. Ed's reluctance to get married and the pressure
   he felt: DW 12/5/94; RZ 12/1/94; CM 8/29/94

3. EAS 7/25/94, 8/22/94, 11/14/94

4. ES 7/25/94; DS 8/9/94

Chapter Three
A Short Honeymoon

1. EAS 7/25/94

2. DS 8/9/94

3. EAS 11/14/94

4. Huntington, Gertrude Enders, "Health Care," Chapter Nine in *The Amish and the State*, ed. Donald E. Kraybill, Baltimore, MD: The Johns Hopkins University Press, 1993

5. BS 8/15/94; RNS 4/11/95

Chapter Four
The Pennsylvania Doctor

1. Huntington, Gertrude Enders, "Health Care," Chapter Nine in *The Amish and the State*, ed. Donald E. Kraybill, Baltimore, MD: The Johns Hopkins University Press, 1993

2. *Ibid.*

3. *Ibid.*

4. Terrell's in-office treatment and diagnostic procedures: EG 7/12/94; LJ 10/18/94; RZ 12/1/94

5. MWT medical records pertaining to EG 8/18/88 to 3/18/93

6. DS 8/9/94; JP 8/23/94

Chapter Five
The New Sawmill

1. JE 8/22/94

2. BS 8/15/94; JP 8/23/94

3. EG 7/12/94; JP 8/23/94; EH 7/25/94

4. LK 8/11/94

5. EAS 8/1/94

6. EAS 10/6/94; DS 8/9/94

Chapter Six
The Sidekick

1. EH 7/25/94; JP 8/23/94

2. DL 10/14/94; JP 8/23/94; DS 8/9/94

3. EG 7/12/94; JP 8/23/94; DL 10/14/94; DS 9/13/94, 11/12/94

4. JCM 7/22/94

5. EG-KG: EAS 11/14/94

6. DS 9/13/94

7. EAS 9/3/94

8. JP 8/23/94

Chapter Seven
Beware of Loggers with Bibles

1. BS 8/5/94, 8/9/94; RNS 8/8/94, 4/11/95

2. LL 8/31/94; DLL 8/13/94; EM 4/13/94

3. DLL 8/13/94

4. *Ibid.*

5. *Ibid.*

6. *Ibid.*

7. DLL to author: "At one time I wanted to be a missionary to the Amish—to save them, to lead them out of their cult."

8. DLL 8/13/94

9. *Ibid.*

10. *Ibid.*

Chapter Eight
The Hard Sell

1. DLL 8/13/94, 8/19/94

2. DLL 8/13/94

3. LL background: DLL 8/13/94, 8/19/94; LL 8/31/94, 4/19/95; DLL-EG: DLL 8/13/94

4. DLL 8/13/94; LL 8/31/94

5. JP 7/28/94, 8/23/94

6. EAS 7/25/94, 9/23/94, 11/14/94

7. RZ 12/1/94

8. MWT medical records

9. LL 8/31/94

Chapter Nine
The Reluctant Witness

1. JP 8/23/94

2. Ed hitting his wife in the garden constructed from: JP 8/23/94

Chapter Ten
Alone and Abandoned

1. JP 8/23/94; DL 8/6/94; DS 8/9/94; JE 8/15/94; RZ 12/1/94

2. On 12/5/94, DW advised the author her relationship with Ed was platonic.

3. JE 9/12/94; RZ 12/1/94; JP 8/23/94

4. EAS 9/23/94, 11/14/94

5. EAS 11/14/94

6. EAS 9/23/94

7. RZ 12/1/94

Chapter Eleven
Evangelists at the Gate

1. DLL-DEG: DLL 8/13/94, 8/19/94

2. DLL-EG: DLL 8/13/94, 8/19/94

3. DLL 8/13/94

4. DLL 8/13/94

Chapter Twelve
New Home, Old Problems
1. JP 8/23/94

2. JP 7/28/94

3. *Ibid.*

4. JP 7/28/94

5. JP 8/23/94; EH 7/25/94, 8/16/94

6. The room-painting scene where Ed pulls Katie up by her hair was constructed from JP 8/23/94

7. *Ibid.*

Chapter Thirteen
Marks of Violence
1. CO 8/27/94. In December 1991, Katie told Joe's wife, Annie, that if anything should happen to her, she didn't want Ed raising the children. She wanted the children raised by Mr. and Mrs. Gingerich. (EAS 9/3/94)

2. CO 8/27/94. In August 1996, Dave Lyle, while driving Atlee Gingerich to a barn sale, asked him when the family first learned of Ed's physical abuse of Katie. "We knew for a long time that Ed wasn't nice to Katie," Atlee replied. (DL 8/19/96)

3. EAS 8/22/94

4. EAS 9/3/94; JM 10/11/94

5. EAS 8/1/94

6. EAS 9/3/94

Chapter Fourteen
Two-faced

1. EAS 8/1/94

2. EAS 7/25/94, 8/1/94

3. EAS 9/23/94

4. DS 9/29/94

5. EAS 8/22/94; EH 8/16/94

6. KG-EAS: EAS 9/3/94

7. The snow-rolling scene constructed from: JP 8/23/94; EAS 7/25/94; BS 7/26/94

8. JP 8/23/94

9. *Ibid.*

Chapter Fifteen
The Sermon in the Machine Shop

1. EAS 8/1/94

2. Ed's Gunk fume symptoms based upon trial testimony of: DLL, JS, LAM, LFB, RZ

3. DLL 8/13/94

4. DLL-EG in machine shop: DLL 8/13/94, 8/19/94

Chapter Sixteen
Ed's Vision

1. EAS 7/29/94, 8/1/94

2. BS 8/15/94

3. EAS 9/3/94

4. Ed's psychotic ramblings: EAS 8/1/94; BS 8/9/94; RNS 4/11/95

5. MWT medical records

6. Ed's dreams: EG 7/12/94; BS 8/9/94; RF interview of DDG 6/11/93; CH interview of SW (no date)

7. EG-JG-DDG: EAS 8/1/94; BS 8/9/94; RNS 4/11/95; RS 8/16/94

8. RNS 8/16/94

9. RF interview of DDG 6/11/93

10. EG-EH: EH 8/16/94

11. LS-KG-EG: EAS 8/1/94; RNS 4/11/95

Chapter Seventeen
Ed's First Spell

1. EAS 8/1/94

2. RNS 4/11/95; RF interview of DDG 6/11/93

3. RNS 4/11/95, BS 8/9/94

4. *Ibid.*

5. *Ibid.*

6. EAS 8/1/94; RNS 4/11/95; BS 8/9/94; RF interview of DDG 6/11/93

7. EAS 8/1/94; RNS 4/11/95

8. According to a 1988 Gallup poll, 66 percent of American respondents claimed to believe in the devil, compared with 30 percent or fewer in France, Great Britain, Italy, Norway, and Sweden.

9. JG-EAS: 8/1/94

10. CDC 8/12/94

11. EAS 8/1/94

12. *Ibid.*

13. EG-KG: EAS 8/1/94

14. EAS 8/1/94

15. *Ibid.*

16. *Ibid.*

17. *Ibid.*

18. CDC 8/12/94

19. EG-KG-CDC: CDC 8/12/94; EAS 7/29/94; BS 8/15/94

20. EAS 7/29/94

21. KG-CDC: EAS 7/29/94

22. BS 8/1/94

Chapter Eighteen
"The English Have Ed"

1. DDG-KG: EAS 8/1/94

2. EG-KG: EAS 8/1/94; RF interview with DDG 6/11/93; RF interview of AG 6/11/93

3. DDG-DEG: EAS 7/29/94; RF interview of DDG 6/11/93; RF interview of DEG 6/11/93

4. In his six-page PSP report, LP wrote: "They [AG and DDG] stated that the suspect would go into what they called spells; that he would go into spasms. The suspect would just sit there and then his muscles would start to stiffen up and he would go out of control."

5. EG-DEG: EAS 7/29/94

6. EAS 7/29/94, 8/1/94

7. DP 7/29/94

8. EAS 7/29/94

9. TM 7/15/94

10. EAS 7/29/94

11. *Ibid.* .

Chapter Nineteen
Waking Up in a Mental Ward
1. DP 7/29/94

2. Emergency entrance scene: DP 7/29/94

3. KG-psychiatrist: EAS 7/29/94

4. EG-KG: EAS 7/29/94

5. KG-EAS: EAS 7/29/94

6. EG-KG-EAS-nurse: EAS 7/29/94

7. EAS 7/29/94

8. KG-Hamot doctor: EAS 7/29/94

9. KG-DEG-EAS: EAS 7/29/94

10. KG-EAS-desk woman: EAS 7/29/94

11. Padded-room scene: EAS 7/19/94

Chapter Twenty
An English Visitor
1. ES 8/16/94

2. EG-KG-LS-EAS hospital visit: EAS 7/29/94

3. DLL 8/13/94

Chapter Twenty-one
Drug-Addled
1. The $8,000 Hamot bill was paid in installments. (EG 7/12/94)

2. EG was interviewed by WSH social worker HP on 3/19/93. On page 8 of his report, HP wrote:

"After his [Ed's] release from Hamot hospital, the patient had been going to the outpatient clinic of Hamot hospital for his regular check-ups. However, after three weeks of appointments, the patient stopped going to Hamot hospital because he did not want to take psychotropic medication because of their side effects such as dry mouth."

3. LL-EG: LL 8/31/94, 4/19/95

4. JP 8/23/94

5. RZ 12/1/94

6. EG 7/12/94. LP PSP report 3/19/93: "After he [Ed] was released from the hospital [Hamot], he gradually got better. He was taking medication when he got out of the hospital and it was pills to rest but not to sleep and the suspect did not agree with taking the pills." (according to DDG)

7. RF interview of DDG 6/11/93; EAS 8/22/94

8. EAS 11/14/94.

9. LAM Neuropsychological Report 1/19/94: LFB report: Independent Medical Examination of Edward D. Gingerich 1/31/94; WSH Discharge Summary Report 7/31/93

10. The fear that EG might commit suicide: RF interview of DDG 6/11/93; DEL interview of RZ and KK 6/11/93; CH interview of SW (no date). EG denied such intentions to author (EG 7/12/94)

11. EAS 8/22/94

12. *Ibid.*

13. Ed's behavior and the events leading to his Jamestown hospitalization: EAS 7/29/94, 8/1/94

14. EAS 8/1/94

15. *Ibid.*

16. *Ibid.*

17. EAS 7/29/94

18. EAS-KG-MG: EAS 7/29/94, 8/1/94

Chapter Twenty-two
Another Spell, Another Stint

1. EAS 8/1/94

2. *Ibid.*

3. *Ibid.*

4. *Ibid.*

5. *Ibid.*

6. *Ibid.*

7. *Ibid.*

8. *Ibid.*

9. WCA report 5/6/92

10. *Ibid.*

11. *Ibid.*

12. EAS 8/22/94

Chapter Twenty-three
Saved from the Bishop

1. EAS 8/22/94; LP PSP report: "When he [Ed] got
   out of the Jamestown hospital, he was still weak
   and sick. He was getting better, but did not stay
   on his medication." Report of FY 3/19/93: "He
   [Ed] knows that they treated him with medication but he said he had 'problems' with the med-

ication and it 'didn't agree with me.' " DEL
pretrial interview of CB re EG quote: "Our people don't believe in medicine and doctors."

2. EAS 8/22/94

3. EAS 8/1/94; 8/22/94

4. EAS-KG: EAS 8/1/94

5. DLL 8/13/94; 8/19/94

Chapter Twenty-four
Out of Step

1. DS 8/9/94; DL 11/14/95; EH 7/25/94; BS
   8/5/94

2. MWT medical records. The nature of MWT's
   business practices, healing philosophy, procedures, and treatment techniques is based on: EG
   7/12/94; LJ 10/18/94; RZ 12/1/94; DEL interview of RZ and KK (no date); LP PSP report
   3/19/93: "The family was not satisfied with the
   way Dr. Terrel [sic] 'doctors.' "

3. EAS 8/1/94

4. EAS 8/22/94

5. MWT medical records

Chapter Twenty-five
Punxsutawney Healer

1. EAS 11/14/94

2. EAS 8/1/94; RF interview of DEG 6/11/93; RF
   interview of AG 6/11/93

3. EAS 8/1/94

4. RF interview of DEB 6/11/93; EAS 8/1/94

5. RF interview of AG 6/11/93

6. BS 8/5/94

7. CH interview of SW (no date)

8. SW trial testimony

9. *Ibid.*

10. *Ibid.*

Chapter Twenty-six
"I Am a Quack"

1. SW trial testimony

2. SW trial testimony; CH interview of SW (no date)

3. *Ibid.*

4. JT 7/21/94

5. *Ibid.*

6. *Ibid.*

7. JT, when questioned by the author, insisted that he did not hold himself out as a physician and that his brand of health care was nothing more than being a dispenser of healthy foodstuff in the form of herbs.

8. KG-DDG-JT 7/21/94

9. SW trial testimony

10. EG 7/12/94; SW trial testimony

11. JT 7/21/94

12. DDG trial testimony

13. SW trial testimony

Chapter Twenty-seven
Liver Pills

1. LP PSP report 3/19/94; WSH report by HP 3/24/93

2. DDG trial testimony; RF interview of DDG 6/11/93, LP PSP report 3/19/93

3. *Ibid.*

4. EAS 8/1/94

5. JG 7/15/94; LP PSP report 3/19/93

6. RZ 12/1/94

7. LP PSP report 3/19/93; EAS 8/1/94; RF interview of DEG 6/11/93

8. RF interview of DEG 6/11/93; DEG trial testimony

9. RZ 12/1/94; RZ trial testimony

10. *Ibid.*

11. MWT medical records

12. EG 7/12/94

13. EG 7/12/94; LP PSP report 3/19/93

14. RZ 12/1/94; DEL interview of RZ (no date)

Chapter Twenty-eight
The Work of the Devil

1. RZ trial testimony

2. RZ 12/1/94

3. EG-KG-RZ: RZ 12/1/94; KK 12/14/94

4. *Ibid.*

5. *Ibid.*

6. KG-EG: RZ 12/1/94; KK 12/13/94; RF interview of AG 6/11/93; DDG trial testimony

7. RZ 12/1/94; KK 12/13/94

8. DDG-EG-KG: RF interview of DDG 6/11/93;

DDG trial testimony; RS 8/16/94; LP PSP report 3/19/93

9. RF interview of DEG 6/11/93; DDG trial testimony; RF interview of AG 6/11/93

10. KG-EG: RF interview of AG 6/11/93; RS 8/16/94; LP PSP report 3/19/93

11. RF interview of DDG 6/11/93

12. LFB report: Independent Medical Examination of Edward D. Gingerich 1/31/94: "Mr. Gingerich believed at that time he was possessed by the devil and that he had to act to save himself and his soul."

13. DDG trial testimony: RF interview of DDG 6/11/93

Chapter Twenty-nine
"You Wouldn't Understand"

1. DDG trial testimony; RF interview of DDG 6/11/93

2. *Ibid.*

3. *Ibid.*

4. LP PSP report 3/19/93; DDG as quoted in *TMT*: "It looked like he would come after me so I left."

5. JO as quoted in *TMT* 3/19/93; RF interview of DDG 6/11/93

6. Details regarding this aspect of the killing: EG's fifteen-page PSP statement to DPL and GB 3/19/93

7. RF interview of DDG 6/11/93; BS 8/5/94; WSH Discharge Summary Report 7/13/93

8. BS 8/5/94; EAS 8/1/94

9. RA trial testimony

10. RZ trial testimony; RZ 12/1/94

11. EG's encounter with Mill Village firefighters: DPL PSP reports 3/21/93, 3/22/93; LP PSP report 3/19/93; RR PSP report 3/19/93; DP 7/29/94; AMcL quotes in *TMT* 3/19/93

12. *Ibid.*

Chapter Thirty
The Wedding Announcement

1. EG-DDG: DDG trial testimony

2. RR PSP report 3/19/93; RR trial testimony; DDG trial testimony

3. *Ibid.*

4. *Ibid.*

5. LP PSP report 3/19/93

6. EAS 7/25/94

7. RR PSP report 3/19/93

8. DPL 10/6/94

9. DPL trial testimony

10. RR PSP report 3/19/93; RR trial testimony

11. DDG trial testimony; RF interview of DDG 6/11/93

12. DS-JH: DS 9/13/94

13. DS-LS: DS 9/13/94

14. EAS 8/1/94

15. *Ibid.*

16. *Ibid.*

17. *Ibid.*

18. DS 9/13/94

19. *Ibid.*

Chapter Thirty-one
From the Killer's Lips

1. The interrogation of Ed is based upon the fifteen-page transcript of the interview with DPL and GB. The dialogue is verbatim.

Chapter Thirty-two
Jail

1. WJB 7/19/94

2. *Ibid.*

3. DS 8/9/94

4. WJB 7/19/94

5. *Ibid.*

6. *Ibid.*

7. Autopsy report #93-023, four pages, Dr. Takeshi Imajo, MD 3/19/93

8. EG-FY: FY Psychiatric Assessment Report 3/19/93; FY trial testimony

Chapter Thirty-three
Cleaning Up

1. EAS 11/14/94

2. The preparation of KG's corpse for burial: DL 3/23/94; Hostetler, John A., *Amish Society,* 4th Edition, Baltimore, MD: The Johns Hopkins University Press, 1993

3. EAS 11/14/94; RH 8/23/94

4. EG-CC deputies: RBS 3/21/94, 3/22/94: interviews of CC deputies who drove EG to WSH

5. *Ibid.*

6. *Ibid.*

Chapter Thirty-four
The Funeral

1. Description of KG's funeral: JCM 7/22/94; KK 12/13/94; EAS 8/1/94; DS 9/13/94

2. KK 12/13/94

3. *Ibid.*

4. *Ibid.*

5. The gravesite ceremony informed by: Hostetler, John A., *Amish Society,* 4th edition, Baltimore, MD: The Johns Hopkins University Press, 1993

6. DDG's speech to family members in the murder house: EAS 11/14/94

Chapter Thirty-five
Loose Talk

1. WSH Psychiatric Evaluation Report for ARAZ 3/19/93

2. *Ibid.*

3. *Ibid.*

4. *Ibid.*

5. DS 8/9/94

6. BS 8/4/94

7. LK and JP denied such activity to the author

8. EAS 7/25/94; BS 7/26/94

Chapter Thirty-six
Shunned

1. EG-DEG: EAS 7/25/94; RF interview of DEB 6/11/93; DEG trial testimony: EG 7/12/94

2. CB 7/14/94

3. EAS 7/25/94

4. BS 7/16/94; 8/5/94

5. EG-EAS: 7/25/94

6. EG 7/12/94; EAS 7/25/94; BS 8/4/94

Chapter Thirty-seven
Hiring the Head Doctors

1. DEL 7/12/94

2. *Ibid.*

3. The Gingerich defense case file was made available by Attorney Donald E. Lewis on April 20, 1994.

4. *Ibid.*

5. TI autopsy report #H01-93-026 3/19/93: "2cm bluish ecchymosis in the right hip area anteriorly"

6. LFB vitae 9/93

7. LFB report: Independent Medical Examination of Edward D. Gingerich 1/31/94

8. *Ibid.*

9. *Ibid.*

10. *Ibid.*

11. *Ibid.*

12. *Ibid.*

13. LAM Neuropsychological Assessment Report 1/19/94 (italics mine)

Chapter Thirty-eight
Beating the Bush for Witnesses

1. PJR letter to JWR 3/18/94

2. DEL 7/12/94

3. *Ibid.*

4. *Ibid.*

5. *Ibid.*

6. LP PSP report 3/19/93

7. EAS 11/14/94

Chapter Thirty-nine
Brainstorming

1. Fifty-three-page transcript of DEL, RF, CH, and KE trial strategy meetings 3/94

2. *Ibid.*

3. *Ibid.*

4. *Ibid.*

5. *Ibid.*

6. *Ibid.*

7. *Ibid.*

8. *Ibid.*

Chapter Forty
Commonwealth v. *Gingerich*

1. Although certain testimony has been transcribed, there is no transcript of the entire trial because there was no appeal, which would have required a written record of the proceeding.

2. GRM 7/31/97

3. ATN

4. DL 3/22/94

5. *EDT* 3/24/94

6. *TMT* 3/24/94; ATN

7. ATN; *PPG* 3/24/94; *TMT* 3/24/94

8. GRM 7/31/97, GRM believes that the drawing of KG's corpse "dehumanized the victim."

9. *TMT* 3/24/94; ATN

10. ATN

11. According to GRM, having an expert other than the forensic pathologist who performed the autopsy testify as to the victim's cause and manner of death is rare in homicide trials.

12. ATN; *TMT* 3/24/94; *EDT* 3/24/94

Chapter Forty-one
Lord Willing

1. Although, according to GRM, the children were not, by law, too young to testify, the prosecution had decided not to put them on the stand.

2. ATN; *EDT* 3/24/94; according to EAS: "He [the prosecutor] didn't ask me enough questions" (EAS 8/1/94)

3. RF interview of DDG 6/11/93

4. According to JWR, DDG was not a good witness because childlike, he didn't read anything into the questions. Questioning him was like "pulling teeth." (JWR 7/20/94)

5. ATN; *PPG* 3/24/94; *EDT* 3/24/94

6. ATN; *EDT* 3/24/94

7. *Ibid.*

8. On the question of Ed's Miranda rights, GRM believes they may have been violated by the PSP. (GRM 7/31/97) JWR doubts that EG knowingly waived his rights that night at the PSP station. (JWR 7/20/94)

9. ATN; *EDT* 3/24/94

10. ATN; *EDT* 3/25/94

Chapter Forty-two
The Gunk Defense

1. Twenty-four-page transcript of testimony of RZ 3/24/94

2. ATN; *EDT* 3/25/94

3. ATN: *TMT* 3/25/94; *EDT* 3/25/94; GRM considered JS a weak witness. In the judge's opinion, the Gunk defense didn't hold water. (GRM 7/31/94)

4. ATN; *EDT* 3/25/94

5. ATN; *EDT* 3/25/94

6. ATN

7. *Ibid.*

8. *Ibid.*

9. *Ibid.*

10. When contacted by the author in 1994, JDM said he did not wish to talk about EG or his case. On 7/11/97, ADM telephoned the author from her home in Arizona to say she was worried about EG getting out of prison soon. Although she had testified as a character witness for the

defendant, she had known from the first day she had met him in 1987 that there was something profoundly wrong with him. There was "something dark beneath the surface," she said. As for EG's relationship with his wife, he, according to ADM, was "extremely indifferent to her." They did not have a good marriage from the beginning, and after the children were born, one could tell, from their hollow-eyed expressions, that they had been affected by this unhappy marriage. ADM said she had called because she had to get the truth about EG off her chest. She believes he is dangerous and should not be released from custody.

11. ATN; *TMT* 3/26/94

Chapter Forty-three
"Whacked-Out"

1. ATN; *PPG* 3/26/94; *TMT* 3/26/94

2. DEL 7/12/94

3. ATN; according to GRM, LFB was a strong witness for the defense. (GRM 7/31/94)

4. ATN

5. *Ibid.*

6. *Ibid.*

Chapter Forty-four
The Verdict

1. ATN; *TMT* 3/27/94

2. GRM believes the jury decision amounted to a compromise verdict. (GRM 3/31/97)

3. *TMT* 3/27/94

4. *Ibid.*

5. *TYV* 3/27/94

6. *TMT* 3/26/94

7. *EAS* 8/1/94

8. WSH Discharge Summary Report #52118 7/21/94

9. *Ibid.*

10. LFB letter to DEL 5/2/94

11. *TMT* 5/3/94

12. *Ibid.*

13. DL 5/3/94

14. GRM Finding and Sentencing Order 5/2/94

15. EAS 8/1/94

Index